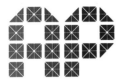 **Architecture in Practice**

Competing Globally in Architecture Competitions

D1258664

Published in Great Britain in 2004 by Wiley-Academy,
a division of John Wiley & Sons Ltd

Copyright © 2004 John Wiley & Sons Ltd, The Atrium,
Southern Gate, Chichester, West Sussex PO19 8SQ, England
Telephone (+44) 1243 779777

Email (for orders & customer service enquiries): cs-books@wiley.co.uk
Visit our Home Page on www.wileyeurope.com or www.wiley.com

This publication is designed to provide accurate and authoritative
information in regard to the subject matter covered. It is sold on the
understanding that the Publisher is not engaged in rendering
professional services. If professional advice or other expert assistance
is required, the services of a competent professional should be sought.

Other Wiley Editorial Offices

John Wiley & Sons Inc., 111 River Street,
Hoboken, NJ 07030, USA

Jossey-Bass, 989 Market Street,
San Francisco, CA 94103-1741, USA

Wiley-VCH Verlag GmbH, Boschstr. 12,
D-69469 Weinheim, Germany

John Wiley & Sons Australia Ltd, 33 Park Road,
Milton, Queensland 4064, Australia

John Wiley & Sons (Asia) Pte Ltd, 2 Clementi Loop #02-01,
Jin Xing Distripark, Singapore 129809

John Wiley & Sons Canada Ltd, 22 Worcester Road,
Etobicoke, Ontario, Canada M9W 1L1

ISBN 0470 86 2130

Cover and book design:
Christian Küsters, CHK Design, London

Printed and bound in Italy by Conti Tipocolor

With the support of the Graham Foundation for the Advanced Studies in the Fine Arts

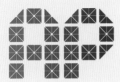
Architecture in Practice

Competing Globally in Architecture Competitions

G Stanley Collyer

With essays by Michael Berk, Carlos Casuscelli,
John Morris Dixon, Larry Gordon, William Morgan,
Roger L Schluntz, Robert G Shibley and Brian Taggart

CONTENTS

6   **Introduction**
       Why Compete? G Stanley Collyer

22   **Chapter 1 Government Buildings** G Stanley Collyer
34   Eugene, Oregon Federal Courthouse (1999) John Morris Dixon
40   Canadian Embassy, Berlin (1998) G Stanley Collyer
46   Contra Costa County Government Center (2000) Mark Tortorich
54   Los Angeles Federal Courthouse (2001) Larry Gordon

60   **Chapter 2 Performing Arts Centres** G Stanley Collyer
72   Rensselaer Polytechnic Electronic Media and Performing Arts Center (2001) W Morgan
78   Tempe Visual & Performing Arts Center (2001) Brian Taggart
84   Jyväskylä Music and Arts Centre (1998) William Morgan
88   Miami-Dade Performing Arts Center (1995) Carlos Casuscelli

96   **Chapter 3 Educational Facilities** G Stanley Collyer
106   Lick-Wilmerding High School, San Francisco (2001) Susannah Temko
116   Chicago Prototype Schools (2001) G Stanley Collyer
124   Booker T Washington Arts Magnet School, Dallas (2001) Mark Gunderson AIA
130   IIT McCormick Center, Chicago (1998) Michael Dulin
136   University of South Dakota School of Business (2000) Tom Reasoner
142   School of Architecture, University of New Mexico (2000) Brian Taggart

148 **Chapter 4 Public Libraries** Roger L Schluntz FAIA
158 **Salt Lake City Library (2000)** Roger L Schluntz FAIA
164 **Kansai-Kan National Diet Library (1996)** Tony Coscia
170 **Brooklyn Public Library (2002)** Michael Berk
178 **Québec Library, Montréal (2000)** William Morgan

184 **Chapter 5 Museums** G Stanley Collyer
194 **Modern Art Museum of Fort Worth (1997)** George Wright
200 **Palos Verdes Art Center (2000)** Larry Gordon
206 **Nam June Paik Museum (2003)** G Stanley Collyer

212 **Chapter 6 Housing** Robert G Shibley AIA, AICP
220 **Chicago Housing Authority (2001)** Rosemarie Buchanan
226 **Europan (1993)** Lucy Bullivant
232 **Sustainable Housing, Lystrup, Århus, Denmark (2003)** G Stanley Collyer

238 Appendix – Competitions by Country
246 Bibliography
247 Photo Credits
248 Acknowledgements
249 Contributors
250 Index

Why Compete?

The Global Equation

In the late 1980s, Rafael Viñoly, a young architect from Uruguay residing in the United States, encountered Japanese architect Fumihiko Maki. When asked by Viñoly about the possibility of gaining a commission in Japan, Maki suggested he might try by entering a competition. A short time later Viñoly followed his advice and entered an open competition for the design of a new Tokyo Forum. To the complete surprise of the Japanese, Viñoly's entry won the competition for the $800 million project. Not only did the large fee he received for the realisation of this project position his office to go after large projects, it enabled the firm to prosper during a period when commissions for large projects were evaporating in both the United States and Europe. Firms from around the world began looking to Asia for commissions, and many large firms – some by way of competitions – managed to keep their heads above water by looking abroad during those difficult times.

Although the scale of the Viñoly success story is one few architects can hope to emulate, it does hold important lessons. Viñoly's professional training took place in a culture where competitions were often staged for the design of major buildings. He had already been part of a team which had won a major competition in Argentina for the design of a large television complex in Buenos Aires. Thus, competing against great odds did not deter him from pursuing a dream – especially when there was a real project at stake. Also, by winning the Tokyo Forum, Viñoly suddenly became a recognised expert in the design of major performance venues, the new concert hall in Philadelphia being one of his latest projects. Now, when a competition for the design of a new performing arts centre is underway, such as was recently the case in Copenhagen, one is hardly surprised to find Rafael Viñoly among the competitors.

Viñoly's success on foreign soil is not an isolated case. The competition for the Pompidou Centre in Paris was not only important because it resulted in a major public museum; the team of Richard Rogers and Renzo Piano which won that competition was not based in France at the time. By winning that competition, Rogers and Piano gained a rapid entrée into the international market. Today, Piano seldom builds in his home country; more often than not his projects are seen in Berlin, Rotterdam, Switzerland, France and, more recently, in New Caledonia and the USA. The same holds true, although to a lesser degree, for Rogers. Because of the Pompidou, he almost immediately began to get work in

Top
Daniel Herren
(Bern, Switzerland)
Thoerishaus Urban Centre,
Switzerland
Competition 1994
Axonometric perspective

Bottom
Paul Chemetoff/Borja Huidobro
(Paris, France)
Ministère de l'Économie,
des Finances et de l'Industrie,
Paris, France
Competition 1981
Completion 1987

One of Mitterrand's 'Grands
Projets', criticised because
it is the only building in Paris
that intrudes into the Seine

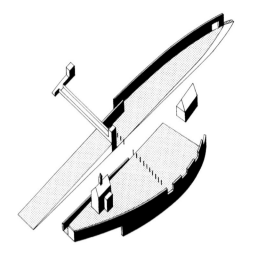

the UK and today is involved in projects throughout the world. Although one of the most well known figures in the world of architecture, Rogers is still a strong advocate of competitions as a way to improve the public realm.[1]

The profession had now gained the same status as that of musicians, artists and filmmakers, all of whom had long ago crossed national boundaries. And it would not be long before foreign architects were even invited to take part in limited competitions in countries where they were not licensed to practice. Now it is hardly unusual for Richard Meier to build in The Hague, or for Meinhard von Gerkan of Germany or Jean Nouvel of France to have projects underway in China or the United States. In many cases, they got their foot in the door by excelling in a competition.

Eero Saarinen
(Bloomfield Hills, MI, US)
Jefferson National Expansion
Memorial, St Louis, Missouri
Competition 1947
Completion 1965

This was a two-stage
competition, the decisive,
second stage with five
finalists being held in 1948.
However, it took 17 years
to complete the project

The Quest for Excellence in Architecture

Starting at the latest with the Greeks, competitions have traditionally been a vehicle for the creation of major civic buildings and public spaces. They have produced high profile projects such as the Spanish Steps, Brunelleschi's Dome, the British Houses of Parliament, Berlin's Reichstag, the Eiffel Tower, Helsinki's Railroad Station, New York's Central Park and the White House in Washington, DC. More recently, this process has been extended to include museums, all varieties of memorials (such as the Jefferson Arch), commercial buildings, schools, housing, industrial parks, infrastructure and even street furniture. In Europe, the proliferation of competitions and the inclusion of so many building types in that process can be viewed as a post-World War II phenomenon. Architectural associations in Germany, France, other European countries and Japan convinced their governments that mandating competitions for public buildings which exceeded a specified budget was the best way to achieve better design.

By the 1980s hundreds of competitions a year were being staged in France alone. Although many outsiders may only recall Mitterrand's 'Grands Projets' during this period, numerous lesser competitions for schools, libraries, railway stations and other projects enabled a whole new generation of young French architects to win significant commissions. The same could be said for Japan, Germany, the Netherlands and Scandinavia, where architects Günther Behnisch, Herman Hertzberger, Toyo Ito, Alvar Aalto and Sverre Fehn stepped to the forefront by virtue of excelling in this métier.

Meanwhile, competitions were few and far between in the United States. A programme by the National Endowment for the Arts (NEA) in the 1980s did serve to encourage the process on a very limited scale, and, due to the efforts of Senator Daniel Patrick Moynihan of New York, the US government initiated an 'Excellence in Architecture' programme which led to competitions for some federal buildings, primarily courthouses.

Today, with the concentration of large commissions more and more in the hands of large architecture offices and the simultaneous reduction in the number of open competitions for large projects, the outlook for rapid advancement by young architects is not as rosy as it was in the 1960s, 1970s and 1980s. According to German architect, Axel Schultes, 'There will be less opportunities for "boutique" firms. In Germany ... there are less and less open competitions, and this is not good for younger architects, who will find it more difficult to get out on their own'.[2]

Deciding to Enter
Because of the extraordinary effort involved in developing an idea which may only have an outside chance of winning, architects view competitions, especially those open to all comers, with mixed feelings. Whereas some European firms acquire up to 90 percent of their commissions by winning competitions on a regular basis, success rates of this magnitude are unheard of in the United States where competitions are the exception, not the rule.[3]

In the European Union, most competitions are strictly regulated and, if limited to a one-stage process, are judged anonymously. The gestation process of competitions differs from country to country. In Finland, for instance, jurors have traditionally been involved in editing the programme as well as in judging. In France, open competitions have given way to invited competitions, with the participation of young architects based on

Renzo Piano and Richard Rogers, (London, UK/Paris, France) Pompidou Centre, Paris, France
Competition 1972
Completion 1977

Piano and Rogers won the Beaubourg competition over 681 entries from around the world. It became the favourite meeting place for an entire generation of young Parisians

portfolios. Germany has even used a lottery system to select a number of architects to take part alongside pre-selected, higher profile firms.

Many architects are aware of pitfalls they may face when entering a competition in their own country and calculate their chances accordingly. Whereas competitions in Europe, which are administered either under the auspices of the national associations or on a non-regional basis according to EU rules, are relatively transparent, one may have to read between the lines before entering a competition in the US or China.

Criteria for Entering

When deciding to enter a competition, most architects agree on what to look for:

- Is the project which is the subject of the competition adequately financed?
- Has the site for the project already been acquired by the client?

- Is the jury known, and are design professionals in the majority? The presence of a large number of laypersons on the jury could be an indication that architects may be engaged in something which has more in common with a 'beauty contest'.
- Is the competition anonymous, or is a presentation in person one of the requirements?
- In the case of a civic project, would a change in government place a project in jeopardy?
- What are the presentation requirements in invited competitions? Are they excessive in view of the amount of compensation which is guaranteed by the client?
- Is there a sharp divergence of architectural language among invited competition participants? Preferences for certain architectural styles, where a client may ignore a jury's recommendation for a modern design in favour of something more traditional, can occasionally lead to bizarre results.
- If it is a two-stage competition with an open first stage, are there paid offices taking part in the second stage, without having to face elimination in the first stage? Since their identity may be known during the second stage, it is possible that they may be favoured over an unpaid team with a lesser reputation.

Architects are sometimes motivated to enter competitions for reasons other than winning:

- Some offices may treat a competition as an exercise to gain expertise in an area, such as school design, courthouses, etc., where they have had little or no experience. Even though they may not be awarded first prize in an open competition, an honourable mention or citation can be enough to raise the profile of a firm so that it may later be seriously considered on a shortlist for a future project in that field.
- The project may be so interesting that an architect will enter regardless of apparent organisational shortcomings in the process. In any case, it may provide a firm with the opportunity to think about ideas it would otherwise not explore on a day-to-day basis.
- Competitions can act as a morale booster within an office, where working on a large project over a long period of time begins to wear on the nerves. Entering a competition during such a period can revive the creative juices.

Behnisch, Behnisch &
Partner (Stuttgart, Germany)
Harbourside Performing
Arts Centre Competition,
Bristol, UK
Competition 1996
Model shot

Although many of the
participants in this competition
produced very elaborate
schemes, BB&P did just
the opposite, relying mainly
on sketches and a design
strategy which the jury
bought into. Due to a change
in the political climate and
reductions in funding, the
project had to be abandoned

And Once You Enter...

To excel in a competition:

- The main idea should be very readable and apparent to the passing juror. The best idea is of no use if it is lost because the designer failed to present it in a clear and striking manner.
- Jurors do look at sections and site plans for ease of circulation and logic in organisation. A clear section and site plan may be more compelling than a complicated – and possibly expensive – rendering which may take several hours to complete.
- Architects should present surfaces in enough detail so that jurors may perceive what the project is actually going to look like. In some cases where the facade treatment on the competition board was vague, jurors passed over that entry in favour of one where the facade presentation was executed in finer detail.
- Pay attention to the rules. Any number of good competition entries have been disqualified for breaking a rule. A good jury may overlook minor offences and assume that they can be resolved in design development, but a strict competition adviser may summarily penalise such an error by disqualification. If a rule is to be broken, the reason better be one that will improve the project exponentially.
- Not only novices, but also experienced architects can hone their techniques and improve design strategies by examining winning competition designs from past years. There are enough examples of large firms referring to past competitions before submitting designs for a

major project. Most say they do not craft their design to respond to the composition of a jury. However, by knowing who is on a jury, it may be an indication of how much an architect may push the design envelope – or not.

Simplicity and clarity usually win out over a complicated scheme, regardless of how sophisticated the presentation. This is especially true in open competitions, where the jurors have less time to spend examining each entry.

Invited Competitions

Once a firm is well established, its principals will probably be reluctant to enter an open competition. But their chances of winning improve dramatically when they are invited to participate in a limited competition with five or less participants. Still, even taking part in invited competitions can pose a challenge to a firm's finances. Charles Gwathmey once remarked that 'one has to win one out of three of these to at least break even'.[4] The pressures placed on Canadian architect Arthur Erickson's firm after several narrow misses in some major invited competitions in the 1980s no doubt contributed to the firm's financial problems and its subsequent reorganisation.

On the other hand, the demands which some clients make on architects to get jobs can only be considered blatant exploitation. According to Ralph Johnson of Perkins and Will, it is not unusual for clients even to ask for a model in a competitive interview process, an effort which he equated with doing an invited competition.[5] Nicholas Quennell of the New York firm of Quennell Rothschild Associates concurs: 'If competitions were the norm, offices might respond the same as they do to RfPs [Request for Proposals]. Writing proposals is an enormous amount of work, too. It takes almost as much work as responding to a competition, maybe more'.[6]

It is important to note that, until recently, American architects have been almost evenly divided in their support or non-support for competitions. The divide has gradually narrowed, however, as high profile firms, used to gaining commissions based on their reputations, are increasingly being asked to participate in invited competitions, both at home and abroad. Although they often grumble about the cost of entering invited competitions, they simultaneously relish the 'star' status which participation conveys.

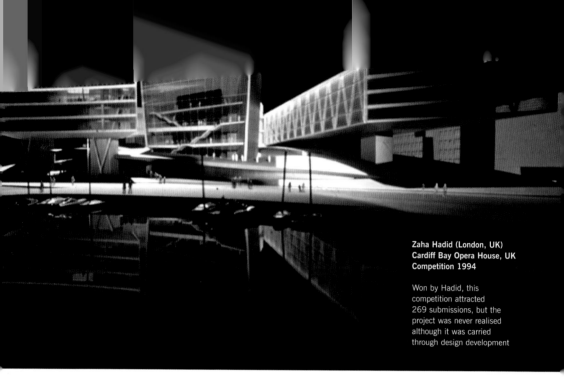

Zaha Hadid (London, UK)
Cardiff Bay Opera House, UK
Competition 1994

Won by Hadid, this
competition attracted
269 submissions, but the
project was never realised
although it was carried
through design development

One of the biggest boosts for the invited competition format occurred with the completion of Frank Gehry's competition-winning design for the new Guggenheim Museum in Bilbao. The accolades which accompanied the opening of that museum were almost unmatched in recent memory. It immediately became a worldwide attraction and in its first year alone drew over a million visitors to a city on Spain's north coast which had not previously been on anyone's itinerary.

The Two-Stage Format

Whereas competitions sponsored by the International Union of Architects (UIA) are still, for the most part, anonymous, more and more open competitions – in the US as well as Europe – are being conducted in two stages. In what one can mainly understand as a concession to clients, the two-stage competition places an additional burden on participants, in terms of both effort and financial resources. The latter is almost always the case in the second stage, as most architects complain that compensation offered by the client seldom covers the cost of expanded presentation requirements. Many architects contend that the design refinement during the second stage – besides the additional hardship it places on the participants – adds little in terms of design improvement. Marion Weiss and Michael Manfredi of Weiss Manfredi Architects, New

York, who have won several competitions, are quite explicit about the downside of two-stage competitions:

> If you win a competition in the first stage, it's about ideas. Often, second stages are excuses to window ideas out on the basis of experience, team make-up and other variables, which really shouldn't be central to the competition... Enormous joy, care, spirit, passion goes into a first stage; second guessing and caution is brought bear in the second stage. That is not what we do competitions for.[7]

The second stage often includes a requirement that teams be formed to substantiate expertise in various areas. When large projects are on the table, cross-pollination takes over and teams consisting of architects, landscape architects, acousticians, engineers of many shades and artists combine to craft a collaborative scheme. The second stage usually requires more detailed drawings, models and cost estimates – even Power Point. Although some architects may go into a big project with the intention of doing 'whatever it takes', a low budget strategy, although risky in the eyes of some, can reap dividends. In the 1996 Harbourside Performing Arts Centre Competition in Bristol, UK, for example, where most of the high profile firms produced a huge number of drawings and even scale models, the Stuttgart firm of Behnisch, Behnisch & Partner won by presenting a number of sketches illustrating the central idea. A number of miniature sketch models were used to show how such a building would work.[8] Although the strategy was successful, the project never advanced beyond the design development stage, as the project was cancelled.

Some Lost Opportunities

The history of architectural competitions abounds with examples where winning designs never see the light of day. In that respect, it is not unlike the construction industry as a whole, where projects begin under the auspices of one architect and end up being realised by another. It would seem, however, that a competition winner's chances of realising a project are better in northern Europe, Canada and Japan than has been the case in the US.

When a competition-winning design for a very high profile project is not built, you may be sure that it will certainly attract more attention from the media than would be the case had it simply been the result of a conventional interview process. One winning design which did not make

**Barton Myers Associates
(Los Angeles, CA, US)
Phoenix Municipal
Government Center,
Arizona, USA
Competition 1985**

A change in city government
after an election spelled
doom for Myers's winning
campus-like plan **(bottom)**
for government offices.

A high-rise office building
by Langdon Wilson **(left)** was
erected instead

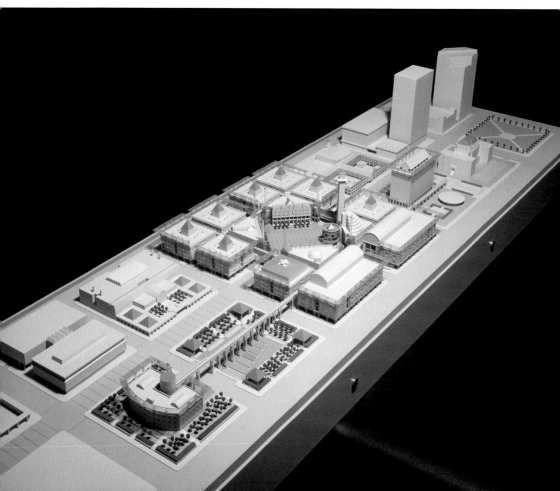

it beyond design development and received intense media coverage in the mid-1990s was the Cardiff Bay Opera House competition, won by Zaha Hadid. A vivid and detailed account of that competition and its aftermath has been given by one of the principal players, Nicholas Crickhowell. His account of the contractual tug of war, hidden agendas and the final cancellation of the project is the stuff of a mystery thriller. Still, because of all the publicity, Hadid emerged as a major voice on the world stage and was subsequently invited to take part in a number of competitions.[9]

Getting a competition-winning design built in the US depends on so many factors, but it usually comes down to the client – and the economy. The Phoenix Municipal Government Center was one of those competitions which produced a very interesting and viable result, but was destined to be scuttled in favour of a less ambitious high-rise project. The competition took place in 1985, at the height of the Post-Modern fad in the US. Thus, it could come as no surprise that the architectural language of the majority of the participants, including the winner, leaned in that direction. As was the case with all of the competition finalists, the winning scheme by Barton Myers proposed a campus plan, integrating the various city agencies in a park-like setting. Instead of embracing the winner, the incoming administration changed the programme and scratched Myers's highly sophisticated civic gestures along with ex-Mayor Terry Goddard's noble urban vision for the west side of downtown. Still, the high-rise building which the city ultimately built in place of the competition winner was one of the few high-rise buildings whose elevations actually responded to the differences in the climate and solar orientation, with views represented by the cardinal points. Moreover, the competition raised the design awareness of the community, as was attested by the quality of the many civic projects which followed.[10]

Another competition where a regime change determined the course of a project was in Rancho Mirage, California. When a two-stage masterplan competition for a new civic centre took place there in 1990, the winner was Arthur Golding & Associates of Los Angeles. Shortly before a contract could be signed by the design architect with the city, a local election took place and a new administration took over – after having campaigned against the design.

Tastes among laypersons have also served to determine the fate of competition winners. In Berkeley, California, where a competition for a public safety building took place in 1996, the winning design of Holt

**Holt Hinshaw Architects
(San Francisco, CA, US)
Berkeley Public Safety
Building, Berkeley,
California, US
Competition 1996**

After the winning competition
design by Holt Hinshaw was
discarded **(top and middle)**,
the commission was
subsequently awarded to a
non-participant, Robert
AM Stern who realised the
project **(bottom)**

Hinshaw of San Francisco (they also won the Astronauts Memorial Competition) was dropped after a two-stage design process. The competition was not only important for the selection of the public safety building; it was to set a standard for the architecture of other buildings which were to follow, including renovation and expansion of the city hall, courts and library. Instead of the modernist design by Holt Hinshaw, the city chose to hire Robert AM Stern, who in turn provided the city with a more traditional scheme.

Although it is hardly surprising to find a large number of European, Asian and South American architects who have risen to the top of their profession by winning competitions, we find an unusual number of US-based architects who have received a real career boost by participating. Besides European and Japanese architects – Snøhetta, UN Studio, Foreign Office Architects, Dominique Perrault, Jean Nouvel, Axel Schultes, Toyo Ito, Heikkinen + Komonen, and Allies and Morrison, just to name a few – North American-based designers like Helmut Jahn (Murphy Jahn), Moshe Safdie, Steven Holl, Craig Hartman (SOM), Ralph Johnson (Perkins & Will), Arquitectonica, Michael Graves, Peter Eisenman, Curtis Fentress (Fentress Bradburn) and Bruce Kuwabara (Kuwabara Payne McKenna Blumberg, Toronto) have found that their stock has risen dramatically after performing well in a competition. Competing may not be the only method of career advancement for an architect, but no award in the profession – with the possible exception of the Pritzker – quite matches the stamp of approval conferred by winning a major design competition.[11]

Notes
1. In his book, *A New London*, Rogers castigated the UK's Thatcher government for its lack of a viable urban design strategy, suggesting that competitions should be widely used in the public realm in the UK.
2. Interview with Axel Schultes, *Competitions*, Volume 7, No. 2, Summer 1997, p 61.
3. Interview with Günther Schaller of Behnisch, Behnisch & Partners, *Competitions*, Volume 12, No. 3, Fall 2002, p 38.
4. 'Competitions in the US; Sending Mixed Signals', *Oculus*, Volume 60, No. 5, January 1998, p 17.
5. Conversation with Ralph Johnson, January 20, 2001.
6. Interview with Nicholas Quennell, *Competitions*, Volume 7, No. 4, Winter 1997–8, p 61.
7. Interview with Marion Weiss and Michael Manfredi, *Competitions*, Volume 13, No. 1, Spring 2003, p 47.

8. Interview with Günther Schaller in *Competitions*, Volume 12, No. 3, Fall 2002, p 44.
9. Nicholas Crickhowell, *Opera House Lottery*, University of Wales Press (Cardiff), 1997.
10. The other competition participants were: Charles Moore/ Urban Innovations Group and HNTB; Tai Soo Kim/Hartfor Design Group; Robert AM Stern Architects and DWL Architects-Planners; Leason Pomeroy Associates and Ricardo Legorreta Arquitectos; GSAS Architects-Planners and Michael Graves, Architect; Hammond Beeby and Babka Architects; Arata Isozaki; Barton Myers Associates; ELS Design Group and Robert Rannkenberger. The four finalists were Myers, Graves, Isozaki and Legorreta.
11. Among the 26 Pritzker winners to date, at least half had already won a competition prior to the award.

Government Buildings

Axel Schultes/Charlotte Frank
(Berlin, Germany)
German Chancellery Building,
Berlin, Germany
Invited Competition 1994
Completion 2001

Interior perspective

Architects are presented with special challenges when designing today's government buildings: how to address security concerns while providing the structures with a 'presence' befitting the status they represent as government symbols.

In replacing feudal princes and ecclesiastical potentates as clients, national, regional and local governments have become the patrons of the modern age. The commissions they provide help sustain the lifeblood of many a firm. When government ministries and municipalities stage design competitions for these projects, it is usually for the express purpose of obtaining better design; but it can also give younger architects the opportunity to compete on a level playing field against more established offices.

Whereas most European countries require competitions for the design of public buildings, only one state in the United States, Minnesota, has such a statute on the books, and even there it is no longer applied in a strict sense. Still, the United States General Services Administration (GSA) has recently staged a number of invited competitions based on a shortlisting process, starting with a Request for Qualifications. These competitions have produced designs for a number of federal courthouses, having the effect of pushing the design envelope and marking a departure from their stolid, neo-classical forebears.

But even the GSA is not immune from parochial tastes when commissioning a winning design. Recently, a competition for the design of a federal courthouse was held in Cape Girardeau, Missouri, a town of 60,000 on the Mississippi River south of St Louis. A previous design by a Chicago firm, arrived at through the regular interview process, was turned down by the town as being too modern. After some time had passed a competition for the same project was organised with a roster of participants which did not include the authors of the original design. Fentress Bradburn of Denver won the competition with a relatively traditional design using red brick – the material of choice in the neighbourhood – as cladding for the facade. Although the firm considered using white or yellow brick for the facade, a phone call from a state politician killed that idea.

Democracy and the Security Issue

Because of security concerns, the design of government buildings – courthouses in particular – has undergone a radical transformation.

Richard Rogers Partners
(London, UK)
Bordeaux Courts Building,
Bordeaux, France
Completion 1998

Perspective illustrating
administrative offices on
right and pods serving as
courtrooms on the left.
Rogers won this competition
after the results of an
initial competition were
overturned because of a
perceived problem with
the construction materials

Especially in the United States, where the traditional county courthouse represented a symbol of openness and accessibility, fear of terrorist acts, both from perpetrators within as well as from without, has heightened security concerns and had an enormous impact on the design process. Gone forever are the days when one could enter government buildings from all points of the compass and roam the halls unimpeded. In new courthouses, there is only one entrance for public visitors, another for judges, and occasionally a third very secure entrance on a subterranean level for those on trial. Where circulation throughout these courts was once a simple matter, it has now become one of the primary issues architects must deal with in order to gain favour with competition juries.

Italy had to deal with security issues during the trials of members of the Red Brigade and later with the Mafia, and Great Britain implemented heightened security during the peak of IRA violence. But, with a few exceptions, the most notable being Paris, European countries still do not require the level of security which is stipulated for government buildings in the United States. As a result, we find new government buildings in cities such as Bordeaux, where a courts building with glass facades borders directly onto a main thoroughfare. That courthouse, by Richard Rogers Partnership, not only extends to the limits of the property line to the sidewalk, but the courts themselves, appearing as suspended pods, are highly visible from an easily accessible entrance from a side street. Thus, we are presented with the illusion of total transparency.

Axel Schultes/Charlotte Frank
(Berlin, Germany)
German Chancellery Building,
Berlin, Germany
Invited Competition 1994
Completion 2001

View of courtyard from east
showing the sculpture by
Eduardo Chillida which has
since been removed to the
interior of the building. This
frontal view is, unfortunately,
only available to visitors to
the Chancellery.

In Germany, where the idea of open democracy has been in the foreground since World War II, the German parliament building in Bonn is a classic case where the architect, Günther Behnisch, endowed the structure with open views into the parliamentary chamber, as if providing the electorate with a direct connection to the proceedings. When the transfer of the German capital to Berlin took place after the reunification of that nation, this idea was carried over with the renovation of the Reichstag building: Norman Foster's dome provides an opening through which the public can have a direct view into the parliamentary chamber below. Axel Schultes's design for the new seat of the German Chancellor next to the Reichstag – the result of an invited competition – anticipated a connection with the public realm. Although the result was a very commendable building, security concerns have had the effect of obscuring the view of the building from most accessible vantage points. Thus, the only real close-up which is accessible to the public is to the rear of the building facing the canal, and this view is available only to those who pass by boat.

In Australia and Canada, where geopolitics suggests that terrorist threats are not top priority concerns, the security issue, when it comes to the design of state government buildings, is hardly on the front burner. Both countries have turned to the competition process to assist in the selection of an architect for major projects. In Australia, one of the biggest competitions in the 1970s was for the design of the High Court of Australia, won by Edwards, Madigan, Torzillo & Briggs in the nation's

Competing Globally in Architecture Competitions

capital, Canberra. Somewhat reminiscent in appearance of the Boston City Hall winner a decade earlier, this building was connected by a pedestrian bridge to the Australian National Gallery of Art.

Public Buildings in the US

After the destruction of the Murrah Federal Building in Oklahoma City, but even more so after 11 September, programmes for the design of courts buildings and US embassies have become even more involved. On the positive side, all this has led to the use of materials such as shatterproof glass, allowing for more flexibility in determining the footprint of such buildings and providing visitors at the very least with a visual illusion of a more democratic structure.

Municipal government buildings, whether city halls or courts, or a combination of both, have been the most frequent objects of design competitions in the US, especially over the past decade. This is in marked contrast to Europe, where population growth has mainly been in existing urban centres, which already have their Rathaus and Hotel de Ville. There, it was usually a case of adding, rather than incorporating, numerous functions scattered in various locations into one brand new structure. Not surprisingly, we find many such competitions in the US occurring in the fastest growing states, California, Arizona, Nevada and Colorado, where new towns spring up and existing villages become small cities at the drop of a hat.

In California, competitions for civic centres began to occur as early as the 1970s in Fremont – later abandoned because it was situated directly on an earthquake fault – and resulted in 1982 in the Beverly Hills Civic Center competition won by Charles Moore and the Urban Innovations Group. Other competitions for community administrative centres in California followed: Escondido (1984), Santa Clarita (1991), Rancho Mirage (1991), Parris (1991), Redwood City (1994), Cathedral City (1995), Foster City (1999) and Contra Costa Government Center (2000). Most of these, located in the fast-growing Los Angeles and San Francisco Bay metro areas, were close enough to the main job markets to allow for commuting. About half of the winners were ultimately built, with the rest falling by the wayside for various reasons – political, economic, and even aesthetic. It was this latter issue – that of architectural expression – which led the Cathedral City Council to overturn the jury's choice of James Alcorn & Associates as the winner of the competition in favour of a neo-

Left and bottom
**Kuwabara Payne McKenna
Blumberg
(Toronto, Canada)
Kitchener City Hall,
Ontario, Canada
Competition 1989
Completion 1993**

This open, national
competition in 1989 drew
153 entries. KPMB of Toronto
won in the second stage with
a design which created a
large, U-shaped plaza in front
of the main entrance to the
building. The top image
shows the rotunda's interior

**Opposite
Golemon/Bolullo Partnership
– Harry Golemon
and Mario Bolullo
(Houston, TX, US)
Mobile Government Plaza,
Alabama, US
Competition 1995**

classical design by MWM Architects with Thomas Smith of the University of Notre Dame. Other major civic projects decided by competitions in the western US were in Las Vegas – the Clark County Government Center, won by Fentress Bradburn Architects – and the Denver Civic Center, which was advertised as a design build competition.

An ingenious solution for the design of a building complex to house both city and county government agencies as well as the district courts was the result of an open competition in 1991 held in Mobile, Alabama – a combined city/county effort. The winning design by Golemon Bolullo Architects of Houston indicated two buildings connected by a great atrium, whereby the courts were located on one side of the atrium and the functions of the city and county government agencies were positioned at the same levels on the other side. This allowed for a seamless fusion of agencies in case the two governments ever became the subject of an administrative merger.

The Toronto City Hall competition of 1958, won by Viljo Revell of Finland, set a standard for design of civic buildings in Canada. It was followed by several competitions for the design of city halls in the 1980s and early 1990s. These included city hall competitions in Edmonton, Alberta (1980); Calgary, Alberta (1981); Mississauga (1982) and Kitchener (1989), both in Ontario; and Richmond, British Columbia (1997). Some of these were open – both in one- and two-stages – and

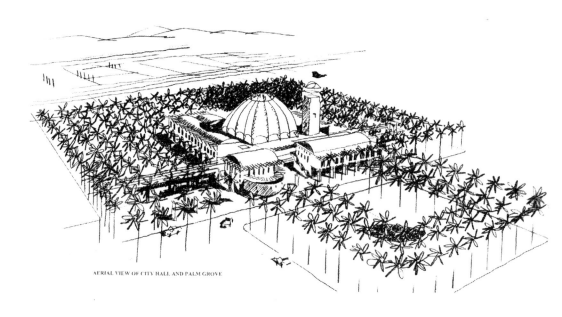

AERIAL VIEW OF CITY HALL AND PALM GROVE

one, although open, was limited to architects residing in the province (Calgary). In contrast to the US experience, almost all of these city halls were completed as designed by the winning architects.

One of the very few great civic competitions which combined planning with architecture was for the design of Brasilia. Much as Peter the Great had created a city out of a swamp on the Neva River on the Baltic Sea, Brazil decided to move its capital from Rio de Janeiro to a barren site in the interior. This was one of the few notable civic competitions in Latin America, as the majority of government offices were in older buildings, only supplemented on the rare occasion by a new government ministry building.

There were competitions for some provincial government buildings in Argentina: Coriado Testa won two competitions for the initial design and then an addition for a new administration building in La Pampa in 1955 and 1995. Odile Suarez also won a competition for a similar structure in Lomas de Zamora and a competition for a new government building in Cordoba was the object of a competition in 1990. In Chile, the highest profile competition for a government project was for the Square of the Moneda Palace in Santiago, also in 1990.

**Cathedral City Civic Center,
California, US
Competition 1995**

**This page
Commission
MWM Architects/
Thomas G Smith
(Oakland, CA, US/
Notre Dame, IN, US)**
Aerial view of completed
project with new facade
treatment (right) which
indicates a strong
Mediterranean flavour as
opposed to the original
competition entry (below).
Although this entry was
ranked lower than the other
finalists by the professional
jury, the team was awarded
the commission by local
authorities

**Opposite
Jury Choice as Winner
James Alcorn & Associates
(La Jolla, CA, US)**
Aerial view of competition
scheme

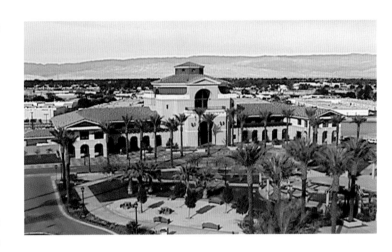

**Lee/Timchula Architects –
John MY Lee/Michael
Timchula
(New York, US)
Shenzhen Citizens Centre,
Shenzhen, China
Competition 1996
Completion 2003**

The American firm won
this invited competition in
1996 as part of a greater
masterplan for the city

Competing Globally in Architecture Competitions

Civic Buildings in Asia

Cultural facilities and transportation-related structures were the subject of most of the competitions which took place in Japan and China in the 1990s. In Japan, these sometimes took the form of multipurpose community buildings, which also included health services as well as police and city administrations. Typical of such a complex was the Kawasato Village multipurpose town centre with a medical facility, library, museum and welfare centre, designed by Takefumi Aida.

The creation of new towns in China has resulted in several competitions for public buildings. In Shenzhen, one of the fastest growing of the cities in China's 'New Economic Zones', an invited, urban design competition which included a new 'Citizens' Centre' was won by the American-based firm, Lee/Timchula of New York in 1996. Their presentation was remarkable for their extensive use of sophisticated computer renderings and was one of many invited competitions which took place in China during the past decade. In the aftermath of the high profile Pudong Masterplan Competition, won by Richard Rogers in the early 1990s, an entire new, western-style city took shape just across the river from Shanghai. Subsequently, the Chinese staged several invited competitions for new towns, most of which were won by European and American architects.

Competing in China does have its downside, however, as their jury proceedings often lack the transparency one finds in Japan and the West. Many firms also have complained that the Chinese are very adept at driving very hard bargains after the competition has been won. And once the construction phase begins, ensuring that the local construction contractors adhere to western construction standards can be a frustrating experience. Chinese architects familiar with the western competition system would also like to see the state promote more open competitions, mainly for the benefit of a new cadre of young architects trained in their home country and abroad.

The worldwide demand for civic administrative structures will probably occur mainly in areas of high population growth – in Asia and, eventually, Africa. It remains to be seen how long western firms will be able to compete for some of these high profile commissions as the architectural professions in those countries narrow the profile gap with the West.

Eugene, Oregon Federal Courthouse (1999)

John Morris Dixon

The General Services Administration's Design Excellence Program continues to search for better ways to encourage design quality. Widely praised for its improved method of qualification-based architect selection, GSA has in a few cases added a competition stage to the process, inviting finalists selected on the basis of qualifications.

GSA recently asked professional adviser Donald Stastny to organise design competitions for two modestly scaled federal courthouses, one in Springfield, Massachusetts, and the other a continent away in Eugene, Oregon. These projects, with six to nine courtrooms each, are considered representative of more than 100 courthouses GSA foresees will be required in medium-sized cities over the next decade. For the most part, previous federal courts in such cities have been embedded in more general federal buildings. As separate structures, the courthouses covered in these competitions are taking along with them closely related functions such as probation offices and US Marshals. In line with broader federal environmental objectives, they are being located to reinforce existing urban cores.

The juries for these competitions were not directly responsible for choosing the design teams. They reported back to an Evaluation Board for each courthouse, which selected the competing teams to begin with, and the board then integrated their rating of the team's capabilities with the jury's rating of the competition concepts. Even after all this expert evaluation, the final decision on the design team rested with GSA officials.

GSA's Chief Architect, Edward Feiner, sees the insertion of a design competition phase into the agency's selection process for such projects as a way to attract firms of design distinction that might not otherwise pursue GSA's commissions. While one of the great virtues of GSA's established selection method is that design accomplishments are adequately weighed in the qualification-based decision, what counts is past accomplishment rather than present potential.

Although past achievement was also a major consideration in determining the shortlist of participating firms, a competition can favour the up-and-coming designers, confident that their current design skills can carry the day, while discouraging firms preferring to be judged on the resources and previous performance of the teams they've assembled. Given these shifts in the odds of winning a commission, several architects who competed for these two projects acknowledged that the competition phase convinced them to pursue these jobs.

In order to test and refine the procedures for such competitions, Stastny was brought in not just to manage these two contests, but to follow them up with a guidebook to architect selection under GSA's Design Excellence Program. It will cover both the two-stage process, which has been more frequently followed to date, and the three-stage strategy that includes a design competition.

Provisionally, the selection sequence to be outlined in this guide can be summarised as follows:
Stage I: Submission of portfolios by firms and 'lead designers' for review by an Architecture/Engineering Evaluation Board to select six to eight designers to advance to Stage II.
Stage II: Assembling of A/E teams, submission of Standard Forms 254 and 255, interviews of selected teams, and evaluations by Board - leading to either (a) a ranking of participants as a basis for awarding

Winning Entry
Morphosis/DLR Architecture
(Santa Monica, CA, USA/
Portland, OR, USA)

The jury found this scheme by far the most efficient from a planning viewpoint. There was no unnecessary duplication of circulation. Although the irregularity of the building's volumes and silhouette may prove to be controversial for a courthouse, the concept would work extremely well from a functional perspective. Thom Mayne, lead designer and principal of Morphosis, observes that the building programme was so demanding that it took virtually all the team's time to work it out. Since, in the jury's view, they managed to resolve it more successfully than any of the others, it was time well spent. Mayne now feels no qualms about starting the design process over, as the situation demands, verifying some competition decisions and revising others. His presentation boards show photos of evolving study models, lined up in a band that suggests that the design could continue to evolve. The jurors were as impressed with the scheme's formal qualities as its functional ones, and the jury chair had to emphasise to the Evaluation Board that they were not seduced by its formal virtuosity

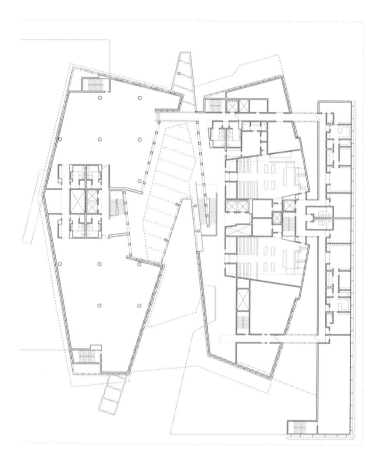

the commission (two-stage process) or (b) a shortlist of three to five finalists to participate in Stage III. Stage III: Finalist teams take part in a 35-day Concept Design Competition, with modest presentation limits. An independent jury evaluates them anonymously and ranks them, submitting written and oral reports to the Evaluation Board as the basis for a final recommendation.

Some of the procedural fine points of these two competitions – not necessarily precedents for future ones – are worth noting. In each case, GSA in Washington appointed an independent jury of three individuals: the dean of an architecture school, an architect who had designed a federal courthouse for GSA, and an architect who is also a journalist. The jury chair (in each case, the dean) presented the jury's recommendations verbally to the Evaluation Board.

Eugene, Oregon

Eugene is a university town sometimes considered to be 'Berkeley North', retaining some of the idealism and the counterculture manifestations of the 1960s. Tie-dyed shirts can still be seen. The judges who will hold court here, however, tend to have more traditional world views. Eugene's relative scarcity of sunshine makes extensive glazing desirable, and its moderate temperatures impose hardly any penalty in terms of heat gain or loss. The site remains undecided in part because of controversy over the first-choice location: it adjoins an historic residential area that would be at the courthouse's back door.

For the Eugene competition, the jurors used a scoring system that awarded up to 50 points for each entry. The final ranking was then based on a weighted combination of the jury's scoring of the entries (counting 40 percent) and the board's rating

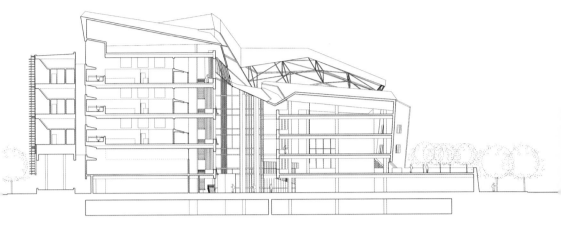

determined in Stage II (counting 60 percent). Statistically, the jury's ranking was likely to carry more weight, because the teams the board selected out of a larger field were likely to be clustered at the upper end of their rating scale. Considering only the board's finalists, the jury was likely to come up with a greater spread between highest and lowest-rated contenders, giving their scores added leverage in the final calculation. It is entirely possible, of course, for the jury to give some entries close scores, in which case the board's prior evaluation could well determine which entry is ultimately rated higher. In this case, at any rate, the jury's highest-ranking firm became the board's first recommendation, even though the board had not initially ranked it first.

Stastny found that the approach 'worked', but the Eugene methodology 'required higher maintenance to ensure equity throughout'.[1] The guidebook's recommendations, he reports, will 'not rely on numbers alone', hewing more closely to the Springfield model.

Everyone involved in this competition stresses that the jury was not selecting a design, as such, but rather rating the potential of each design team. The objective of competitions is often said to be for the choice of architects, not designs, but here everyone seems especially aware that the commissioned team may scrap the competition concept and start over. For one thing, everyone realises that the competition was deliberately carried out on a tight schedule (35 days) for relatively modest compensation ($25,000 for each competing team), with limited presentations (four 30 x 40 inch boards, no text except on the boards and no models, although model photos were permitted).

Detailed functional programmes tested the planning ingenuity of the designers, who also had to give special attention to symbolism, urbanistic relationships and environmental considerations. But in this case the local circumstances were not fully resolved. Either of two full-block sites could be the final one, although this was not a critical drawback, since the city's blocks are identical. Finally, GSA was not the ultimate client, but essentially the developer and landlord for these facilities, so the wishes of the judicial staffs occupying (who were represented on the Evaluation Boards) would undoubtedly figure strongly as the designs evolved. Compromises between owners, tenants and architects on where money would be spent are almost a certainty. (As one GSA official puts it, the judges are often ready 'to eliminate the foundations' in favour of features dear to them.)

Jury Criteria

Of particular interest to jurors was the relationship of the courthouse to its urban setting. Low ratings went to concepts that seemed unaffected by their surroundings, as if they could have been dropped into any city. The jurors were put off by schemes that established symbolic fronts but turned forbidding walls towards neighbours on the other three sides. Some subtlety was required in the configuration of garage entrances, truck docks and sally ports for prisoner vans.

The main test of courthouse planning is how the architects sort out the various types of circulation – public, jurors, judges, prisoners, etc. – without excessive elevators and corridors. The movement of

Left
**Koetter, Kim &
Associates/GBD Architecture
(Boston, MA, USA/
Portland, OR, USA)**

Pedestrian perspective of
courthouse

The jury was much impressed
with this scheme's exceptional
presentation, which clearly
addressed each of the design
criteria. The full-block site is
divided, one half for the
courthouse and the other for
a Courthouse Square. A
'Public Porch' with trellises
and a glass roof is integral
to both the square and the
building. A glazed lobby
at one end of this porch
introduces visitors to an
unusually simple, readable
circulation system. Dropping
at one end from four stories
to two, the building includes
a skylighted atrium as a
circulation node in the lower
portion and a gardened roof
terrace opening from the
judges' chambers. The
chimney effects of the tall
lobby and the lower atrium
form part of the low-energy-
demand environmental
systems

Finalist
**Thomas Hacker & Associates
(Portland, OR, USA)**

Middle Model perspective
Bottom Lighting strategy

The architects felt that the
building should look very open,
yet have a commanding
presence, so they broke it up
into visible blocks of
courtrooms and vertical
circulation elements, with
glassed-in lobby and concourse
spaces in between. The
prominent front stairway would
have quotations on the law
inscribed on its glass walls.
Views towards the two buttes
that bracket downtown Eugene
were considered crucial in
laying out the public spaces.
The major courts, located on
the third and fourth floors,
appear to rise from a two-storey
elevated 'ground plane',
encompassing a broad terrace
on top of the entry portico.
Landscaping would represent
the wild and cultivated terrains
of Oregon, with a swatch of
evergreen forest to one side of
the front and a cherry grove on
the other. (The architects note
that an especially high
proportion of cases heard
in this courthouse will involve
forests and other environmental
resources.) An effort was made
to give neighbours on all sides
a non-forbidding view of
the building. The jurors were
concerned that splitting
the courtrooms into groups
increased the number of
elevators and stairwells
required.

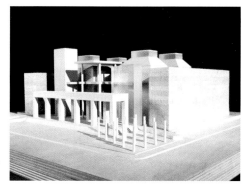

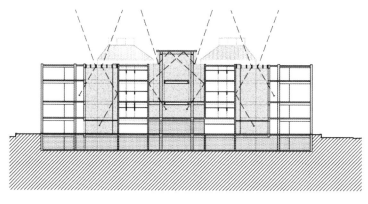

Right
Finalist
Antoine Predock Architect
and Yost Grube Hall Architects
(Albuquerque, NM,
US/Portland, OR, US)
'Oregon Room' perspective

The 'Oregon Space' is the heart – or better yet the lungs – of the scheme developed under lead designer Antoine Predock. Natural convection within this space is used to introduce fresh air and expel heat-gain through ports at roof level. Photovoltaic cells supplement these currents by powering heat-port fans at times of maximum need. In much of Predock's work, architecture as an expression of natural terrain features is a prevailing theme: here the symbolic mountainside of terraces in the Oregon Room recycles roof-collected rainwater through tiers of vegetation to a reflecting pool outside in the plaza, dubbed the 'Northwest Space'. Along its route to ground level, the water is diverted through pipes to cool the structure's thermal mass. Elsewhere in the building, glazed corridors along the exterior thermally buffer the occupied spaces, while also admitting daylight

prisoners into and through the building has security implications, which are generally dealt with in proven ways. Whereas terrorist acts have to be considered, the need to make the building a welcoming symbol of the law precludes fortress-like treatments. The designs presented to these juries show controlled entry points, of course, but generally have ample lobbies and porticoes on the public front, outside security, to effectively buffer the more sensitive and populated courtrooms and offices in case of assault. Sustainable environmental strategies called for in the programme were met with a variety of measures such as the use of ground water and night air for cooling. Daylighting is stressed in several designs, with courtrooms offering outdoor views or, alternatively, skylights or clerestories. In most of the schemes, only the courtrooms and offices have precisely controlled air-conditioning, allowing for more variable conditions in lobbies, for instance, with untreated outside air used whenever possible.

Although not to be regarded as preliminary designs for the courthouses in question, effective handling of these complex design issues clearly established the teams' capabilities in the eyes of the juries. Jurors for the Eugene courthouse competition were: Michael Fifield (Chair), head of the architecture department at the University of Oregon, Eugene, William Pedersen of Kohn Pedersen Fox & Associates, New York, and Robert Ivy, Editor, *Architectural Record*, New York.

Conclusion

Introducing a competition stage to the GSA selection process has not and will not open up the field of federal courthouse design to emerging firms (though such firms may win smaller GSA commissions). For these buildings, the judging of a team's capabilities based on past accomplishments necessarily limits the range of firms invited to compete. But the competition process favours 'lead designers' such as Antoine Predock or Morphosis, winner of the Eugene competition, who are known for design originality in actual built work. As for team capabilities, Mayne's firm, Morphosis, has complemented its proven design skills with the resources of a joint venture firm. Reviewing these competing courthouse schemes, it is striking how divergent the concepts are for one site. Though every entry presumably responds to its physical context, along with a programme and environmental demands, little pressure towards conformity is apparent. Participation in a competition usually pushes architects towards more idiosyncratic design than they might otherwise come up with. It will be interesting to see whether the selected team will produce a building close in character to their competition scheme. Morphosis's approach to form, with much subtle folding of surfaces, is appreciated in the architectural community but may encounter resistance in Eugene. Public attitudes towards avant-garde design are now being altered, however, by the popular appeal of Frank Gehry's Bilbao museum, much as past breakthrough structures altered expectations (Richardson's Trinity Church, for instance, or the pavilions of the 1893 Chicago Fair). GSA's commitment to the design excellence of its completed courthouse projects has been impressive, so we can expect support for creativity in Eugene. We can only hope that GSA's efforts to lift the curse of drab expediency from federal work will continue and will encourage comparable efforts at every level of government.

Notes
1. All quotes in this essay are from its original publication in *Competitions*, Volume 9, No. 4, Winter 1999.

Case Study
Canadian Embassy, Berlin (1999)
G Stanley Collyer

In what was a radical move for the Canadian government, the Department of Foreign Affairs and International Trade (DFAIT) decided on a competition for one of Canada's most prestigious public projects – the new Canadian Embassy in Berlin. The high-visibility location – on Berlin's Leipziger Platz in the midst of a giant, ongoing construction site near the location of the former wall – posed a serious challenge to the participating designers. Because of the awkward configuration of the parcel, the teams had to come up with some creative solutions which could deal with a skewed footprint. In the words of the winning team's lead designer, Bruce Kuwabara, 'It's an impossible site'.[1]

Added to this were the perceived limitations imposed by the urban design guidelines of the Berlin city government, which included the results of a Leipziger Platz planning competition from 1994. Participants must also have been aware of the results of an earlier chapter in embassy design, when a William Alsop entry for the new British Embassy preferred by the professional jury – featuring a large expanse of glass as the street facade – was set aside in favour of a less flamboyant scheme by Michael Wilford.

In the case of the Canadian Embassy competition, the architects were asked to use 'Canadian materials to the extent possible', suggesting stone and wood as major design elements. Although not explicitly mentioned in the competition brief, recent history of construction in the centre of Berlin indicates preference for 'punched' window facade treatments. (The rigid guidelines imposed by former City Building Director, Hans Stimmen, would seem to have been relaxed somewhat during the new regime of his replacement, Barbara Jakubeit, a jury member.) Thus, the focus of creative energy of the competing firms was directed more towards a circulation plan for the site which could provide exceptional interior spaces.

Bordering on a northwest corner location of an octagonal section of Leipziger Platz, 'Canada House' is to accommodate three distinct activities: a) the Embassy itself, with all its functional requirements (c 6,000 square metres) b) commercial offices (c 5,000 square metres) c) residential quarters (2,700 square metres).

In addition, underground parking for 90+ cars was to be included, not only for staff, but also for visitors (something strictly forbidden in the construction of any US State Department structure). Provision was to be made for different levels of security in four different 'zones' in the new Embassy. The highest level 'Secure Zone' was the only area without windows, and it could not have a common wall with the lower level – public and semi-public – zones. Some space in the public zone would be reserved for private sector commercial, even retail, use. The brief required three entrances to the Embassy, with entrances lending themselves to various clientele – formal, business, consular, immigration, cultural and information. The image the building would project was also important: it should somehow present 'a Canadian face' to the outside world.

A Jury Favourite
As is the case in many competitions, this one is also not without controversy. When the jury report submitted by the competition's Professional Adviser became public (as part of the 'Executive Summary'),

**Winning Entry
Kuwabara Payne McKenna
Blumberg (KPMB)
(Toronto, Canada)**

Top Interior perspective
showing 'Timber Hall'
Bottom View of model from
Leipziger Platz

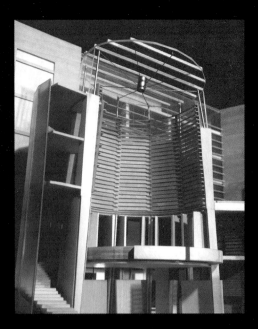

Left
Ebertstraße facade
of 'Canada House'
Opposite
Ground floor plan

There were long discussions
between KPMB and the
government as to the
necessity of 'Timber Hall'
as a symbol of Canada.
The architects finally prevailed
on this issue. Using timber
as a Canadian symbol was
not new. Arthur Erickson
had used it as the principal
material in the design of
his pavilion for the Tokyo
Trade Fair in 1965

it revealed that six of the eight jurors on the final jury (including two German jurors) preferred the entry of the Montréal/Toronto team of Saucier + Perrotte/ Dunlop Farrow over the winning Kuwabara Payne McKenna Blumberg (KPMB) design. But according to the Department of Foreign Affairs, the 'design review committee' was only one of four hurdles that each of the finalists' designs had to clear. Sean Rowan, a spokesperson for the Department, declared that in terms of cost effectiveness and function, the KPMB design was superior.

Gilles Saucier of Saucier + Perrotte felt that their use of a risky facade treatment – 'breaking the rules' by avoiding punched windows in a critical area – may have placed their scheme at a disadvantage. But the preference by two German jurors, Professor Barbara Jakubeit (Berlin) and Professor Christoph Sattler (Munich) for the Saucier + Perrotte scheme suggests that this risk was not the deciding factor in the Department's final decision. Sean Rowan, according to an article in the *National Post* commented, 'While it [the KPMB design] was less inspired, the space worked better for the embassy's facilities. It was the least expensive and functionally superior'.

The Process
The competition, which was run in three stages and administered by Dr Essy Baniassad of the Dalhousie Polytechnical Institute, Halifax, attracted 31 entries in the initial stage. Those firms were asked to provide a 'suitably illustrated statement of 5,000 to 7,000 words on the philosophy, vision and approach to the design and development of the Canadian Embassy'. This list was reduced to 16 firms in the second stage by a Technical Advisory Committee, which included

five design professionals, and then to five firms who participated in the design competition:
- AJ Diamond, Don Schmitt (Toronto)
- Saucier + Perrotte (Montréal)/Dunlop, Farrow (Toronto)
- Dan Hanganu Architect (Montréal), Bregman + Hamann (Toronto)
- Kuwabara Payne McKenna Blumberg (Toronto)
- Moriyama and Teshima (Toronto)

The 'Design Review Committee' established by DFAIT to evaluate the submissions, none of whom served on the Technical Advisory Committee were: Douglas R Gillmor (Calgary); Dr Barbara Jakubeit (Berlin); Ernst Keller (Winnipeg); Jacques Rosseau (Montréal); Christoph Sattler (Munich); Kim Storey (Toronto); Wilfried Wang (Frankfurt); Terry Williams (Victoria); Dr Essy Baniassad (non-voting Chair).

The new Embassy is to incorporate three main functions: the Embassy, private commercial facilities, and residential accommodation for staff. In the words of the brief, 'the challenge for the building is to express the international associations, national aspirations and cultural characteristics through the architectural language of built-form'. To those approaching the Embassy, it was supposed to present 'a building of distinct identity', offering visitors an 'open spirited space'. In addition, the interior of the building was supposed to have flexibility for internal redesign 'in response to changing ideas, circumstances and functions'.

Thus, the Design Review Committee was charged with the task of looking beyond the specific functional requirements to examine the designs, first in terms of their essential strategy, then the manner in which they handle the primary access to the building, how

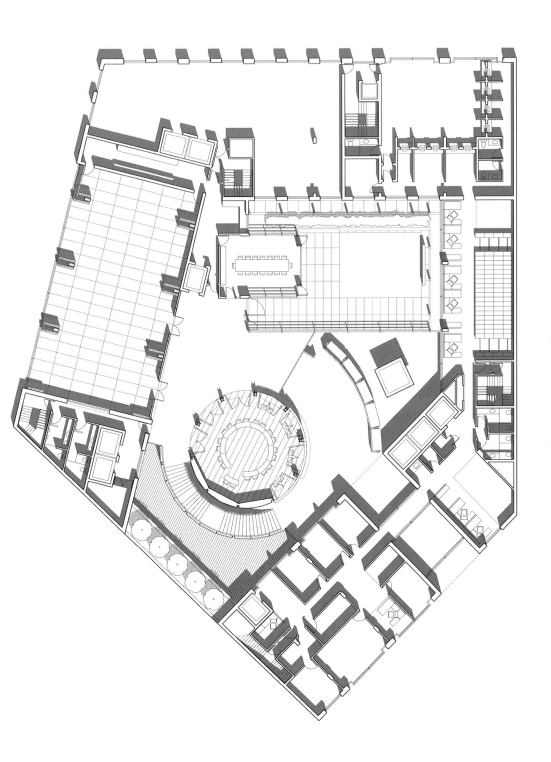

**Finalist
Saucier + Perrotte/
Dunlop Farrow
(Montréal, Canada/
Toronto, Canada)**

View from catwalk

This entry was a jury
favourite, receiving six of
eight possible votes. As it
turned out, this adjudication
exercise by professionals
was only one step in the
selection evaluation process

Finalist
Dan Hanganau Architect/
Bregman + Hamann
(Montréal, Canada/
Toronto, Canada)

Views of interior
sculpture court

Hanganau and Bregman
+ Hamann also utilised
the symbolic element of
trees in their courtyard,
although in a more whimsical
and lighthearted fashion.
They were included more
as a suggestion than as
a dominating force

they organise the public spaces and access to various main parts and the approach adopted to the material expression of the design. Canadians paid less attention to the security issue, which has necessitated fortress-like considerations in the construction of recent US missions. The open approach of all the submissions and even the existence of a public passageway under the building would be strictly off limits for any US State Department building.

In determining the suitability of the 'design strategy', numerous factors were considered:
• Does it meet the local planning requirements?
• Does it have potential approval where it varies from such requirements?
• Does it offer a clear resolution of required parts and functions?
• Does it offer a constant framework for flexibility and future internal changes?
• Does it altogether support the proper image and cultural identity of the building?

Trying to express the Canadian image was resolved by most of the architects as an interior matter, reserved for the courtyard areas or, by the winning KPMB team, with a large conical room, 'Timber Hall'. Saucier + Perrotte's answer to this was more

theoretical – creating a feeling of spaciousness, referring to the great expanses of the Canadian landscape, whereas Dan Hanganau created an interior 'sculpture court'. Of the three entries which received support from jurors as best design, Dan Hanganau's entry got one vote, as did KPMB.

The fear expressed by some that the KPMB design will look too much like other corporate structures in the immediate area may be unfounded. The original competition drawings of KPMB's Kitchener City Hall could not fully communicate the impact which detailing had on the final product. The question remains as to whether or not the $52 million allotted by the Canadian government for this project will be sufficient to allow KPMB to work its magic here as well. As one of KPMB's strongest hands lies in organisation and detail, one may only hope that budget will not place undue limitations on the designers. Presently under construction, 'Canada House' should be completed in late 2004.

Notes
1. All quotes in this essay are from its original publication in *Competitions*, Volume 9, No. 1, Spring, 1999.

Contra Costa County Government Center (2000)

Mark Tortorich

The competition to select an architect for the new Contra Costa County Government Center was an attempt to introduce the contemporary design philosophies of established architects to a community that long ago felt betrayed by modern architecture and civic planning. The object of this controversy – an unwelcome neighbour in the community – was the 12-storey County Administration Building which had finally reached the end of its useful life. County planners therefore hoped that a new structure would do more than simply replace obsolete and dysfunctional office space.

The planning and design process had the potential to establish a new architectural direction for county facilities and demonstrate the new partnership between city and county governments. Martinez, California, a San Francisco Bay community of 35,000 residents, has been the Contra Costa County seat since 1850. County facilities dominate the downtown, but residents viewed the modernist administration tower as a symbol of government arrogance. Standing in stark contrast to its historic predecessors and the adjacent two- and three-storey commercial buildings, the tower provided little value to the Martinez landscape. As of 1998, the tower was also becoming a liability to the county. Failing mechanical systems and suspicions of seismic instability justified a comprehensive Building Evaluation Report. This analysis provided the catalyst for the new government centre by concluding that it would be more cost effective to construct a replacement structure than to renovate and modernise the existing one.

Community leaders, including the Martinez City Council, were eager to support a new building as an economic and aesthetic boost to their downtown. In fact, the Council expressed a willingness to incorporate city offices with the new centre. Conversely, the County Board of Supervisors was less than enthusiastic about financing a $50 million capital project. Regardless of the economic justification, some Board members argued that constructing a new building would come at the expense of other, more desperately needed programmes. However, despite their misgivings, the Board agreed to begin the search for an architect.

With the hope of galvanising the Board's support for new construction and generating community interest in the project, the County Capital Facilities Director, Laura Lockwood, authorised a design competition to augment the qualifications-based architect selection process which was modelled on the federal GSA Design Excellence Program.

The competition programme, developed by the SmithGroup, identified an initial structure of approximately 130,000 square feet along with a masterplan for additional buildings of 40,000 and 30,000 square feet. The programme identified space requirements and essential adjacencies for county offices, city offices, and a combined City Council and Board of Supervisors chamber. The programme also established a height limit to alleviate citizen concerns that the county would construct another high rise. The site for the project was a two-block parcel and intersecting street that formed an edge to the downtown. To one side were the railroad tracks that separated the town from a regional park and marina, and, on the other side, the 1901 courthouse.

To aid the public outreach process, the county commissioned a scale model of the downtown

Winning entry
Dworsky Associates Cannon Dworsky
(Los Angeles, CA, US)

Competition model

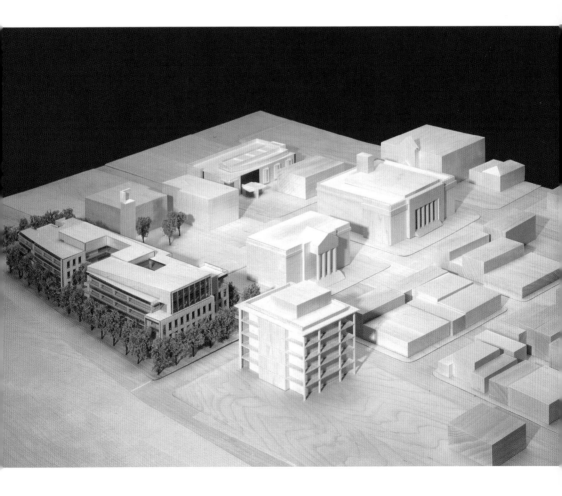

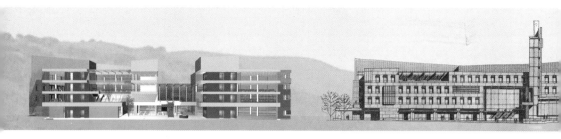

government and commercial districts. This model, when displayed at board meetings or council sessions, sparked public discussion regarding future downtown development. The model also provided a template for the competition submittals.

The 18 January 2000 request for qualifications led to responses from 25 firms. The selection panel including Ms Lockwood, County Managers, the Martinez City Manager, the Project Manager, and a professional advisor (David Meckel FAIA) evaluated these proposals and established a shortlist of four architectural firms. These four firms, Dworsky Associates (now CannonDworsky), Moore Ruble Yudell/Fisher Friedman (MRY), Fentress Bradburn, and Hellmuth Obata & Kassabaum (HOK) each demonstrated the technical capacity to accomplish the project, but, more importantly, represented distinct philosophies towards making public buildings. For example, Mehrdad Yazdani, Dworsky's lead designer, provided a decidedly contemporary portfolio of public buildings emphasising bold forms and colours, while John Ruble FAIA offered community oriented structures based on a more traditional palette of forms and materials. The Fentress Bradburn and

HOK teams each presented a strong collection of projects for other county governments that ranged from the heroic to the contextual.

Each shortlisted firm received a $25,000 stipend and was allowed six weeks to develop the competition submittal. Requirements included four 30 x 40 inch boards depicting plans, sections, elevations and renderings of the scheme. Additionally, a wooden model of the proposed development (to align with the county provided template) and a construction cost estimate were required.

An independent professional jury evaluated the architectural concepts before the unveiling to the selection panel. This jury, composed of Craig Hartman FAIA, Mary Margaret Jones ASLA and David Meckel, appraised each scheme and agreed on a rank order. However, the jury acted only in an advisory capacity to the panel and therefore did not have final authority to make a selection. The panel (except for Meckel and the Project Manager) did not view the competition submittals before the interviews, and were not aware of the jury comments until their conclusion.

Although evaluated separately, the selection panel and jury agreed on the rank order of the four

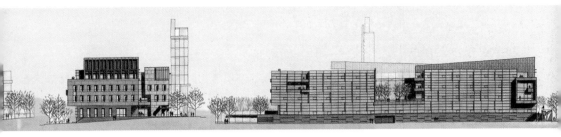

Winning Entry
Dworsky Associates – Cannon
Dworsky
(Los Angeles, CA, US)

Opposite Rear of building
Top Elevations
Bottom Perspective

Although this project is not
yet underway, in the interim,
Cannon has recently been
commissioned to design a
facility for the county sheriff
by the local government –
a contract they would never
have received had they not
won the competition

schemes. Dworsky Associates ranked first with MRY a close second, while Fentress Bradburn and HOK tied for fourth. The Dworsky and MRY schemes demonstrated superior qualities in site planning, massing and place-making when compared with the other submittals. These two schemes also conveyed a modern civic presence that complemented the historic government structures, yet incorporated contemporary forms and materials. The Dworsky scheme, in particular, was an inspired response to the competition programme. The floor plan provided flexible and open office space, interior atria that brought natural light into the building cores, and a multifaceted facade that responded to solar orientation.

After considering the jury comments, the interview and qualification statements, the selection panel endorsed both the Dworsky and MRY teams, leaving a final decision up to the Board of Supervisors. This allowed the board time to consult with constituents and develop a financing plan before making a final commitment.

To collect these community opinions and reactions, the City and County hosted a series of town hall meetings. Understandably, the comments centred rather more on the development impact than on architectural merit. Issues such as construction quality, noise, traffic and parking dominated the conversation. Some members of the community had difficulty embracing the contemporary architectural language of the proposals, but others saw it as an opportunity to look towards the future. Residents whole-heartedly supported the project and appreciated the consultation during the earliest stages of design.

The rapidly deconstructing economy and California's energy crisis are making budget analysts sceptical about capital expenditures, so the project is on hold while the Board of Supervisors grapples with the financing plan. However, the competition achieved its intended results. First, by involving Martinez residents in the architect selection process they became project advocates instead of opponents. Second, board members who once challenged the wisdom of new construction have since embraced the idea. In fact, the board established a special task force to study sustainable architectural concepts. Finally, the city and county forged the strong partnership necessary for a successful building campaign.

Postscript

Although the approval for the government centre has not been granted, another related project, a sheriff's headquarters building, has been commissioned. And the design firm carrying out the project is none other than the winner of the original competition: Cannon Dworsky.

Second Place
Moore Ruble Yudell/Fisher Friedman Associates
(Los Angeles, CA, US)

This page, top Aerial view
This page, bottom
Porch perspective
Opposite page, top Site plan
Opposite page, bottom West elevation

Although technically ranked second to Dworsky, the call was close enough that the jury felt it could recommend both the first and second place entries to the client

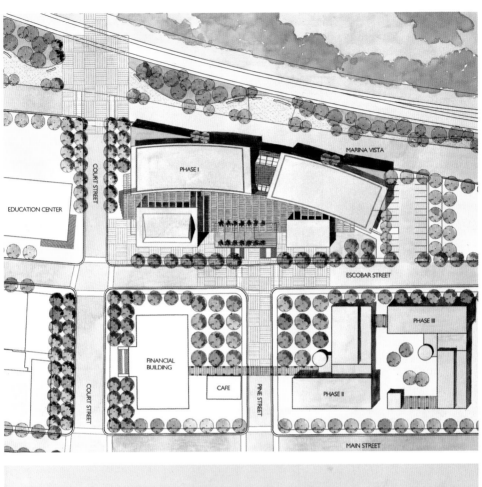

EDUCATION CENTER

COURT STREET

PHASE I

MARINA VISTA

ESCOBAR STREET

FINANCIAL BUILDING

CAFE

COURT STREET

PINE STREET

PHASE II

PHASE III

MAIN STREET

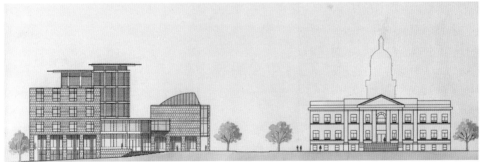

Finalist
Helmuth Obata & Kassabaum
(San Francisco, CA, US)

Competition board

Competing Globally in Architecture Competitions

**Finalist
Fentress Bradburn
Architects
(Denver, CO, US)**

Top Competition model
Bottom Perspective of
building with San Francisco
Bay in the background

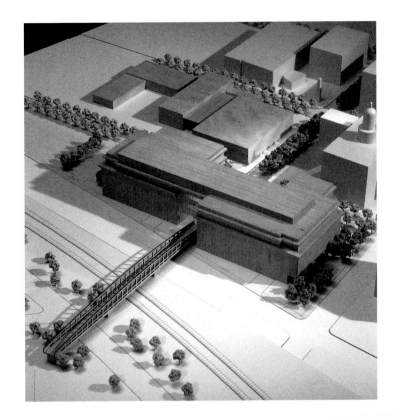

Case Study
Los Angeles Federal Courthouse (2001)

Larry Gordon

The four finalists in the competition to design a new high-rise courthouse in downtown Los Angeles faced, above everything else, a location problem. The site for the one million plus square feet building is at a transition juncture in the depressed but starting-to-stir-again area close to the landmark City Hall. It is a confusing spot, a sort of a no-man's-land occupied by a seismically weakened state office building and made more difficult by being on a hillside. It marks the end of the bustling Broadway shopping quarter, which attracts mainly low-income Latino immigrants, and has a host of partly empty historic structures.

Its Hill Street side is a block or two from the newer cultural and architectural jewels of Bunker Hill, including Frank Gehry's Disney Concert Hall and Rafael Moneo's new Catholic Cathedral. And its First Street edge, the most prominent facade, forms a boundary for the downtown Civic Center, the largest conglomeration of government buildings west of Washington, DC, most notably City Hall, the beloved 28-storey tower that has starred in many films and television shows.

Ed Feiner, Chief Architect for the US General Services Administration, explains:

The site is so important. Disney Concert Hall, the cathedral and City Hall are already icons. We wanted to establish a presence of the federal government in the Los Angeles Civic Center which would not diminish the Civic Center, but represent in a very positive way the commitment of the federal government to the people and city of LA.[1]

The final judging – in which the identities of the finalists and jurors remained hidden from each side – focused on aspects such as the need for security since the Oklahoma City bombing and the desire to tap California sunshine in environmentally friendly technology. Jurors, however, stressed that the handling of location was what put the eventual winner, Ralph Johnson in the Chicago office of Perkins & Will, over the three other finalists: Craig Hartman of the San Francisco office of Skidmore Owings & Merrill; Rafael Viñoly of Rafael Viñoly Architects, New York; and Mehrdad Yazdani of Cannon Dworsky in Los Angeles.

Johnson proposed an L-shaped, 16-storey structure with a breathtaking curved wall at its elbow along Broadway. An ornamental tower peaks at the First Street corner, a kind of friendly echo of City Hall. The glass wall containing a photovoltaic energy system to help run the building's utilities services acts as a great interior wall for a huge public atrium, with views on many floors to the Civic Center. And a sawtooth configuration along the Hill Street side allows for all the courtrooms to receive natural light, also helping with the circulation needed to accommodate and separate judges, jurors, the public and prisoners.

Jury chairman Thom Mayne of Morphosis, who designed the proposed new federal courthouse in Eugene, Oregon, praised the Johnson submission for the way it responded to the immediate environment.

While construction of the $300 million building has been delayed by a slow economy, completion is now envisioned for about 2009. Then, when the glass wall is lit from the inside, what is now a drab corner of Los Angeles will be a glowing nighttime reminder of federal justice.

Note
1. All quotes in this essay are from its original publication in *Competitions*, Volume 11, No. 3, Fall 2001.

Winning Entry
Perkins & Will – Principal
in Charge: Ralph Johnson
(Chicago, IL, US)

The huge glass facade
incorporates photovoltaic
panels which will serve
to make the building
self-sufficient in energy
consumption. Ralph Johnson
even maintains that it can
contribute to the city grid
under favourable conditions.
Juror Thom Mayne said,
'The Johnson submission
responded best to the
intersection of its urban
response and the response of
the courtroom. Instead of
turning its back on Broadway,
as some of the other finalists
did, Johnson's was appealing
in the way it incorporated
open space on Broadway and
connected well to the street.'

This page
Finalist
Rafael Viñoly Architects
(New York, US)

Top right Model showing
site with Los Angeles City
Hall at lower left
Middle right Section
Bottom right East elevation

The Rafael Viñoly plan calls
for a "Space of Justice"
within a series of monumental
columns topped by a giant
louvered canopy. Within this
open-air box, the courthouse
itself is a curved 11-storey
structure with much glassy
horizontal patterns and great
views of the region

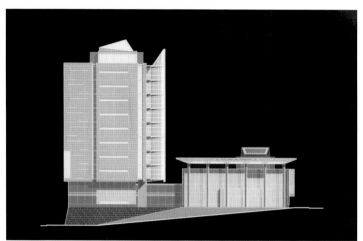

Finalist
Skidmore Owings & Merrill –
Design Principal: Craig
Hartman with Michael
Duncan (San Francisco, CA, US)

Top and centre Elevations
Bottom left Night view,
aerial perspective

The SOM team proposed
an 11-storey rectangular
limestone building along
Broadway and a low-rise,
dramatic pavilion structure
with a glass enclosed
ceremonial entrance and
garden at the higher elevated
corner of First Street and
Hill Street. A lagoon-like pool
stretched between those
buildings, crossed by a series
of bridges and walkways.
Hartman said he wanted
to connect the court to the
hilltop's cultural resources
and to the Subway station on
Hill Street. The civic garden,
topped with a breathable and
louvered roof, 'suggests that
the justice should be open
and transparent and that the
lines between private space
and public domain could be
blurred, not drawn so strictly.'

Finalist
Dworsky Associates – Cannon
Dworsky – Principal in
Charge: Merhdad Yazdani
(Los Angeles, CA, US)

Top Model perspective
Middle right Elevation
Middle left Entrance
from street
Bottom Typical floor plan

A Los Angeles resident,
Yazdani had a strong desire
to create a hometown civic
garden along Broadway from
First Street, with a reflecting
pool, leading to a low-rise
courthouse pavilion for a
cafeteria and other public
functions. His main 12-storey
courthouse is formed by
a series of six limestone
columns, marking entrances
to the courtrooms, all
behind a curtain of wall.
The hallways are visible
from the exterior

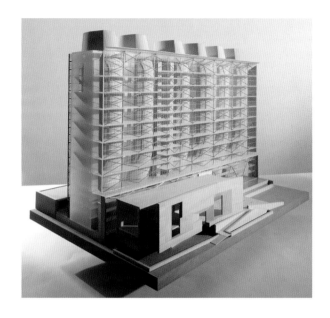

1. JUDGES CHAMBERS
2. RECEPTION
3A. SHARED LIBRARY
3B. SHARED LOUNGE
4. JURY ROOM
5. ANCILLARY FACILITIES
6. EQUIPMENT STORAGE
7. DEFENDANT ELEVATOR / HOLDING
8. JUDGE / STAFF SERVICE ELEVATORS
9. PUBLIC ELEVATORS
10. LIGHT MONITOR (TYPICAL)

Performing Arts Centres

Hans Scharoun
(Berlin, Germany)
Berlin Philharmonic,
Germany
Competition 1956
Completion 1963

Population growth and the need to update facilities have spawned a demand for more performing arts centres, in North America as well as Europe and Asia. The existence of icons in this genre such as the Sydney Opera House, the Berlin Philharmonic and the Cité de la Musique in Paris – all the result of competitions – has led many communities to pursue this avenue in the architect selection process.

The years 1956 and 1957 turned out to be milestones in the design of performing arts centres. When Hans Scharoun and Jørn Utzon won competitions for the Berlin Philharmonic Hall and the Sidney Opera House, respectively, no one could have foreseen the impact those buildings would have on the world of architecture. Although it took Australia 16 years to finally complete Utzon's Opera House, construction went at a faster pace in Berlin. The 'Zirkus Karajani' (Karajan's Circus), as it was dubbed by Berliners because of its tent-line form, opened in 1963 to critical acclaim – and a few dissonant voices.[1] In contrast to the Sidney Opera House, which became a symbol of Australia to the rest of the world because of its striking exterior form, Scharoun's masterpiece was more important for what happened once one was on the inside, not only when the visitor encountered various catwalks and winding stairways upon entering the foyer, but in the auditorium itself. There, the juxtaposition of different levels of tiers surrounding the performance area made it seem the perfect venue for ushering in a new age of music. Frank Gehry's early model for the Disney Music Hall in Los Angeles 40 years later was in many respects a paean to both designs – Utzon on the exterior, Scharoun on the interior. In any case, those two competitions rendered the traditional concert hall 'shoe box' configuration a thing of the past.

By the 1990s, performing arts centres were in high demand, and not only in regions where population growth had pushed up demand for more and larger cultural performance venues. Older cities were beginning to regard the arts as an essential building block in the rejuvenation of their downtowns. America's rust-belt cities, in particular, were looking for ways to lure new businesses to their localities. Even cities such as Newark, New Jersey, where going downtown could be downright dangerous, regarded such venues as the key to bringing life back to their city centres, long in decline.

Supporting the arts was now beginning to be viewed differently by the cities; they began to be regarded as an industry which could create jobs and attract tourists, not just in New York, London, or Paris. In places like

Top
Carlos Ott
(Toronto, Canada)
Bastille Opera, Paris, France
Competition 1983
Completion 1989

Jurors believed that the winning design might have originated from Richard Meier's office

Bottom
Jørn Utzon
(Copenhagen, Denmark)
Sydney Opera House,
Sydney, Australia
Competition 1957
Completion 1973

Juror Eero Saarinen was instrumental in bringing this design back into consideration after arriving late for jury duty. Previously, the other jurors had not advanced Utzon's concept to the next round

**Arata Isozaki
(Tokyo, Japan)
Shenzhen Cultural Centre,
Shenzhen, China
Competition 1998**

This was one of the elements
of the Shenzhen masterplan,
establishing the cultural and
administrative centre of a
new city in southern China.
The building not only includes
facilities for the performing
and visual arts, but is also
to house a large city library.
The arts are located on one
side of the road running under
the platform, the library on
the opposite side. According
to one source, the architect
has questioned the installation
of the mullions which are
being installed along the
curving facade, possibly
having an adverse impact
on the appearance of the
building. In any case, the
structure is scheduled to
open by 2005

Competing Globally in Architecture Competitions

Atlanta, Birmingham, and Dijon (the latter won by Arquitectonica), competitions for the design of performing arts centres started to become more frequent. It was also becoming clear that the highly skilled people working in the new high-tech industries, which cities were trying to attract, preferred communities where the arts were a high priority.[2] If you wanted to attract new businesses to your town, and the arts were one of the selling points, what better way to do it than show off a new performing arts centre?

A 'Grands Projets' competition for the Bastille Opera House in Paris in 1983 resulted in one of the more controversial projects under Mitterrand. The winner of the competition was a young architect from Uruguay, Carlos Ott, who was living in a walkup in Toronto. In this anonymous competition with over 700 entries, the jury surmised that the author of the winning design was probably Richard Meier. Finished in 1989, the Opera has never been an attraction to match Spreckelsen's La Defense, Pei's pyramid, or even Dominique Perrault's controversial Bibliothèque de France. Those who anticipated that the competition would result in

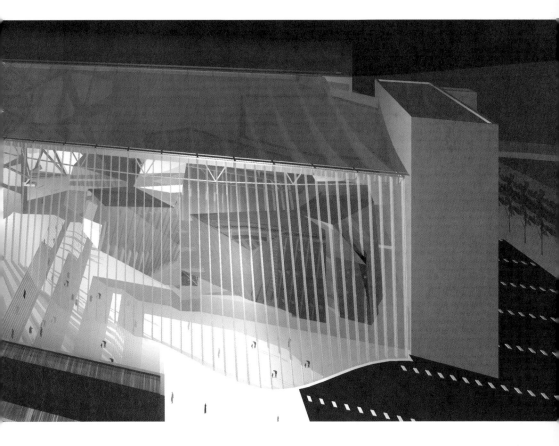

Arquitectonica
(Miami, FL, US)
Dijon Performing Arts Centre,
France
Competition 1990
Completion 1997

Left Masterplan model
Bottom Pedestrian perspective
of concert hall

This was a limited
competition where local
authorities had some input
as to who should be invited.
The French, much like the
Germans, were inviting foreign
firms to participate in these
competitions. The central
government could say little
against this practice, as
Mitterrand had commissioned
a foreign architect, IM Pei,
to design the pyramid at
the Louvre

another Sydney Opera House were to be disappointed, for it would be
another seven years before another arts project competition, this time in
Bilbao, Spain, could make such a claim. As for the fate of Carlos Ott, he
now has offices in both Toronto and Uruguay and is involved in projects
in Germany, China and elsewhere.

A competition for a new Music and Conference Centre in Lucerne,
Switzerland, ushered in the last decade of the 20th century. Won by the
French architect, Jean Nouvel, who previously had quickly risen to the top
of the profession by virtue of winning the Arab World Institute (Institut du
monde arabe) competition in Paris a few years earlier, the building was,
in a sense, an inverted platform with a large, sweeping roof as a great
symbol of shelter for what was transpiring underneath.

Dominique Perrault
(Paris, France)
Mariinsky State Theatre,
St Petersburg, Russia
Competition 2003

Right Pedestrian perspective
along canal
Bottom Site model

Perrault won this second,
invited competition for this
project, when the winning
design from the first
competition, won by the
American, Eric Owen Moss,
was dropped

An Entrée into the Asian Market

The Tokyo Forum competition, co-sponsored by the International Union of Architects (UIA), reflected a growing trend for global participation in the profession. Not only was the international aspect of the competition reflected in the composition of the jury – Arthur Erickson (Canada), IM Pei (US), Vittorio Grigotti (Italy), joined by Japanese architects Fumihiko Maki and Kenzo Tange – the top four places featured the Uruguayan-born winner Rafael Viñoly and the UK-based office of James Stirling Michael Wilford. The size of the fee received by Viñoly – in excess of $56 million – served as a wake-up call for European and American architects.

Two Chinese competitions for performing arts venues also deserve special mention: the Shenzhen Cultural Centre competition won by Arata Isozaki, and the Beijing Opera House competition in 2000 won by Paul Andreu of Paris.

Getting Invited

Of the six competitions for performing arts centres held in the us during the 1990s, only one was an open, anonymous competition, and that was for a smaller facility on a college campus. And of these six, three were sponsored by American universities. Why were there not more open competitions, considering the number of performing arts centres which were built over this period? And why were almost all invited?

Almost all performing arts centres in the us lack government funding and are almost entirely dependent on private donations. Their boards of directors are usually made up of scions of the corporate world. Only in the rarest cases do we find an architect on one of these boards. Thus, it can come as no surprise that such committees in charge of architect selection often are swayed by arguments which have little to do with the intrinsic value of the design. Fortunately for them, the shortlists for these competitions are usually drawn up by a committee which does include architects. But why not have an open competition? These boards normally want a direct voice in the selection process, because it is, at least in part, their money which is being spent. They want to be involved at an earlier stage, not just at the end, where they might have the option either to accept or reject a decision made by a panel of design professionals. In these situations, the presentation may be of equal importance; a psychological misstep can mean a lost commission.

Demise of the Wild Card?

When four firms were shortlisted for the University of Maryland's Performing Arts Center competition in February 1994, it must be said that the two eastern firms invited – Cesar Pelli & Associates from New Haven, Connecticut and Pei Cobb Freed from New York City – had to be the favourites. The two western firms were relatively young and didn't have nearly as many commissions under their belts. One, Antoine Predock, had won an important competition to design a Fine Arts Center for Arizona State University; the other, Moore Ruble Yudell of Santa Monica, California, had won a prestigious planning competition in Berlin, built an arts centre in California, and designed some academic buildings on the west coast. But one of the chief partners and founders of the firm, Charles Moore, resided in Texas and was in poor health. To the dismay of the firm's other partners, Moore suffered a heart attack on the airport tarmac just as he was about to board a plane for Los Angeles to review the competition designs. However, this tragedy did not slow the firm down, as they won the competition and went on to build the Arts Center. And, by winning the competition without their senior partner, they announced to

**Atelier Jean Nouvel
(Paris, France)
Ørestaden Concert Hall,
Copenhagen, Denmark
Competition 2002**

Following the Ørestaden planning competition, which was described by Paul Spreiregen as a most exemplary model, one of the major building blocks in this plan, the concert hall, was the subject of an invited competition with a list of star architects as participants. Nouvel won this competition with a 'box', much to the surprise of local pundits, who thought they would finally get something with curves

Competing Globally in Architecture Competitions

the world that they were designers to be reckoned with in their own right. They subsequently went on to win a number of competitions, some in urban planning and others in academic settings.

As invited competitions were becoming the preferred format for large arts projects, the young architects who were without a track record of completed projects were seeing their chances to compete dwindle. A phenomenon such as Carlos Ott was becoming an ever more remote possibility. So the only way a firm might receive an invitation to participate in such a competition would be as a result of the authorship of other high profile buildings. In France, where it was determined that all architects should be paid for their work, the limited competition also became the norm. But here, young architects were brought into the process via the 'Album' system, whereby an architect was selected to participate by virtue of doing well in a portfolio competition.

American-based architects will again have to look abroad for an opportunity to pad their résumés. The Oslo Opera House competition was one such opportunity; however, it was won by Snøhetta, the Norwegian firm that had earlier come out of nowhere to win the Alexandria Library competition. Now they were being asked to take part in all kinds of invited competitions. Although no US-based architects were finalists in that competition, two non-Scandinavian firms did receive recognition: Alsop & Stormer of the UK and Maria José Araguren Lopez/José Gonzalez of Spain.

A more recent concert hall competition in Denmark returned to the invitation format. Jean Nouvel won out over an impressive list of participants, including Rafael Viñoly, Schmidt Hammer Lassen, Rafael Moneo, Henning Larsen, Arata Isozaki and others. The Danes were hoping that this competition would produce something other than the ubiquitous 'box'. Although Nouvel's winning design was hardly a 'box' on the inside, it certainly will be to those approaching it from the street. In any case, the concert hall interior certainly paid homage to Hans Scharoun. Even more recently, Dominique Perrault became the beneficiary of a second competition for St Petersburg's Mariinsky Theatre when the winning design by Eric Owen Moss was dropped.

Notes
1. Herbert von Karajan was the conductor of the Berlin Philharmonic when the building opened.

2. Richard Florida, *The Rise of the Creative Class*, Basic Books (New York), 2002, p 17.

Rensselaer Polytechnic Electronic Media and Performing Arts Center (2001)

William Morgan

In setting out guidelines for an architectural competition for an Electronic Media and Performing Arts Center (EMPAC) at Rensselaer Polytechnic Institute (RPI), a university task force declared: 'We want the building to energise the campus ... to make bold and intelligent statements about who we are and where we're going'.[1] This group – students, faculty, staff and a trustee – further defined their architectural vision by refreshingly asking competitors to 'Make this a memorable place ... embody a new spirit in Rensselaer'.

RPI has an image problem shared with most technical institutes, not to mention their location in a classic gritty city (their literature refers to Troy as the 'cradle of the industrial revolution'). Even though Rensselaer has a respected architecture school, they lack a cultural magnet: 'Every first-tier university with whom we wish to compete has a performing arts center and a vibrant arts community'. RPI also believes that an arts centre will 'offer a more appealing environment to attract and retain the highest quality faculty'. Whether or not EMPAC will really become a 'beacon of promise' overlooking the Hudson River, the smoothly run competition for the centre has injected an element of excitement in the university's hitherto somewhat drab public persona.

This is the first competition that RPI has engaged in its 178-year history, and was put on a fast-track from the start. The campus task force held open meetings with various constituencies on campus in January 2001. They visited buildings like the Wexner Center at Ohio State and Arizona State's Nelson Fine Arts Center, and by March published competition rules. Roger Schluntz, Dean of Architecture at the

University of New Mexico and fresh from advising Cornell on a competition for a school of design on the Ithaca campus, was hired as the competition advisor. The selection committee consisted of the president, the Director of Campus Planning & Facilities Design, various vice presidents, a student, Alan Balfour, dean of RPI's School of Architecture, and three external advisers – Bruce Fowle, Michael Hays and James Thompson. The winner was announced in June.

The clear, sensible and unambiguous brief for a 'campus living room' outlined a 130,000 square foot building with two theatres, a gallery, and a 1,200-people space for convocations. The centre, to be filled with all sorts of electronic and other media, will occupy a prominent bluff overlooking Troy. The selection committee noted that EMPAC would 'require a thoughtful artistic programme, excellent acoustics, and intelligent design'.

Ranking of the competitors' entries would be on contextual appropriateness, respect of the site, commitment to work with the stated budget of $33 million (this was increased during the competition to over $50 million just a few weeks before submissions were due, creating considerable consternation among the participating firms for the changes which had to be implemented), and an ability to stay on task for a projected September 2003 completion date. Most important of all, the building must 'instill pride, enrich the campus environment, and enhance the expectations of the broader academic community'.

RPI's architecture faculty recommended approximately 30 architects, who not surprisingly included 'some of the most admired and respected in the world'. Seven firms from those who responded to

**Winning Entry
Nicholas Grimshaw &
Partners (London, UK)**

'The EMPAC design is an appropriate one for RPI at this time, and typical of Grimshaw's so-called "Victorian" approach to architecture, wherein a lot of small, mechanistic details contribute to an overall high-tech identity. The Grimshaw scheme was certainly the most musical and clear in its expression of purpose.'
— William Morgan.

By premiating the Grimshaw scheme, RPI has committed itself to a considerably higher budget than was originally anticipated. But none of this seems to deter the college, as it recently received one of the largest donations for capital projects of any university to date

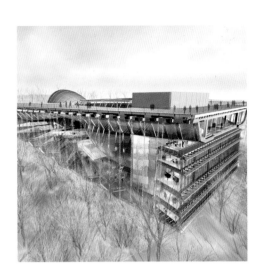

the competition announcement were interviewed. Four of those were chosen to participate in the design competition for EMPAC (Scogin, Elam & Bray, UN Studio, and Smith-Miller + Hawkinson did not make the cut). Bernard Tschumi, Davis Brody Bond, Nicholas Grimshaw and Morphosis provided interim presentation of first ideas, a design report and a final presentation.

Max Bond, in collaboration with RPI professor Thomas Leeser, produced a scheme with a plethora of ideas. Their long and narrow steel 'bar building' dramatically cantilevers over the site, very reminiscent of a competition-winning design for the French Ministry of Culture in Paris. Incorporating the library (somewhat alien itself) into the complex was one of the strong points. Still, much of the circulation remained unresolved. The idea of the hanging rehearsal hall seemed very forced – why would that be the featured space?

Bernard Tschumi, on the other hand, is an architect who has been winning competitions all over the world. The Columbia dean has recently won competitions in Athens, São Paolo and Geneva, and his competition-winning design for the new School of Architecture at Florida International University is nearing completion. His entry for this competition, a big glass cube – a 'crystal beacon', was an intriguing solution to the hillside location: instead of going out horizontally, Tschumi packed everything into a vertical envelope, providing lots of views for the occupants. It was ingenious in the manner in which it fitted so neatly into the cube – like a Chinese block puzzle. His flexible scheme, and especially the wooden interior container, made the Tschumi project a very strong contender.

The most far out, and easily the most fun, proposal was that of Morphosis. In their entry, the Santa Monica studio sought to reflect the 'softened and eroded boundaries, the instability and flux' of contemporary performance arts disciplines. Citing relaxed distinctions between audience and performance, Morphosis created a 'continuous surface with no discrete edges', an undulating shell wrapped in glazed foil. It is hard not be amused and delighted by the idea of a centre which would be a 'physical and disciplinary incubator for hybridisation in engineering and the arts'.

It seemed to have the strongest and most exciting parti with the most room to play and makes a perfect match to the needs of the school. Although visually strong, the exterior form was the weakest element; but Thom Mayne seemed very flexible and was willing to work with the school. The advantage was that the form, while an evolution of the function, was not as driven by it. Strangely, while seemingly expensive, in reality it could be very cost effective since the volumetric elements of the programme didn't necessarily have to make perfect architecture – there was a kind of interstitial space between the skin

and the function. The interplay of the penetrating circulation elements with the exterior form was exciting and connected well to the campus. The concern was the relation of the building's form to the city. What could be seen as a giant egg may have required too large a leap of faith for the university administration. One can too easily hear the wisecracks about the futuristic world of Woody Allen's *Sleeper* or *The Invasion of the Body Snatchers*. Yet, the combination of seriousness and whimsicality might have proven a tremendous asset.

The winning design by Nicholas Grimshaw & Partners represents a compromise: superficially, it shares some of the brave new world of Morphosis, but it provides a very workable design cleverly masked by the requisite flash. The EMPAC design is an appropriate one for RPI at this time, and typical of Grimshaw's so-called 'Victorian' approach to architecture, wherein a lot of small, mechanistic details contribute to an overall high-tech identity. The bulk of EMPAC lies down and into the hill, and appears to be suspended from the planted, terrace-like roof that extends out from the campus. The two largest elements, the auditorium and recital hall, are huge shells – one round side down, the other round side up (the architects liken these shapes to the hull of a ship or the rounded belly of a stringed instrument). These counterbalanced ovoids form the central mass of a building that otherwise appears transparent from the campus side.

The Grimshaw scheme was certainly the most musical and clear in its expression of purpose. While the main auditorium would be a terrific experience, and the metaphor of the cello very sensuous, I questioned how appropriate it was for its purpose – too refined perhaps for its multipurpose/academic use. Much of the programme, like the studio and faculty space, as well as the circulation, seemed to be unresolved. One could be more optimistic that these elements would be resolved better in the other schemes, as they were not working with such a singular icon. Also, the use of a wafer as an extension of the campus quad is debatable. The presentation did not show how this seemingly unnecessary surface would be developed, and it seemed to conceal the auditorium feature from the campus, reducing it to something that could only be enjoyed by the users and the passers-by at the street.

There was no question that this was going to be an expensive scheme. It was chosen in the end because it seemed to be the most contextual with regard to the city – a welcome feature on the hill – and it would have the least impact on the existing campus while still being a strong architectural statement. It also showed the most connectivity to the city with the ramped auditorium lobby that was so beautifully integrated into the hillside – one of the strongest elements of the scheme.

Unfortunately, Grimshaw was not there to present

Finalist
Davis Brody Bond Architects/
Leeser Architecture
(New York, US)

Top Sections
Middle View to cantilevered
feature from the road
Bottom View along arts corridor

Finalist
Morphosis
(Santa Monica, CA, US)

Left Model perspective
Bottom View to entrance

In their entry, the Santa Monica studio sought to reflect the 'softened and eroded boundaries, the instability and flux' of contemporary performance arts disciplines. Citing relaxed distinctions between audience and performance, Morphosis created a 'continuous surface with no discrete edges', an undulating shell wrapped in glazed foil

Competing Globally in Architecture Competitions

Finalist
Bernard Tschumi Architects
(New York, US/Paris, France)

Top Functional diagram
Bottom View from ravine

FOUNDERS ROOM   RECITAL HALL   GALLERIES   MUSIC ROOMS

MUSIC PRACTICE ROOMS

MUSIC LEVEL

LOBBIES

1200 SEAT THEATER

CAMPUS ENTRY

AUDIO-VIDEO COMMUNICATIONS

THEATER SUPPORT

BLACK BOX THEATERS

DANCE REHEARSAL

TOWN ENTRY

his plans. Clearly, President Shirley Jackson and he had hit it off during her tour of his work, and thus she was very optimistic that the problems mentioned above could be resolved and that his scheme could be made to work. Since the jury's reservations were mainly about the practicality and the unresolved issues of the scheme, and she, as the owner, was willing to take that risk, the committee happily gave her their support.

In spite of the late programme changes mandated by RPI, the participating firms, in the words of adviser, Roger Schluntz, all managed 'to jump through these hoops' and submit challenging designs. Due to the fast-track approach to the competition, it is certain that many changes to the winning design will have to take place, but that is often the nature of the process.

Ground breaking for the Electronic Media and Performing Arts Center had been scheduled for spring 2002 but has been delayed. All in all, however, Rensselaer Polytechnic Institute's bold foray into the rarified world of architectural celebrity – made possible by the competition process – has been a remarkably fruitful experience.

Notes
1. All quotes in this essay are from its original publication in *Competitions*, Volume 11, No. 4, Winter 2001.

Tempe Visual & Performing Arts Center (2001)

Brian Taggart

Tempe lies on the south shore of the dry Salt River in the shimmering desert southeast of Phoenix. Home to Arizona State University, the city aspires to become a cultural oasis. A major step towards this ambition is a new Visual & Performing Arts Center to be built on the banks of the Tempe town lake, created in the early 1990s by damming the Salt River. Barton Myers's striking design, with its high angular roof forms covering a circular compound beneath, will be a cultural icon rising out of the harsh terrain to embrace that unexpected surprise in the desert ecosystem – a vast expanse of water.

The 24-acre site selected is far from idyllic: it is barren open desert crossed by power lines, degraded by gravel extraction to a depth of 40 feet, and later used as a landfill. Only half of the area is on the lake with the remainder lying below the dam. When the lake was created, a channel for the Salt River was also built. Prior to this the site was periodically flooded. Across Rio Salado Parkway, which borders the site to the south, is an industrial area. A freeway runs along the north side of the lake. The site itself is also somewhat isolated. Downtown Tempe is across the tracks half a mile to the southeast, with Arizona State University just beyond. But the overwhelming attractions of the setting – its unique location on the lake and its ownership by the city – overcame all objections. Tempe has allocated $6 million for site remediation and will bury the power lines.

The Competition Format
The first stage of the competition involved a particularly rigorous analysis of the submissions of the 16 firms that had responded to the Request for Qualfications (RfQ). This review reduced the list to six. These initial phases were not based on the programme because it had not yet been issued. The City of Tempe regarded the start of the competition to be when the three finalists had been selected. This occurred after the jury had visited the offices of the semi-finalists and had travelled the country to look at their prior work. Only after this review were the three finalists chosen:

- Barton Myers Associates
- Skidmore Owings & Merrill
- van Dijk Pace Westlake Architects with Hodgets + Fung and Hargreaves Associates

The programme for the 80,000 square foot building with a budget of $35 million was now presented to the finalists, each one of which received an honorarium of $25,000 to prepare a schematic design. The process was concluded in early 2001 with two seminars at which the teams had the opportunity to meet with the jury, the design committee, user groups, the technical committee and members of the public. In terms of public input Barton Myers and Paul Westlake ran neck and neck. Final designs were presented to the jury at a one-day session on 19 March where the three teams each had 90 minutes to present their concept. The competition concluded on 29 March when the Tempe City Council unanimously approved the jury's selection of Barton Myers Associates Inc. and ARCHITEKTON as the winning team.

The Process
The nine-member jury was composed almost entirely of laypeople, including the Mayor of Tempe and city

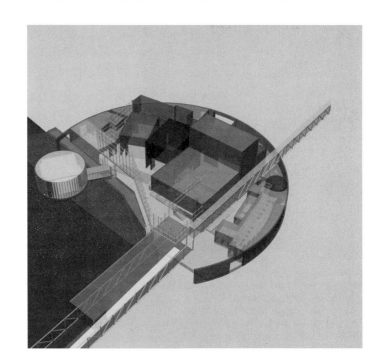

**Winning Entry
Barton Myers
Associates/ARCHITEKTON
(Los Angeles, CA, USA)**

Top Aerial view of
computerised model
Bottom Plan showing
Salt River and, on the
south bank of the river,
the site outlined in white

employees from the arts, community and construction sectors. There were also two representatives from the community. The Tempe city architect, Mark Vinson, was the lone professional on the jury and, while he thought that the lay jury had been effective, he said he would have preferred a more flexible initial analysis because the rigorous standards adopted by the city favoured large firms who were associated with landscape architects and acousticians. As a result of this, submissions by noted architects such as Antoine Predock and Will Bruder were eliminated in the RfQ phase.

Barton Myers felt that the competition process in Tempe was probably as good as any. He said:

I would tell people, make your shortlist, spend the money to go and see the work, go see the architects' offices, and then choose the guy you think is going to be best, and start working with him. The big problem with a competition is that the users, the clients, tend to be totally cut out of it. Competitions where they have tried to integrate the users through the competition process were so difficult and created such confusion that it wasn't so successful ... The problem with Tempe was that we would go off on our own and didn't sit down with the client every couple of weeks and say, 'Well what do you think of this?' ... We did go back, and we talked about a lot of our ideas, so we were trying to use them as a sounding board, but it's hard with such a lot of people to get direct feedback from that.[1]

In the end most of the dialogue had to take place during the presentation of the final design. Myers said he always asks if a competition is to choose a scheme or an architect. But he observed, 'It's often hard to undo the scheme; it's hard to go back to square one again. We get emotionally caught up in it, and the jury is affected by what they have seen'. Every time Barton Myers does a competition he says it's the last one he's going to do. He stated, 'Now we won't do them unless they are paid – we don't do open competitions anymore'. But he also said this:

A competition is a terrific way to mobilise interest,

it's like going to war – you learn how to do things quickly, working against the gun, getting your team working together, exploring a whole series of ideas quickly, being able to focus and move ahead. These are excellent drills for offices, and you do learn something from them.

On the question of what he should have presented to a lay jury such as this, Myers said:

In this case models were probably the way to go and our model was breathtaking, but I think we lost a lot of points on our drawings - too architectural, too hard-edged, too computer generated. The jury was taken aback by this high-tech, hard-edged look after they had seen the warmth of Newark and Portland. In Toronto we had Howard Sutcliffe, one of the greatest watercolour touches I have ever seen, very close to the 19th Century. I can't remember ever losing a competition if Howard was doing the painting.

He expressed the opinion that competitions should stress the techniques of the visual presentations and how these crucial techniques contributed to the winning and losing of competitions.

Paul Westlake of van Dijk Pace Westlake Architects was frustrated by the competition format because it only allowed 90 minutes to present what was a very complex design. He noted that the development of the design had involved hundreds of hours of work, dozens of drawings on 32 feet of 8-foot high boards, 80th and 20th scale models, cost and phasing data – an effort that could not be adequately presented in just 90 minutes. He said:

This was one of the most difficult and tense things I have ever tried to do because, having worked on this for months, there was so much to explain. I didn't feel that we had a real opportunity to discuss the issues in enough detail given the investment the firms had made in the process.

Notes
1. All quotes in this essay are from its original publication in *Competitions*, Volume 11, No. 4, Winter 2001.

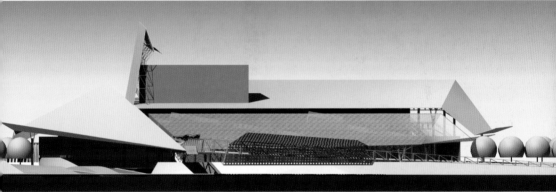

**Winning Entry
Barton Myers
Associates/ARCHITEKTON
(Los Angeles, CA, USA)**

Opposite Night view
This page Elevations

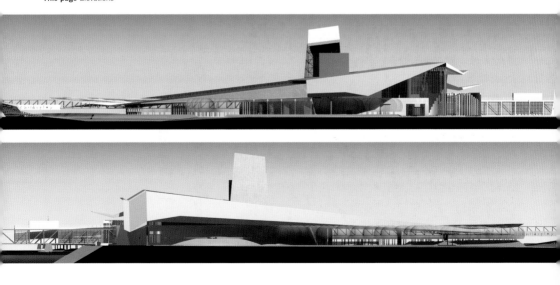

Finalist
Skidmore, Owings &
Merrill – Design Principal:
Leigh Breslau
(Chicago, IL, US)

Left Aerial view of site
Bottom Aerial view of
model showing organisation
along spine with bridge

**Finalist
van Dijk Pace Westlake
Architects with Hodgets
+ Fung and Hargreaves
Associates
(Cleveland, OH/Phoenix,
AZ/Los Angeles, CA/San
Francisco, CA, US)**

Right Perspective of front
entrance
Bottom Aerial view of model

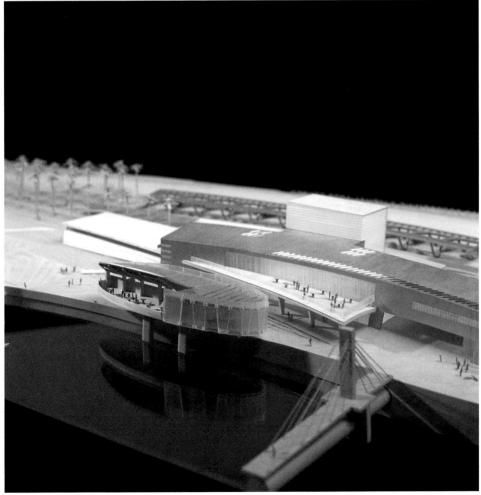

Jyväskylä Music and Arts Centre (1998)

William Morgan

Jyväskylä, a university town of only 75,000 people 185 miles north of Helsinki, is perhaps most significant as the boyhood home of Alvar Aalto. The architect's first office was in the town and there is a number of both early and late works by him here, including the university and the museum dedicated to his work. His masterpiece, the civic centre at Säynätsalo, as well as his summer home at Muuratsalo, are nearby. The annual Aalto Symposium held here attracts architects from around the world. And, not least of all, 1998 marked the Centennial of the mythic Finnish designer's birth with celebrations across Finland, as well as a major exhibition at the Museum of Modern Art.

The programme called for a city arts museum and a concert hall for the Jysväskylä Sinfonia (the Finns are as serious about music as they are about design) in the centre of downtown, very close to an early building by the master himself, the Defence Corps Building. The competition, open to European architects, was printed in Finnish newspapers, mailed throughout the EU, and, like the Starr Report, was distributed on the internet. 4,000 programmes were issued, 970 background information kits sold, and 359 entries were received by the September 1997 deadline.

In addition to local arts and music dignitaries and two Jyväskylä architects, the working jury was composed of an incredibly respected foursome: Finnish architects Juhani Pallasmaa and Simo Paavilainen, the Swede Gert Wingårdh, and 1998's Carlsberg winner, Peter Zumthor of Switzerland. In awarding three prize winners, three purchase prizes, and half a dozen honourable mentions, they took their work extremely seriously. The Jury Report is straightforward, without any slick public relations hype; it is a thoughtful commentary on the problem at hand.

The design of a Music and Arts Centre for Aalto's home town was a difficult one. The complexities of the building's dual functions – really two different buildings, plus the very civic nature of the site in downtown Jyväskylä ('several entries, however, project a scale which is entirely alien to the urban context of Jyväskylä'[1]) – created the chief hurdles. Not surprisingly, the entries themselves helped define the jury's expectations: 'The complexity of the task has meant that the jury has not been able to judge a single proposal to have fully satisfied all the requirements of the programme, in spite of the high number of entries and the serious professional effort in general'.

Furthermore, the site's 'demanding meditative position between two Aalto's buildings' – the Defence Corps (1924–29) and his Civic Centre (1964–83) created an obligation of honour that overshadowed the entire process. Nevertheless, an 'Aaltoesque vocabulary' was considered inappropriate, although 'an overly dynamic, expressive and overscaled structure' would have a negative impact on the sainted master's work.

While the jury hoped to emphasise 'architectural ideas' rather than functional or technical aspects, they seemed surprised at the high number of entries that did not consider climate (Finland!). Yet, as might be expected, the most technically feasible entries were often those with the higher artistic merit. Predictably given the make-up of the jury, the best proposals

Winning Entry
'Rhododendron'
Zita Cotti/Martina Hauser
(Zürich, Switzerland)

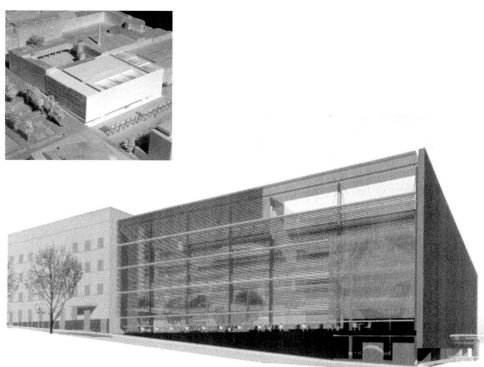

Opposite top
Winning Entry
'Rhododendron' Zita
Cotti/Martina Hauser
(Zürich, Switzerland)

Opposite top Computer
rendering of interior
Opposite insert
Competition model

Opposite middle and bottom
Second Place
'Solat' Antti Iskala/Jouko
Salonen/Olli-Pekka Keramaa
(Tampare, Finland)

Opposite, middle
Competition model
Opposite, bottom
Perspective from square

Right
Third Place
'Woods' Adam Caruso
and Peter St John of
Caruso St John Architects
(London, UK)

Right Competition model

were those that exhibited 'a strong, clear concept that provides a sense of coherence at all levels of the project'.

The winning design, by Zita Cotti and Martina Hauser of Switzerland, is praised for its 'clear concept of composition ... classical urban behavior ... clear structural discipline'. In a sort of backhanded compliment, the Cotti-Hauser scheme is called 'almost in a classical mode', while the proposed building 'does not act like a prima donna'. In fact, the other two finalists – Finnish architect Antti Iskala and the English team of Caruso St John Architects – produced equally understated box-like solutions to the urban context conundrum. The purchase prizes were won by Switzerland's Daniel Frick and Ivo Stalder; Tuomo Siitonen – perhaps the best known of the finalists; and Honjo Kunihiko of Japan, with honourable mentions to three Finns, another Swiss, a Dane, and Americans Robert Claiborne and Richard Abramson. There is no information on 300 non-winning firms (the entries are listed only with their entry pseudonyms), but that is a small shortcoming of this otherwise complete study of one particular competition in a faraway land.

Like the clarity the chief jurors so much admire, the Jury Report is a model of architectural writing (and it was written in English, with a Finnish translation). It is incredible to think that Europeans routinely produce entire books like this for any number of architectural competitions. Whether one has any interest in a small city along the shores of a lake in central Finland, the Jvyäskylä competition and subsequent book provide an exercise in architectural education. Imagine such briefs for American buildings!

One amusing note in an otherwise serious business is in the competition names, clever and less so, employed by the entrants. While the Finnish habit of naming a building after its winning entry label probably won't happen with Cotti-Hauser's 'Rhododendron', the names are revealing in themselves. There are a lot of references to Aalto: 'Alvaro', 'Alvarus est altissimus', 'Ave Alvar', 'Für Aino' (Aino was Aalto's first wife), 'Nemo propheto in patria' (the name of Aalto's boat). Others recall that Aalto means wave in Finnish: 'New Wave', 'Make Wave', and 'Tsunami'. Aside from the predictable, like 'Metamorphosis', 'Red Yellow Blue', 'Chaos' and 'Agora Cultura', there is any number of musical monikers: 'Con brio', 'Dongiovanni', 'Grand Piano', 'Grieg', 'Stradivarius', and 'Symphony in architectural movement', and three entries called 'Built sound'. Finnish, winter and forest names appear, of course: 'And the Forest is Singing Behind', 'Lemminkäinen's Return', and 'Slabs of Ice'. And, then the names that are so personal or so clever that their meaning is known only to the competitors: 'Armadillo', 'Banana', 'The Lord of the Flies' and 'Uncle Scrooge'.

Note
1. All quotes in this essay are from its original publication in *Competitions*, Volume 8, No. 4, Winter 1998.

Performing Arts Center of Greater Miami (1995)

Carlos Casuscelli

A decade ago, the Summit of the Americas made Miami more than ever aware of the importance that nations south of the border attach to it as the economic and cultural gateway to the United States. One only need travel through one of the area airports – Miami International or Fort Lauderdale – to feel the vibrant economic pulse of that booming region. And there is, too, a certain self-assurance about the strides the city has made in design. One of the more visible symbols is the new Brickell Bridge in downtown Miami, itself the result of a design competition which was staged back in 1990. This complements the preservation effort on Miami's South Beach as well as a successful public art programme, which has left its mark on the city's streets and skyline.

Competitions such as Brickell Bridge proved to members of the community that other ways could be explored in the selection of designers for important projects. Therefore, when it became apparent that the development of a cultural complex of international stature was long overdue, the way had already been paved for a process which would determine the design for Miami's most important new cultural symbol, the Miami-Dade Performing Arts Center. The rationale for a competition was simple: it was to be a very public process with active participation from various community interest groups such as artists and preservationists.

It was probably for this reason that the Performing Arts Center competition aroused little controversy and appears to be well along the approval track. And this seems to have taken place without a hitch, in spite of a complex and lengthy organisational scheme for the competition. The selection process actually lasted over a period of several months. Among the initial guidelines imposed was one which prohibited joint ventures. On the other hand, a dispensation was obtained from the state which allowed for the participation of out-of-state firms. Still, the rigid rules led many Miami firms, some of them wellknown, to the conclusion that participation was an extremely complicated matter.

A lengthy screening process, initiated by RfQs and interviews of 25 leading architectural firms, led to the selection of three finalists: Cesar Pelli and Associates, New Haven, Connecticut; Rem Koolhaas/The Office of Metropolitan Architecture, Rotterdam, Holland; and Arquitectonica with Duany Plater-Zyberk of Miami. Hometown architect, Jorge Hernandez, who served on the technical jury which had the daunting task of screening the architectural firms, said that Arquitectonica/Duany Plater-Zyberk and Koolhaas were unanimously agreed as finalists from the very beginning, while Pelli came up from the middle of the pack. The initial stage saw these three firms take part in a week-long charrette with public participation and input. The firms submitted their final plans in Miami a month later. There they reconvened for their final presentations and jurying.

The quality of all the entries validated the process, despite the strains it placed on the competitors. Hernandez says there was 'complete agreement on the part of the participants that the week spent in Miami - especially for the out-of-town competitors – to gather information and sense of the will of the community'[1] was very helpful. The downside was the burden which is placed on the firms – the time spent away from the home office and the financial implications. Pelli agrees with the observation, noting

that 'this kind of charrette process is fine as long as the participants are adequately compensated'.

Although the 'technical jury' was involved intimately in the selection process through the first two stages of the competition, it was not given a mandate to express its opinion on the value of the entries during the final stage, being relegated solely to the role of technical advisers. This, found Hernandez, was rather 'ironic' considering the extent to which the professionals had been involved up to that point.

The Site

The site on which the Performing Arts Center is to be built is directly across the street from Knight Ridder, which publishes the *Miami Herald* and donated the parcel of land. Hernandez said that the choice might have been a different one: the Center might have been a 'jewel' on one of the unused islands. However, he acknowledges that the present choice does present the possibility of neighbourhood revitalisation, which another venue might not have. As it is, the site for the Performing Arts Center is part of a larger vision of the city that considers the linkage of Miami's main nodes, i.e. the airport, the downtown/Cruise Port area and Miami Beach. The site's immediate surroundings do not differ significantly from the downtowns of other American inner cities: derelict buildings, historical

structures, recently built office buildings and hotels, huge parking lots and the modern paraphernalia of routes and connectors, including an elevated transit system. It all coexists as living proof of what has been and has yet to be, so as to bring back the urban qualities that this area used to possess in the past.

Amidst this panorama, the healing and organising potential of a $140 million structure in a two-square-block, inner-city area cannot be overestimated. Still, a blighted zone in Miami does not have the same visual impact it may have in Midwestern and other inland cities. The proximity of water, the striking vistas and a myriad of visitors combine to soften the impression of urban decay which is common to the Overtown District. Thus, the site configuration and relative location of the project are of absolute importance, not only to the Center's own success, but also to the revitalisation of the whole neighbourhood.

Only in this broader urban context can an analysis of the three finalists be understood. The two theatre buildings will be located on two adjoining blocks, facing each other across a main thoroughfare. This street is an important one, and it is impossible to ignore it. Moreover, a former Sears store, Miami's first art deco building, is on the site and is regarded by preservationists as an element worth saving. If local preservationists had not made such an issue of this

Winning Entry
Cesar Pelli & Associates
(New Haven, CT, US)

Opposite
Competition model with
Biscayne Boulevard passing
between the two buildings.
The opera house is at the left

Below
Aerial view of Performing
Arts Center with existing Sears
tower as signpost directly on
Biscayne Boulevard

during the charrette, it is possible that not even the
tower would have remained from the historic
structure; aside from nostalgia and some cultural
interest, there is in fact little historical value in the
Sears structure, and too much would have been
jeopardised by keeping the entire building. So, due to
the presence of the preservationists, all of the
participating architects kept the tower as part of their
schemes in what might be understood to be an
equivocal sense of history.

The Design Proposals
Arquitectonica and Duany Plater-Zyberk's strategy
was to treat the two main halls on opposite sides of
the street as separate entities, thus creating two
internal lobbies. For a city whose inhabitants cannot
imagine life without air-conditioning, this solution had
a sound logic. In wrapping the site with the perimeter
of the urban block – a necessary mechanism to
regenerate the lost urban fabric of the area – the two
main volumes exude a strong urban image. Due to
their similarities, the halls generate a gateway,
especially when approached from the downtown area,
to which both glass facades make a strong gesture
and thereby achieve the desired linkage with the city
centre. This is supplemented by a series of guidelines
for the development of the neighbourhood which will

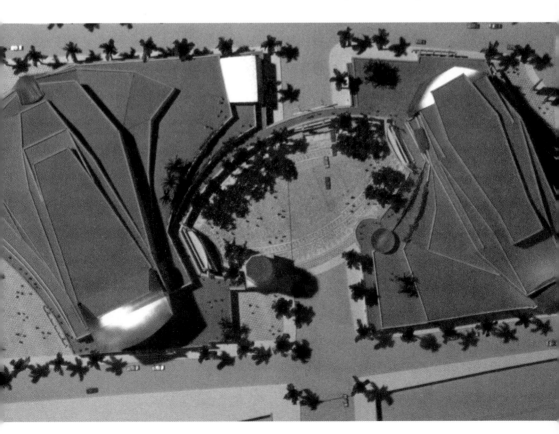

Finalist
Arquitectonica
(Miami, FL, US)

Opposite page, top
Model shot
Opposite, bottom
Looking north on
Biscayne Boulevard

This page, top
Crossing Byscane Boulevard
to the main theatre
This page, bottom
Night view from east
over water

prove to be very useful in the future, for, regardless of how the project is finally realised, it represents a valuable piece of urban analysis and strategy.

If there is a surprise in the scheme presented by Dutch architect Rem Koolhaas, it is the desire to not deal with the context as it is, but to reform it considerably. Nevertheless, in its ambitious but reasonable attempt to make the complex work as a whole, the building looks almost intrusive and out of scale compared to the other two designs. Although very creative in his attempt to generate a 'mixing chamber' and public arena, Hernandez feels Koolhaas may not have made enough of its interesting concept. The scheme, in broad terms, is similar to Rafael Viñoly's Tokyo Forum, a classic solution to the same programmatic needs that has, in the past, turned out to be a successful formula.

The winning entry by Cesar Pelli, unlike Koolhaas's and similar to Arquitectonica's, positions a performance hall in each block. In Pelli's design, the massing is diminished considerably, creating a friendly image with the main volumes stepping down. This ingenious solution seems very appropriate for generating a pedestrian-oriented space: two outdoor public plazas to either side of the boulevard will act as open forums. As opposed to Arquitectonica's

gesture towards the city, Pelli's scheme is more introverted, probably with the understanding that this complex is so huge that one can hardly drive by without noticing it. The formal internal unity of the plan is achieved by the linkage of its separate parts with an elliptical void, whose footprint crosses the boulevard as an ethereal organiser of the surrounding volumes. To connect the two sides physically, Pelli has a bridge crossing the street linking the two complexes. Whether that element will remain is questionable. But should it be missing, it will still be a silent reminder that air alone may not do the trick.

What long-term effect this project will have on the renewal of the adjoining neighbourhood is an open question. Pelli's idea that the plaza might be a gathering place is somewhat hard to follow when one thinks of the great plazas and why they function so well. San Marco (Venice), Breitscheid Platz (Berlin) and those in downtown Baltimore, for instance, all have one thing in common: they are heavily travelled way-stations for pedestrians, on their journey from one point in the city to another. Moreover, they are in high density areas which are famous for their monuments and functions.

Overtown, by itself, would certainly not be a popular destination for downtown workers and

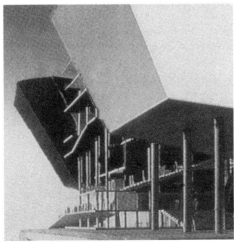

tourists in the immediate future. To what extent the
Arts Center will become a magnet will depend in part
on what happens around it. Looking back at the
South Beach of 20 years ago, hardly anyone except
the most inveterate optimists would have predicted
its present popularity. One may only hope that a
similar fate awaits the Performing Arts Center a
decade or so down the road.

At present the centre is nearing completion, and it
is scheduled to open sometime in 2005. There have
been – as there always are – changes from the
original design. But the idea is still intact, and it
might well turn out to be the catalyst for the area
which the city has sorely needed.

Note
1. All quotes in this essay are from its original publication
in *Competitions*, Volume 5, No. 2, Summer 1995.

Educational Facilities

Winning Entry
Pfau Architecture
(San Francisco, CA, US)
Lick-Wilmerding High School,
San Francisco, California,
US Competition 2001
Completion 2003

The need for new school types has been spurred by the advent of high technology and an emphasis on more flexibility in the organisation of large spaces. New school types, such as Performing Arts High Schools have also led to competitions for this building type.

Schools have been, and probably always will be, regarded as one of the most essential community assets. Kindergarten is actually an orientation exercise for that first job – First Grade. It is about being attentive and good attendance, putting your 'stuff' in a secure place, competing against your fellow students, completing tasks on time, and fitting in. Schools, which prepare you for the bigger jobs in life, are essential to your understanding of place and how the job environment works. Those municipalities and government institutions that recognise the role which good design plays in crafting the ideal learning environment will often turn to competitions for the best solution.

Especially in the US, where many urban school systems are in trouble, good design is often regarded as an essential ingredient in bringing about positive change. This is often the rationale for using competitions as a way to create the best possible learning environment. Thus, it should come as no surprise that metropolitan school districts such as New York City, Chicago and Atlanta have turned to competitions for better design solutions. In 1997, the New York City School Construction Authority staged two ideas competitions which focused on two areas common to all schools, one for the design of the 'Classroom of the Future', primarily for Fourth and Fifth graders; the other was for a 'Commons', a large space to function as auditorium, gym and cafeteria. The Fulton County School System (Atlanta) staged two invited competitions for prototype elementary and middle schools, the first in 1997–8. As might be expected in the latter case, more emphasis is placed on vehicular circulation due to parent 'drop-off' zones and school buses than would be the case in New York City or Europe, where students depend largely on public transportation.

Some of the more imaginative competitions for school design in the US have been the result of competitions staged by private schools. A privately funded high school in San Francisco, Lick-Wilmerding, staged a competition for a new complex which resulted in a below-grade design solution. A downtown high school in Louisville, Kentucky, staged a limited regional competition for an arts/sports centre complex which is to complement an existing, renovated Beaux Arts structure – a former YMCA

Right
Premiated Entry
Richard Dattner Architect
(New York, US)
New York City 'School
Commons of the Future'
Ideas Competition 1998

'The Commons' challenged
architects to think creatively
about a method to conserve
space in elementary schools
by manipulating large spaces
for a variety of functions –
assemblies, sports, cafeteria
and events such as
performances

Bottom
Winning Entry
Riken Yamamoto & Field
Shop
(Yokohama, Japan)
Iwadeyama Junior High
School, Iwadeyama
Township, Miyagi Prefecture,
Japan
Competition 1993
Completion 1996

This school was typical of
those built in less populous
districts in Japan, as it
had only nine classrooms

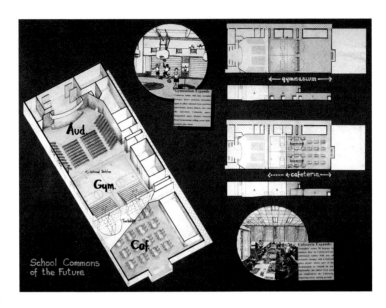

building. In middle America, communities often restrict the design language of infill architecture, asking for a building which they can understand as being 'contextual'. In the latter case, the administration of this high school opted for a more progressive solution, mixing the modern with the traditional.

The Role of Nonprofits

In the absence of strong underwriting support for competitions by government in the US, nonprofits (i.e. organisations and institutions of non-profit making or charitable status) often play a key role in their organisation. This has been very pervasive in the affordable housing sector, but also occurs on occasion with the design of educational facilities. Participation by US-based nonprofits can have a positive impact on the organisation of competitions, as jurors are more likely to be design professionals, instead of bureaucrats. On the other hand, once the competition is concluded, the lack of a strong connection to the funding entity, whether it be city, state, or a developer, may result in the winning design being stripped of some of its most important features or, worse, being abandoned altogether.

One competition funded by a nonprofit in the educational sector was the 1995 'Head Start' prototype competition, a facility for early childhood education. Although specific to a site in Windsor, New Jersey, the aim of the competition included establishing patterns of design for a facility adaptable to other locales. Sponsored by the nonprofit Early Childhood Facility Fund (ECFF), the competition, which had 143 entries, resulted in some very innovative winners, the most impressive being an entry by a young team from Cambridge, Massachusetts led by Homu Fardjadi. But again, the nonprofit client was never able to deliver a finished product. A competition for a Montessori school in California had a more fortunate outcome. This competition, for an addition to an existing Montessori school in Berkeley, is scheduled to be completed by 2004.

A competition for inner-city prototypes, 'Big Shoulders, Small Schools', – in this case, it was site specific – was the brainchild of a Chicago-based nonprofit organisation, Business and Professional People for the Public Interest (BPI). Staged in 2001, the challenge was to imagine a school where at least 20 percent of the students are handicapped. This competition also suggested that the image which the school of the future wants to project is hardly that of a fortress. Light and whimsy were high

Winning Entry
Behnisch, Behnisch & Partner
(Stuttgart, Germany)
St Benno Gymnasium,
Dresden, Germany
Open Competition 1993
Completion 1996

Below Atrium perspective
Right View to front entrance

priorities here. Although security was certainly a concern, no high fences to keep out the drug dealers were in evidence.

Atlanta also staged two competitions for elementary and middle schools in the 1990s. The results indicate that the structures now being built have taken a very sensitive approach to the hillside sites where construction is presently taking place.

European competitions for school design were in high gear in the 1960s and 1970s – the baby boom years. A competition for the design of 16 middle schools in Berlin in the late 1960s was not all that unusual. In the meantime, most of the schools resulting from that competition have been shut down, mainly due to the use of asbestos in the steel construction. The former Communist East Germany was an area where some new school construction in that country might have been a high priority. However, new schools such as the St Benno Gymnasium in Dresden have been the exception to the rule. The exodus of young people from east to west in Germany because of the lack of job prospects in their home towns and a low birthrate has dampened demand there. Most of the competitions taking place in Germany at the moment have been occurring in the south, where both population growth and the economy have been strong.

In Asia, where the work ethic of schoolchildren is a notch above standards in the Western democracies, and their duties may even include cleaning up the classroom, design of educational facilities is hardly neglected, but is not necessarily informed by the US and European model. Still, some significant architecture has resulted in Japan as a consequence of competitions for school design. One such competition was for the Iwadeyama (township) Junior High School, Miyagi Prefecture by Riken Yamamoto. This rural school, although only having nine classrooms, was certainly a model for other outlying regions.

Academia

The expanding student population worldwide has resulted in massive building programmes on many campuses around the world, providing fertile ground for competitions. Aside for fulfilling the need for more facilities, it is a vehicle for academic institutions to suggest that they represent the cutting edge in this information age. In Europe, where most institutions of higher learning owe their existence to state funding, the design of most large-scale projects has been the result of competitions. Two examples from the 1960s which attracted international attention were for the design of major academic facilities in Berlin – at the Technical University and the Free University. In Canada, a 1963 competition for the design of a completely new facility for Simon Fraser University in Vancouver, British Columbia, jump-started the career of a young Canadian architect, Arthur Erickson.

Two competitions for campus structures which took place at the University of California at Berkeley in the 1960s – for the Lawrence Hall of Science (won by Anshen and Allen Architects) and an arts centre (Mario J Ciampi with Richard L Jorasch and Ronald E Wagner) – placed that university in the forefront of progressive institutions. Utilising the competition process for the design of two new schools of architecture in the late 1960s – at Ball State University and the University of Tennessee – would seem to be a logical step for any new architecture programme. And a competition for the law school building at Washington University in St Louis in the 1970s produced a truly fine building for that institution. But, as usual, it took a lot of lobbying on the part of the faculty of those departments to convince administration officials, used to letting contracts in the usual manner, to pursue this avenue of design selection.

Aside from the competition for the Roger Williams University School of Architecture in the 1980s, there was a prolonged lull in the design of

academic buildings by competition until the past decade. Then, in the 1990s, universities again began to show more interest in competitions as a method to achieve better campus design. This was motivated in part by the realisation that high design was a way to raise the profile of the institution and thus attract students with high expectations. It could not have escaped the attention of some college administrators that entire new campuses such as Ithaca College, University of California at Santa Cruz and even little Lake Erie College in Painesville, Ohio had built entirely new campuses which, in architectural language, marked a significant departure from the traditional architecture of Ivy League universities. Also, a number of older institutions were turning to modernists such as Louis Kahn (Yale Center for British Art) and IM Pei (Indiana University Art Museum) for the design of landmark structures.

Clemson University in South Carolina staged a competition for a university performing arts centre in 1990. An open, two-stage competition which was won by Sert Jackson of Boston over Graham Gund of Boston and Amy Anderson, a young faculty member at Columbia University, it was one of the few competitions where the second stage did matter, as Sert Jackson modified its scheme considerably to make it a better fit for the campus. Finished in the early 1990s, it represents one of the better university buildings resulting from a competition. It also came in under budget.

Winning Entry
Leers Weinzapfel Associates
(Boston, Massachusetts)
University of Pennsylvania
Chiller Plant, Philadelphia,
Pennsylvania
Competition 1998

This limited competition was
contested by four high profile
firms, with Leers Weinzapfel's
simple, yet innovative,
approach winning the hearts
of the jury. The metal mesh
facade, when illuminated at
night, dominates the skyline
next to the Scuykill
Expressway

University competitions in the past decade were not restricted to individual buildings. Dartmouth University has undertaken a large expansion project, using a competition for ideas to integrate it physically and visually into the present campus setting. The invited competition which ensued was won by Moore Ruble Yudell of Santa Monica, California. Whereas one of the competitors, Bob Stern, used very traditional language in his entry to mimic the earlier architecture, the jury liked the MRY submission, which did stick to brick as the main facade material, but moved away from a strictly traditional approach in favour of more glazing and transparency.

Invited competitions for schools of architecture, a student centre, and even a chiller plant have recently grabbed the headlines: almost all of the invitees were high profile architects who had either won competitions previously, or were prominent at a local or regional level. Here, names like Bernard Tschumi, Rem Koolhaas, Antoine Predock, Helmut Jahn, and Peter Eisenman were more often than not on the table. In one of the more interesting competitions, a firm headed by two female architects came up with a simple, but elegant solution for a chiller plant at the University of Pennsylvania – giving us just a glimpse of the inside workings of this industrial type facility through a metal mesh skin which glows in the night for passing motorists.

The United States is presently the country with the most ambitious plans for spending on educational facilities. Most of this will come from the individual states and municipalities, rather than the federal government. But with states like Ohio projecting $6 billion in K-12 (kindergarden through to 12th grade) spending over the next few years, there should be plenty of work for architects in this sector. Unfortunately most of this will be commissioned without the benefit of design competitions. Still, those that do occur help to raise the bar in school architecture – at least for those who are paying attention.

Lick-Wilmerding High School, San Francisco (2001)

Susannah Temko

Competition adviser William Liskamm maintains that, 'Interaction with the clients during competitions can sometimes bring surprising results'.[1] And that is precisely what happened when the San Francisco firm, Pfau Architecture, came up with a below-grade design during a competition for the Technology and Design Center of San Francisco's Lick-Wilmerding High School.

A crucial element of the surprise had to do with the sophisticated philosophy of the sponsor, Lick-Wilmerding. In 'Lick's "Design Moment" of the Century', Head of School Albert M Adams emphasised that the competition would represent the school's 'head, heart, hands approach to education'. The four interrelated design goals were:

- To revise the 1997 masterplan by Principal Cathy Simon of SMWM, with extra attention to open space and building relations.
- A new Technology and Design Center over the parking lot housing wood, metal, machine, glass and electronic shops.
- Expanding the original Science Lecture Hall into a theatre.
- To renovate the shop building for larger music space and a new cafeteria/student centre.

To achieve these goals, the client shortlisted five architecture firms. Three of them came from the San Francisco area: Pfau Architecture, Leddy Maytum Stacy Architects, and Lundberg Design. The remaining two firms were from the east coast Kennedy Violich/Kuth Ranieri (Boston/San Francisco); and William McDonough and Partners (Charlottesville, Virginia).

After interim design meetings with the client where the finalists' concepts and schemes could be

Winning Entry
(Limited competition)
Pfau Architecture
San Francisco, California

Aerial perspective to east
from interstate

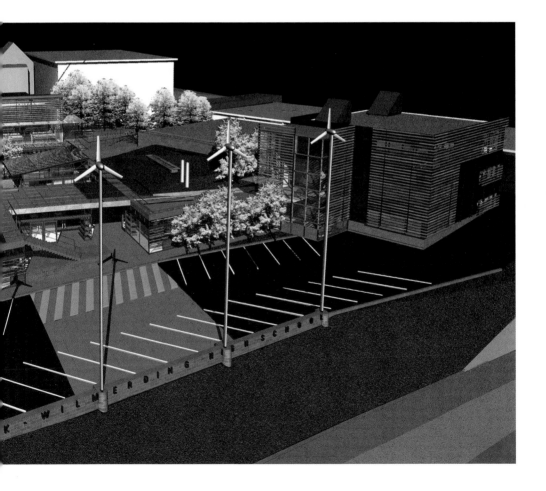

**Winning Entry
(Limited competition)
Pfau Architecture
San Francisco, California**

Left Grade level plan
Opposite top View of finished
building illustrating the
below-grade structure and
same view as illustrated
on the original competition
entry board. The wind
turbines, which were not
in the budget, have not
yet been incorporated into
the final project
Opposite, middle
Cafeteria after construction
Opposite, bottom
View to express-way
(competition board)

'tested' on the client, a public exhibition of the
entries was held before an oral presentation of the
designs to the jury, Board of Trustees, and the public.
The sponsor understood that the future relationship
with the winning team would be an intimate one,
and the school wanted to get to know each team
better before entering into such a relationship.

Everyone, including the non-voting technical
advisers, assumed that all the schemes would
honour the guidelines for an above-ground
Technology and Design Center. Following Simon's
masterplan, they called for building on the open end
of the playing field, thereby preventing a year-long
loss of shop space. But Pfau Architecture had reason
to sink the shops of the proposed Design Center
underground – down to a single level of shops
situated around a yard. From a visual standpoint it
was obvious that it would maintain the field's
eastward view. Secondly, the far side of the proposed
above-ground Center would place it in the immediate
proximity of I-280 interstate highway and its
attendant noise. Even though the underground Center
seemed logical, the firm thoughtfully included two
other schemes for the committee and board.

However, it was the underground scheme that
won the day. 'Their concept was so out of the box

that it just took our breath away. It had never
occurred to us to go underground', according to Head
of School, Albert M Adams. Unlike the other firms,
Pfau Architecture's lowering of the shops put the
outlets on the same level as the parking lot, with the
consequence that elevators would not be needed. The
design retained a lift from the scene shop to the
theatre's stage.

Light can be a concern from below grade, but
Pfau incorporated bump-up window skylights,
doubling as benches at the field level. Waterproofing
turned out to be pretty standard for this type of roof
deck system. The crucial factor was a sufficient two-
foot depth in the roof construction, which allowed for
the drainage slope and the proper depth of
lightweight soil for a landscaping and paving system
at field level.

Construction began the following year and the new
Technology and Design Center opened for business at
the Lick-Wilmerding High School in the fall of 2003.

Note
1. All quotes in this essay are from its original publication
in *Competitions*, Volume 11, No. 3, Fall 2001.

Finalist
Kennedy Violich/Kuth Ranieri
(Boston, MA, US/San
Francisco, CA, US)
Competition board

The rectangular 'Design
Center' had upper-floor MAC
labs and lower-floor shops;
the computers would have
had additional capacity
to direct shop equipment

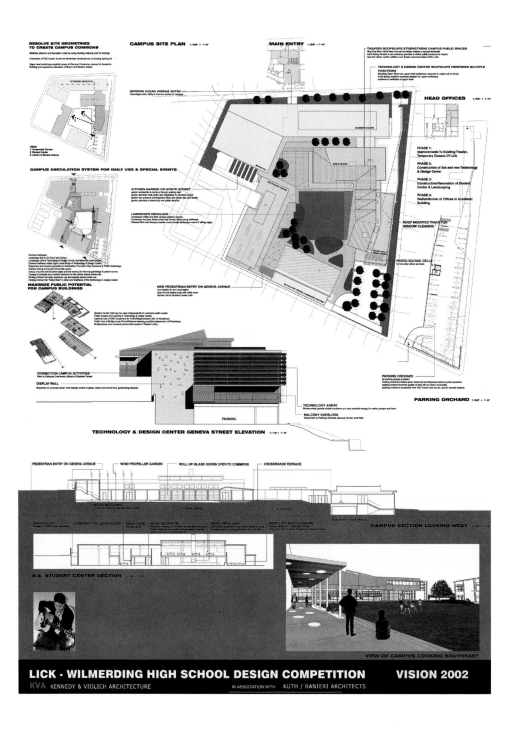

LICK · WILMERDING HIGH SCHOOL DESIGN COMPETITION   VISION 2002
KVA KENNEDY & VIOLICH ARCHITECTURE   IN ASSOCIATION WITH   KUTH / RANIERI ARCHITECTS

**Finalist
William McDonough
and Partners
(Charlottesville, VA, US)**

Right Interior courtyard
Bottom Aerial view of site

In keeping with their national
reputation for sustainable
architecture, McDonough
created an underground
theatre with a verdant
amphitheatre above it.
The two-storey Technology
and Design Center had shops
over a multipurpose level

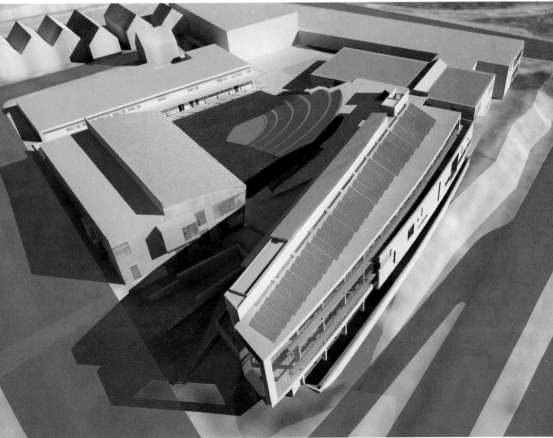

Leddy's design featured a
series of steel frames for the
Center, straddling the existing
theatre to provide additional
seating. The transparent
Center would have the view
as the backdrop

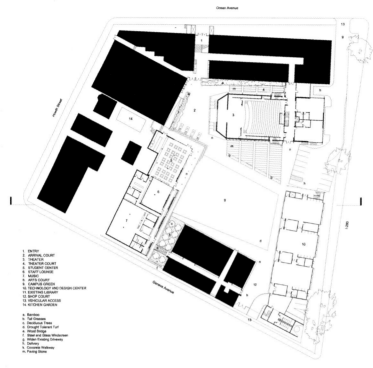

1. ENTRY
2. ARRIVAL COURT
3. THEATER
4. THEATER COURT
5. STUDENT CENTER
6. STAFF LOUNGE
7. MUSIC
8. ARTS COURT
9. CAMPUS GREEN
10. TECHNOLOGY AND DESIGN CENTER
11. EXISTING LIBRARY
12. SHOP COURT
13. VEHICULAR ACCESS
14. KITCHEN GARDEN

a. Bamboo
b. Tall Grasses
c. Deciduous Trees
d. Drought Tolerant Turf
e. Wood Bridge
f. Steel and Glass Windscreen
g. Widen Existing Driveway
h. Delivery
k. Concrete Walkway
m. Paving Stone

MASTER PLAN

Finalist
Lundberg Design
(San Francisco, CA, US)

Top Grade level plan
Bottom Section of exterior
perspective

Lundberg located the
technical shops at the
parking level and connected
them to the theatre

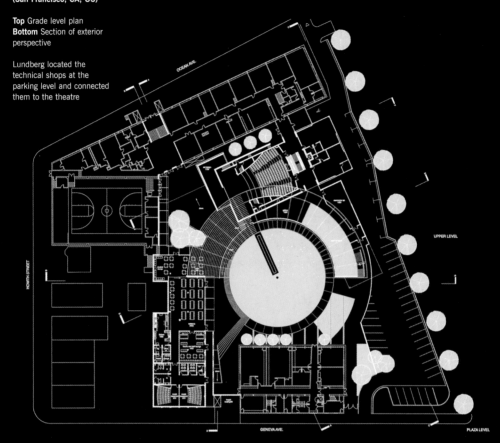

Chicago Prototype Schools (2001)

G Stanley Collyer

In an era of mergers and consolidation, the small neighbourhood school would seem to be a relic from the past. But recent studies indicate that children perform better in more intimate settings. So how does one avoid 'bigness' with all its problems, an all too common characteristic of the US's present schools? Judging from the entries which were submitted to the 'Big Shoulders, Small Schools' competition held recently in Chicago, it is all about clustering. A medium-sized elementary school organised physically into smaller entities, each almost a school within a school, can aspire to recreating a feeling of 'smallness'. Add to this the fact that at least 20 percent of the students are in some manner handicapped and a budget limit of $200 per square foot (the average cost in Chicago is $150 per square foot), you have all the ingredients for a formidable design challenge.

In an effort to relieve overcrowding and improve learning conditions, many school systems have recently embarked on large capital improvement programmes. Whereas Chicago may have been dragging its feet on this issue, various organisations within the city have been focusing attention on it for some time. One of the highest profile non-profit organisations leading this charge has been the Business and Professional People for the Public Interest (BPI). Together with Leadership for Quality Education (LQE) and the Small Schools Coalition (SSC), in partnership with the Chicago Public Schools (CPS) and the Mayor's Office for People with Disabilities, a national design competition was launched in January 2000 for the design and eventual construction of two prototype schools based on universal principles at two sites in the city – one in the south side Roseland

community, and one in the north side Irving Park community.

The competition, which was hybrid in nature, was supported in part through a new programme initiated by the National Endowment for the Arts (NEA) under its Director of Design, Mark Robbins. The hybrid feature of the competition resulted from the NEA's insistence that at least four firms of national stature be invited to participate in a second stage with two winners from the first, open stage for each site. The inclusion of invited firms was stipulated to ensure high design quality.

When the entries in the open competition section were unveiled – just under 60 entries a piece for each site – it was clear that the fears of the NEA were hardly justified. From the theoretical to the architecturally exuberant, the entries exhibited a high degree of creativity and professionalism. Arriving at a decision on a winner in the open section was not going to be an easy matter.

As was the case here, mixing laypersons and design professionals on a jury is often a tricky business. The jury process is slowed somewhat by the inclusion of non-designers, for they often have to go through a learning curve to understand what it is exactly that they are looking at. On the positive side, they are the ones in the community who have to be the advocates for the winning designs after the competition.

Since the two sites were dissimilar – the south side site was square, the other elongated – the architects first had to decide which site best fitted their intended approach. Moreover, the south side site was single level, the north side site two-level. Karen Fairbanks, south side site winner, stated that after

Winning entry
Southside site,
Marble Fairbanks Architecture
(New York, New York, US)

The winning design for this
site was chosen from amongst
the open entries who
made it into the finals, not
one of the "invited" and
compensated finalists.
It prevailed in the first
round over 59 other entries.

Right Aerial perspectives
Bottom Circulation plan

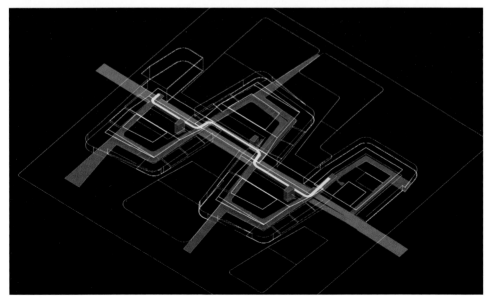

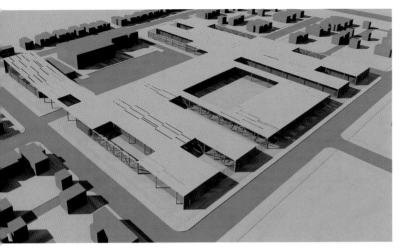

Finalist
South Side Site
Ground Zero Design Studio
(Open stage winner)
Ann Arbor, Michigan

Below View from entrance
Left Aerial view of model

looking at both sites, only the south side matched their criteria. This supports the argument that schools, especially in the inner city, can seldom be the result of a standard footprint; each site has its own set of conditions.

The criteria sounded much like those one would find for most competitions, one difference being the strong emphasis placed on handicapped accessibility and sustainability:

• Innovative: bringing architectural creativity and imagination to educational spaces
• Feasible: buildable for approximately $200 per square foot, which includes soft costs and furniture but not land, utilities, remediation, or medical equipment
• Sensitive to Neighbourhood Context: reflecting the ethnic, geographic and social culture of the neighbourhoods where the schools will be built
• Sensitive to Universal Design: accessible, functional and usable by people of any age, ability or background – including elements of green design and sustainable design
• Sensitive to Small School Design: breaking large structures down into two or more 'schools-within-a-school' to create intimate educational environments

The Winning Designs
The Jury picked two winners for each site in the open section.
South Side Site:
Ground Zero Design Studio, Ann Arbor, Michigan
Marble Fairbanks Architects, New York, New York

North Side Site:
Jack L Gordon Architects, New York, New York
Lubrano Ciavarra Design, New York, New York
These winners were joined by invited architects.
South Side Site:
Mac Scogin Merrill Elam Architects, Atlanta, Georgia
Smith-Miller + Hawkinson Architects, New York, New York
North Side Site:
Koning Eizenberg Architecture, Santa Monica, California
Ross Barney + Jankowski Architects, Chicago, Illinois

When the open section winners had been selected, preliminary designs from the four invited architects for the two sites were unveiled. The initial impression of the jury, according to several present, was the unenthusiastic response the new designs elicited. This was, of course, before the final stage, which would take place several weeks later. In the interim, architects were to meet with neighbourhood leaders and discuss the community's needs. These forums turned out to be extremely useful for both sides. Karen Fairbanks said, 'We made changes in our design as a result of community feedback, including turning the site around, creating a single entry for the school, creating more gently sloping landscaping and ramping system and increasing the amount of outdoor play space'.

As a result of the final evaluation by the jury, Marble Fairbanks was declared the winner of the south side site and Koning Eizenberg was selected for the north side site. Construction has been put on hold because of budget cuts in education.

Finalist
South Side Site
Mac Scogin Merrill
ElamArchitects,
Atlanta, Georgia, US

Right Corner rendering
Below Aerial perspective model
Below, right Hearth rendering
Bottom Ground floor plan

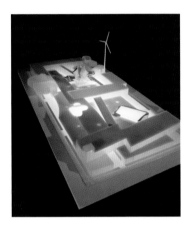

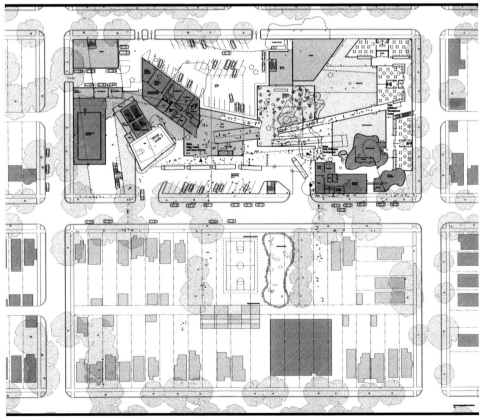

Finalist
South Side Site
Smith-Miller + Hawkinson
New York, New York
(Invited Finalist)

Left Aerial perspective of
school with view to entrance
Below Model interior
Bottom Elementary school
classroom

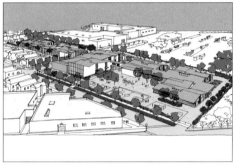

Above
Winner
North Side Site
Koning Eizenberg Architecture
Santa Monica, California
(Invited Finalist)

Similar to the winner of the
South Side site, Koning
Eizenberg chose a cluster
approach for their proposal.
Their scheme was
appropriately labeled, "learning
neighborhoods."

Top Section
Above left Interior Corridor
Above right Aerial perspective

Below
Finalist
North Side Site
Ross Barney + Jankowski
Architets
Chicago, Illinois
(Invited Finalist)

Carol Ross Barney chose
to place much in the way
of sports activities on the
top of the buildings – not
so unusual in Chicago

Bottom left Aerial perspective
Bottom right View of Chicago
skyline from school

Left and below Interior
and exterior perspectives
Bottom Birdseye view of
site model

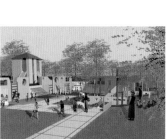

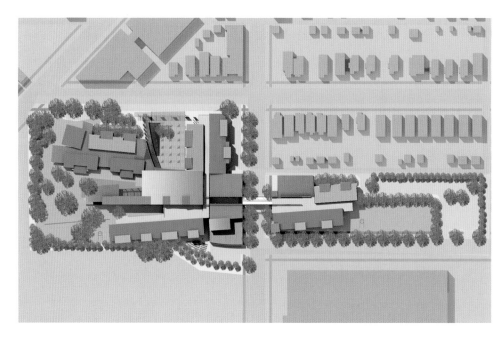

Finalist
North Side Site
Lubrano Ciavarra Design
New York, New York
(Open Stage Winner)

Right Aerial view of model
Middle Ramping and corridor
system
Bottom View to interior
courtyard

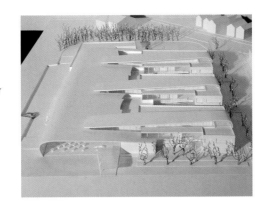

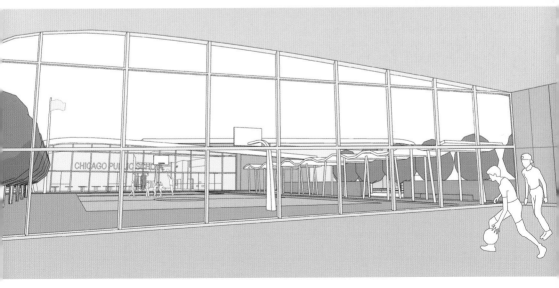

Booker T Washington Arts Magnet School, Dallas (2001)

Mark Gunderson AIA

Allied Works Architecture of Portland, Oregon was selected from four finalists in a competition to provide architectural design services for the $40 million expansion and remodelling of the Booker T Washington High School for the Performing and Visual Arts (BTW) in Dallas. Finalists included Carlos Jimenez Studio of Houston, Charles Rose Architects (formerly Thompson and Rose) of Cambridge, Massachusetts, and Mac Scogin Merrill Elam Architects of Atlanta, Georgia. Steven Holl had been on the original shortlist but withdrew after winning a separate competition. The competition adviser was Lawrence Speck FAIA.

Sited two blocks east of the Meyerson Symphony Center in the Dallas Arts District, the school will anchor the eastern end of the district which includes the Dallas Museum of Art and the Nasher Sculpture Garden designed by Renzo Piano. It is anticipated that the school will be adjacent to a future 150,000 square foot, 800 seat Multiform Theater Center to the west and a future 250,000 square foot, 2,400 seat Center for the Performing Arts to the south. Each adjacent project now has shortlisted firms – all from Europe – including Nouvel, Foster, Libeskind and Koolhaas. Estimated to be between 200,000 and 220,000 square feet when completed, the BTW project is part of a capital improvement programme by the Dallas Independent School District (DISD) and its Board of Education.

The original school building was built in 1922 and was the first African-American high school in Dallas. It was designated as the 'arts magnet' high school in 1976 and has subsequently received acclaim as a prototype for other magnet schools across the country. Of the school's graduates, 99 percent continue on to

college. It is expected that this project will also serve as an example for numerous other such schools in the United States.

The announcement of the competition resulted in expressions of interest by over 80 firms from around the world. RfQ submittals received in March 2001 were reviewed by the jury, which selected the finalists. A stipend of $25,000 with another $5,000 for travel expenses was given to each finalist and an additional $25,000 was awarded to the winner. In addition to representatives of the DISD, BTW and Arts District, the jury included arts supporters Howard Rachofsky and Deedie Rose with Carol Brandt, Dean of the Meadows School of the Arts at SMU, architects Julie Eizenberg of Koning Eizenberg Architects of California, George Miller FAIA of Pei Cobb Freed & Partners of New York and Ron Skaggs FAIA with HKS Architects of Dallas.

Presentations by the finalists took place on 5–6 September 2001. Each firm was given 45 minutes to present its scheme; then the jury was given 45 minutes to ask questions of the architects. Models and presentation boards were placed and removed in the 30 minute breaks between competitors.

Allied Works

The Allied Works scheme consisted of several concentric and overlapping L-shaped bars which defined both interior and exterior spaces with a specific emphasis on 'protection of the existing magic' of the present situation in which students occupy any conceivable corner and residual space of the 1922 building for their artistic activities. 'Loft' spaces and upper level exterior balconies are by-products of this 'centrifugal-centripetal' tension. The hybrid courtyard

Night view of school entrance
with existing school building
to the right

roof 'tent' topography and its possibilities as a 'talisman' for the district.

Mac Scogin Merrill Elam Architects
The Scogin-Elam proposal was predicated on locating a 'non-systemic order' or 'out-of-order order' within the problem. Merrill Elam stated that artists occupy the space between rigour and fantasy and that it was this 'space' for which they were searching. Ribbon-like study models hinted at this attempt to create a 'non-hierarchical space' in which artistic cross-fertilisation would be encouraged. Dual ramp systems rising obliquely from the existing school as an 'entry' were sliced laterally by 'work courts' on their way to activities overlooking the freeway. The original building was emptied of all structure, floors and roof and provided a free form metal scrim-like wall-lining in order to make it the primary presentation and performance space. Their 'exuberant, expressive' scheme 'sprinkled programmatic elements' throughout this complex volumetric network. Scogin noted that the materials were not indicated yet, but that the forms should 'glow'.

Charles Rose Architects
Charles Rose presented concepts which, in some aspects, had a much higher degree of resolution those of the other competitors. The scheme included two levels of below-grade parking which was not required in the programme but which Rose had (correctly) determined to be a crucial component of any actual building on the site. He stated that his favourite building in Dallas was Pei's Fountain Place high-rise and that it was his intention to play off the laconic angularity of this structure by making his proposal a horizontal version of this same aesthetic.

Roofs of his scheme were to be sloping, turf-covered exterior courts – a kind of glass-to-grass conversion of the Pei building. The maintenance considerations inherent in this concept caused several questions from the school representatives during the question and answer phase. The Allied Works scheme was also quite clearly phased for construction, and the presentation included the names of preferred consultants as well as other fairly specific information not given by the other firms. It's 'blunt sculpturalism' and hard materials were intended to reinforce the shard-like, almost monolithic geometry of the open courtyard typology.

The jury met formally on the morning of 7 September and, after a relatively short review of the presentations of the day before, voted unanimously for Allied Works. The jury clearly was impressed by the emotional openness of the presentation together with the high regard and attention paid to the life and work of the students.

morphology allows the school to have both an internal focus and to be permeable to other activities and its neighbours in the Arts District. Allied Works principal Brad Cloepfil described the concept to the jury as a 'city in itself, humming at night' with 'raw interiors' and 'exuding the life of the place'.[1]

Carlos Jimenez Studio
The concept proposed by Carlos Jimenez formed a simple, 'figure of eight' circulation scheme around two open courts, the primary court being an exterior amphitheatre. The overall massing was a box-like shell which stepped up from the height of the existing high school towards the adjacent freeway to the north. Lower level classrooms with exterior work courts were provided for ceramics, metalworking and similar activities while upper level spaces were allocated to dance, painting and music, thus invoking a poetic reading of gravity to the concept. Unlike the other three competitors, Jimenez placed the major performance spaces along the east side of the site. This was a result of his saving an existing 1952 structure on the site for reuse which other competitors found no reason to save. His presentation stressed the 'tapestry' of pedestrian paths within the

Note
1. All quotes in this essay are from its original publication in *Competitions*, Volume 11, No. 4, Summer 2001.

Opposite
Winning Entry
Allied Works – Design
Principal: Brad Cloepfil
(Portland, OR, US)

Top Aerial perspective of
model indicating L-shaped
configuration of scheme
Middle View
of inner court yard
Bottom
Night aerial view of site
showing existing school
building at lower right

This page
Finalist
Carlos Jimenez Studio
(Houston, TX, US)

Top Aerial view of model
Bottom Interior courtyard

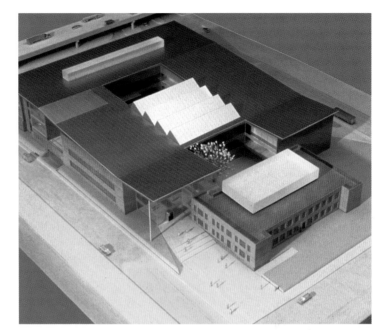

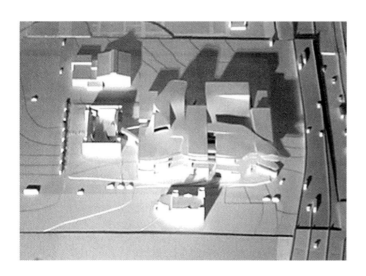

Competing Globally in Architecture Competitions

Opposite page
Finalist
Mac Scogin Merill Elam
Architects
(Atlanta, GA, US)

Top Courtyard perspective
Bottom Model

Finalist
Charles Rose Architects
(Cambridge, MA, US)

Top Aerial view of
computerised model
Bottom Section

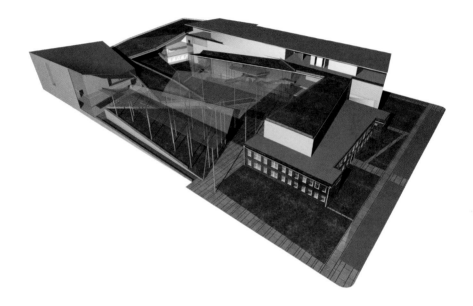

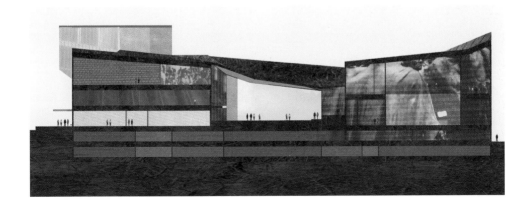

IIT McCormick Center, Chicago (1998)

Michael Dulin

There is an audible change to the grounds of Illinois Institute of Technology – a welcome relief to almost all the faculty, staff and students who have had to endure the deafening rattle of the passing Chicago Transit Authority trains for decades, as well as brave the giant void under the famously elevated tracks. After four-plus years, the Office of Metropolitan Architecture (OMA) has completed the McCormick Tribune campus centre – Rem Koolhaas' first stand-alone building in the US and one of the first new buildings on the IIT campus in over 25 years. Both are impressive feats considering the dramatic site constraints and the widely known campus pedigree.

The winning entry submitted by OMA for the 1998 competition was a huge departure from the crisp simplicity of the original structures – a departure that created considerable controversy within the ranks of the campus's diehard followers of Mies van der Rohe, who designed the original campus. When asked about the nay-sayers who had challenged his design, Koolhaas responded by explaining he believed the structure would ultimately 'undo the entropy' that had fallen on IIT's central core. The 'entropy' he was referring to was the dramatic decrease in student enrolment in the 1980s and early 1990s and the ensuing loss of density that left the campus feeling lonely and somewhat dangerous. Buildings were in disrepair, the population was down and the overall spirit of the school was low. OMA had been charged not just with designing a new building, but also with reversing what Koolhaas himself referred to as 'the doomed life of the Mies campus'.[1]

The final product certainly aims to be as anti-entropic as possible and it is every bit as dynamic as the original competition model suggested. When approached from the main campus quad, the McCormick Center reads as a continuous building topped with a 530 foot long stainless-steel tube. The tube has naturally become the 'instant icon', but it is the interior spaces that truly define the building. The original design strategy capitalised on the paths formed by the students travelling between the dorms and the classroom buildings to create the template into which the greater programmatic elements could be inserted. Things like meeting rooms, lounges and recreation areas weren't necessarily assigned to specific, unchangeable locations within the plan. In fact, the main auditorium was rotated 90 degrees and an entire retail section was eliminated with only minimal adjustments to the basic floor plan – the student paths remained essentially the same throughout the development of the project.

Jeffrey Johnson, the project manager who oversaw the completion of the building, explained that the primary goal was to build the urban experience within the building: to re-energise the core of the campus by making it feel and behave more like a city. The building is designed in such a way as to almost force the kind of random encounters one generally expects in a busy urban area. The angles at which the pathways intersect seem to suggest an urgency of movement, either between classes or to a meal with friends: movements that wouldn't necessarily read in a modern glass box. This was essential in order to develop the sense of density that had previously been missing from the campus. By articulating the movement of students, and not simply framing spaces for them to move to and from, the building has a

**Winning Entry
Office of Metropolitan
Architecture – Design
Principal: Rem Koolhaas
(Rotterdam, Netherlands)**

View of tube from south to
the downtown. The glass
facade reflecting the tube
belongs to a new dormitory
by Helmut Jahn

Winning Entry
Office of Metropolitan
Architecture – Design
Principal: Rem Koolhaas
(Rotterdam, Netherlands)

Left Front entrance to the
McCormick Center with
Mies's image on door
Bottom Interior hallway, with
bottom of tube penetrating
ceiling

Competing Globally in Architecture Competitions

Office of Metropolitan Architecture

Top Original competition entry
Bottom Elevations and sections

In the original competition entry, Koolhaas' plan for the corridor pattern corresponded to the destinations of the students passing from the dormitories on the east side of State Street and the classroom buildings on the west side. The scheme was modified in design development, however, whereby the auditorium was rotated 90 degrees and the space for retail on the right side was eliminated completely

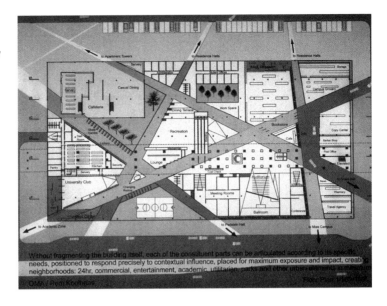

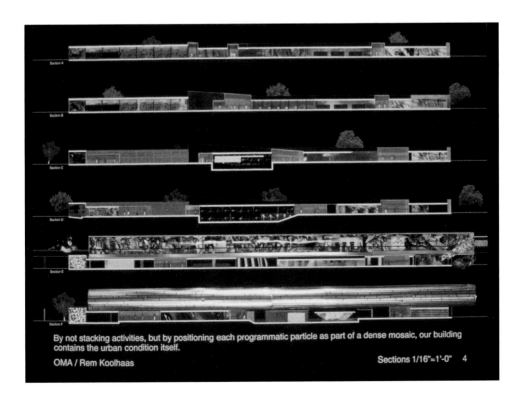

By not stacking activities, but by positioning each programmatic particle as part of a dense mosaic, our building contains the urban condition itself.

OMA / Rem Koolhaas   Sections 1/16"=1'-0"   4

constant energy, even when the crowds are thin.

In true Koolhaas fashion, the materiality and textures of the building are extraordinary. As Dean of Architecture Donna Robertson explained, Mies was very much into materials that reflected the 'spirit of the age', and considering the new building is a campus centre for a leading technology institution at the dawn of the 21st century, the materials chosen by OMA seem very appropriate. The vertical structural elements appear attenuated – almost ghostly – in the reflections on the shiny surface. As for the student pathways the building was originally conceived around, OMA chose to use rectangular aluminium panels. The hope was that the aluminium, being a soft metal, would wear over time and continue to register the student movement in much the same way as the bare earth had done before.

As the floors are almost all made of highly reflective surfaces, it is fitting that the walls are a mixture of clear and coloured glass. Much this Strawglass, a Panelite product which is essentially plastic drinking straws cut in quarter-inch sections and sandwiched – on end – between two sheets of glass. The result is a honeycomb effect that allows one to see through the glass at only a 90 degrees angle, with the straws creating increasing levels of opacity the more extreme the viewing angle. Aside from creating an interesting texture, this material reenforces the 'urban experience' by allowing passers-by views into spaces, but nothing is fully revealed unless the 'pedestrian' stops to get a closer look.

Another dominant feature both on and within the building is the signage and way-finding system. Together with 2 x 4, the NYC based graphic design group led by Michael Rock, OMA created what Dean Robertson referred to as 'the lexicon' of the building – the universal figure reinvented as the 'everystudent' engaging in a variety of school-centric activities.

Students fortunate enough to be enrolled in the architecture programme over the last four years have had a true taste of the competition process and the kind of buildings a successful competition can generate. Professor Jerry Horn has taught a competition studio at IIT for a number of years – exposing his students to a wide variety of themes and programmatic problems in the competitive environment. Dean Robertson added that IIT has always had a competition-savvy curriculum and didn't think the completion of the new campus centre would do anything but accelerate the interest in Professor Horn's studio. Futhermore, in a city renowned for pieces of significant architecture, students now have one more building to analyse, critique and dissect, although this one is much closer to home.

Note
1. Quoted in *Competitions*, Volume 13, No. 4, Winter 2003.

Opposite
Finalist
Helmut Jahn/Werner Sobek
(Chicago, IL, US/
Stuttgart, Germany)

Competition model

Right
Finalist
Zaha Hadid
(London, UK)

Interior perspective

Bottom
Finalist
Peter Eisenman
(New York, US)

Competition model

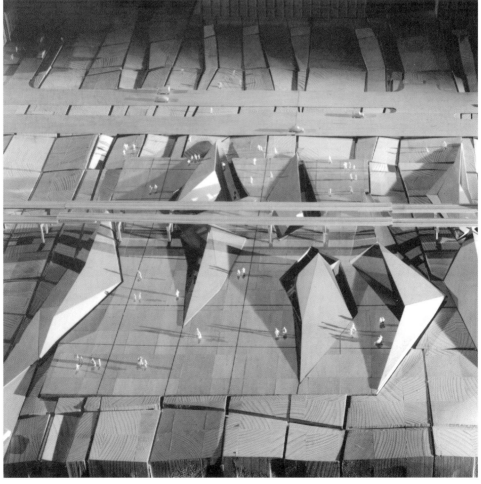

University of South Dakota School of Business (2000)

Tom Reasoner

On 4 January 2001, four nationally recognised firms threw their business cards into a facilities management hard hat at the University of South Dakota to determine the order of their presentations in a competition for the design of a new business school. One of the participants, Charles Rose, of Thompson and Rose Architects had to use his hotel keycard in the absence of a business card. As a result, the keycard came out first, and Thompson and Rose became the first presenter. They were followed by Julie Snow Architects of Minneapolis, Leers Weinzapfel Associates of Boston and Smith-Miller + Hawkinson of New York. As the luck of the draw would have it, the jury, over the course of the afternoon, narrowed the field to two: Thompson and Rose Architects and Smith-Miller + Hawkinson. Although the Smith-Miller + Hawkinson model tipped the scales in their favour as far as the jury was concerned, this hardly marked the end of the selection process. As juror William Conway stated, the jury 'had only made its recommendation'[1]; subsequent ratification of their finding by the Building Committee was hardly automatic.

The Building Programme

When the administration of the University of South Dakota set out to build a new School of Business on their campus, they expressed the wish that it be a 'signature' building. To obtain a design worthy of such lofty expectations, it was determined that the best vehicle for achieving such a goal would be a design competition. Thus, during the summer of 2000, the university advertised for expressions of interest from architecture firms with previous experience designing academic buildings. After receiving over 50 responses, they shortlisted the above-mentioned four firms as finalists, each of which was to receive $18,500 for its efforts. To arrive at a design for the new building, the participating firms had to consider a number of pre-existing conditions. One was a campus masterplan that had been developed by Sasaki Associates. Another was a recent renovation programme envisioned for the neighbouring Telecom building – known as the Al Neuharth Media Center. Its renovated presence had already become a factor in site development by the time the competition was underway. It was a little like putting the cart before the horse. There was talk in the vision statements and site visit discussions with the business school faculty about synergies and programmatic links, but the question of how these would manifest themselves was left to their imaginations. Although two of the participating firms paid considerable attention in their schemes to the Sasaki masterplan, it did not turn out to be a major factor in inhibiting site development for the winning design(s).

The programmes and spaces of the business school read like a full service menu. With an aspiration to engage in the global economy, the services reach across and beyond the academic community to include traditional as well as distance and continuing education learning facilities, outreach programmes and state-wide databases. Some programmes maintain a larger presence within the university fabric, such as auditoriums and classrooms, while others, perhaps smaller in scale, are more specialised, but are essential elements for a business school, such as faculty and administrative offices. Other programmes serve the needs of the business community here and abroad.

Jury Choice
Smith-Miller + Hawkinson
(New York, US)

Interior perspective

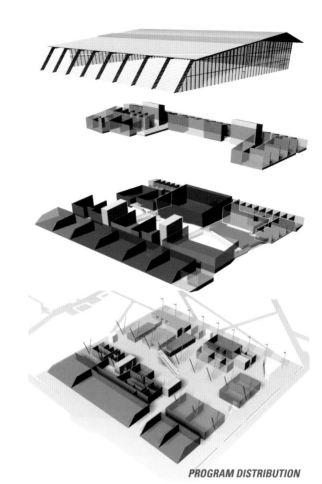

LEGEND

Teaching and learning
- Tiered lecture spaces
- Classrooms
- Computer labs/outreach
- Meeting rooms

Academic resources
- Outreach
- Directors
- Centre for economic education

Office areas
- Administration
- Faculty
- Graduate student centre

Common areas
- Common areas
- Circulation
- Service
- Cores

PROGRAM DISTRIBUTION

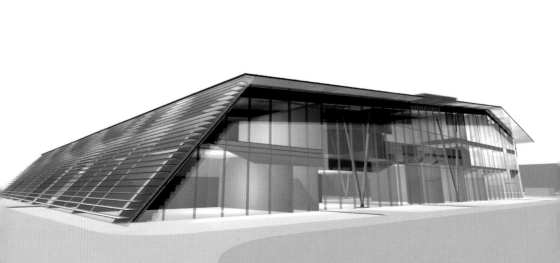

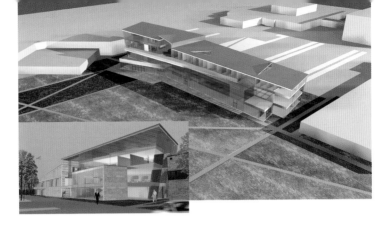

Bottom Elevation perspective
Top Programme distribution

Although the Smith-Miller +
Hawkinson entry, called
'Agora', was the jury choice,
its 'techno' language got a
mixed reception from the
university administration.
Its detailed organisational plan
for the interior – in view of
the lack of such by Thompson
and Rose – failed to tip the
balance in its favour

Commission
Thompson and Rose
(now The Office of Peter Rose)
(Cambridge, MA, US)

Above Aerial view of
computerised model

The architects' declaration
that the campus is composed
of free-standing buildings
and should remain so was
reinforced by a modelling
coup that exposed the tragic
flaw in the masterplan's
suggestion that the new home
for the School of Business
on the south side of the site.
That opportunity to create
and frame a new formal open
space on campus had been
wasted on a parking lot
frontage (**insert right**)

Reaching a Final Decision

On the morning of 4 January 2001, the jury
recommended the scheme of Smith-Miller +
Hawkinson. Sometime on 1 February 2001, the
Building Committee, in the silenced motions of a
conference call, selected Thompson and Rose to be
the architects of the New School of Business at the
University of South Dakota. Smith-Miller +
Hawkinson won the competition, but lost the
commission.

Was it agoraphobia or just fear of the unknown?
The risk involved and the signature that went with it
were more than the university was willing, and
perhaps able, to take. As the selection decision waxed
and waned within the circles of building and advisory
committees, the dean of the business school said that
he wished we had never used the words 'signature
building' anywhere in the competition language.

During those weeks of flux, Smith-Miller +
Hawkinson and Thompson and Rose were asked to
provide more examples of their work and project
references were contacted. What emerged in this
exercise was a concern on parts of the larger
committee about the apparent 'style' of Smith-Miller
+ Hawkinson. The 'Techno' label was in print and the
question of 'Were they flexible?' was a background
echo to the dialogue. Here is the signature issue
again: Smith-Miller + Hawkinson got to where it is by
developing a language of form and place that does
carry a signature, a mark. Its work is recognisable.

Thompson and Rose has a different, multilingual
vocabulary – a history of successful site planning
inhabited by a range of building styles. One of the
client contacts for Thompson and Rose said he felt
one of their strong points was their ability to draw the
brightest talent out of the top schools in their area.
Whose signature will be on this building? Will it sell
in South Dakota? Thompson and Rose offered a
handsome solution and the prospect of a working
relationship that would let the building evolve in a
boardroom climate. A more comfortable fit on many
levels ... Perhaps more of a working relationship.
Business as usual.

Note
1. Quoted in *Competitions*, Volume 11, No. 1, Spring 2001.

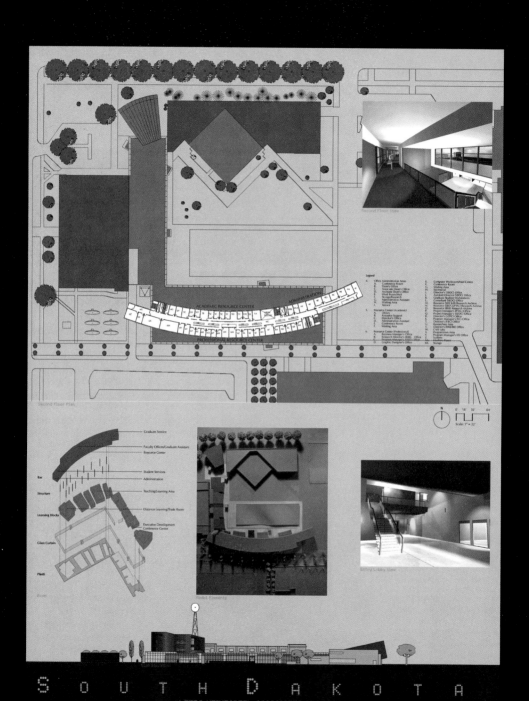

SOUTH DAKOTA

LEERS WEINZAPFEL ASSOCIATES ARCHITECTS

Competing Globally in Architecture Competitions

Opposite
Finalist
Leers Weinzapfel Associates
(Boston, MA, US)

This page
Finalist
Julie Snow Architect
(Minneapolis, MN, US)

Competition board

Exterior perspective

Leers Weinzapfel followed the precepts of the masterplan and located their building on the south edge of the available site while making physical connections to the two neighbouring buildings, the Telecom Center and School of Law. Using the Executive Conference Center to bridge that physical and professional void was indeed risky business

This trabeated playground of box and bay is satisfying to the eye, yet the dynamics of these forms are already available on campus. This complex has a second sense of being more of a connector building poised to continue linking rather than focusing on issues of presence. The 'scenes' inside the building help belay the fears of dead-end corridors and are filled with the joy of reflected light

School of Architecture, University of New Mexico (2000)

Brian Taggart

The site of the new School of Architecture at the University of New Mexico (UNM) in Albuquerque is right on Route 66, a garish strip immortalised in the old song. Although much of Route 66 is now a faded memory, in Albuquerque it is still a vibrant street – running right past the UNM campus. Now lined by a string of nondescript parking lots that front the campus edge to its north, the famous street will soon be graced by a new School of Architecture and Planning. This building, designed by Antoine Predock, will provide a bold welcome to the campus, and the 24/7 activity of an architecture school will contribute to the eclectic life of Route 66. Predock's design triumphed in a competition where four very strong finalists all presented winning ideas in their solutions; but Predock had the edge, indicating the most persuasive approach to facilitating the pedagogy of architecture education.

The Programme

There was a very detailed programme specifying exactly what facilities should be included in the 68,000 square foot building and what space should be allocated to each. It emphasised that the design should encourage a high level of interaction among students and faculty and should create a strong awareness of the activity within the school. The programme also required that the building support the interdisciplinary nature of architecture education and focus on the design studio where instruction was both tutorial and communal in nature. Overall the presumption was that 'the completed complex and site will anticipate both formal and unplanned gatherings' and the programme advised that 'The inclusion of one or more carefully articulated out-door

courtyards and/or indoor atria may contribute to the desired result'.[1] In addition the site chosen for the building would form the pedestrian gateway to the campus.

If this was not enough, the competition rules also required that the building has, 'a visual character and form appropriate to the site, campus, and Route 66 context'. This was no easy task because the campus had been constructed very deliberately in the Santa Fe–Pueblo style, to the extent that the original Victorian buildings had been remodelled in the 1920s to conform to this appearance. But the building to be on a fairly tight site on the southern edge of the campus and fronting on Route 66, so conforming to these disparate elements was inevitable. Roger Schluntz, Dean of the School of Architecture and Planning and a member of the jury, conceded that these requirements were somewhat contradictory in terms of the design having to be 'part of the university fabric but a landmark building, address-in Route 66 and also the Santa Fe–Pueblo style'.

Initially, all this was to be achieved with a budget of $8 million. (It now has been increased to due to the inclusion of the Art Library.) To test the feasibility of the programme, a design charrette was held involving three teams of faculty and students, each led by an architect from another school.

The Charrette

The programme was tested on three different sites including one that was larger and one that was further to the east of the site finally selected. The charrette produced several excellent concepts, including one which blended the Santa Fe style with that of Charles Rennie Mackintosh, and resembled

Winning Entry
Antoine Predock Architect
(Albuquerque, NM, US

View from southwest

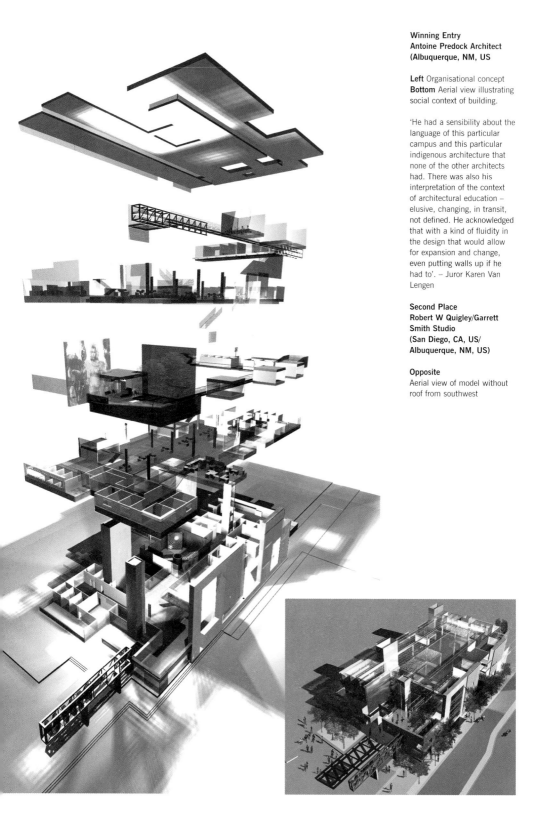

Winning Entry
Antoine Predock Architect
(Albuquerque, NM, US

Left Organisational concept
Bottom Aerial view illustrating
social context of building.

'He had a sensibility about the
language of this particular
campus and this particular
indigenous architecture that
none of the other architects
had. There was also his
interpretation of the context
of architectural education –
elusive, changing, in transit,
not defined. He acknowledged
that with a kind of fluidity in
the design that would allow
for expansion and change,
even putting walls up if he
had to'. – Juror Karen Van
Lengen

Second Place
Robert W Quigley/Garrett
Smith Studio
(San Diego, CA, US/
Albuquerque, NM, US)

Opposite
Aerial view of model without
roof from southwest

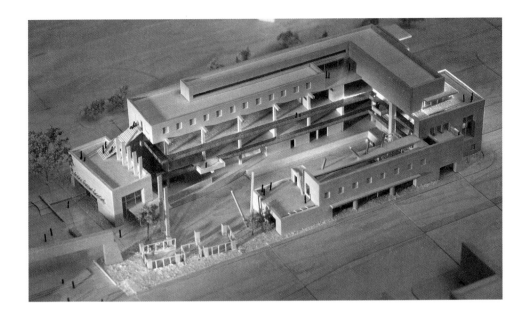

the architecture school at the University of Arizona. But the object of the exercise was to refine the programme, not to design the building. This was achieved and a number of changes were made to the programme as a result of the charrette. However, the most significant outcome was a clear preference among the faculty and students for the site finally selected for the competition. On Route 66, it was immediately to the east of the campus bookstore and to the southwest of the 3,000-seat campus auditorium. This site had not previously been considered by the Board of Regents or the UNM Facilities Planning Department; so its selection arose directly from the charrette.

Process and Jury
The competition was carried out under rules developed by Dean Roger Schluntz. The Phase I jury included Schluntz, Gabriella Gutierrez and Steve Schreiber – faculty members from the School of Architecture – student representatives, and staff from Physical and Facility Planning. Phase I selection was based on the qualifications of the architects who responded to the RfQ, and four finalists were chosen for Phase II. They were:
- Leers Weinzapfel Architects of Boston with SMPC Architects of Albuquerque
- Barton Myers Associates of Beverly Hills, California/Ellis Browning Architects of Santa Fe
- Antoine Predock Architect of Albuquerque
- Robert W Quigley of San Diego California with Garrett Smith Studio of Albuquerque

The next step was public presentations by each lead architect focusing only on their past work. A full-day initial briefing session was then held with the owner/user group and all the finalists. Having received the programme, the architects came well prepared to ask relevant questions.

The next stage was a formal workshop with each team individually. These half-day sessions involved UNM Facilities and Faculty representatives and were designed to mirror an actual architect/owner meeting. Any new information which arose in individual workshops was transmitted to all the competing firms. Schluntz noted that 'The process was informed greatly by the interim workshop. A criticism of competitions is that they cut off dialog between owner and architect'.

For the final stage outside jurors were added to the selection committee - Karen Van Lengen, Dean of Architecture, University of Virginia, and Garth Rockcastle, former Dean of Architecture, University of Minnesota. Jurors were given reductions of the design submissions of the finalists and then each architect presented his solution to the jury in a public session. Architects were not allowed to attend the presentations of competing firms. After much discussion the jury selected the winner by vote. The final placing was Predock first and Quigley second, with Barton Myers and Leers/Weinzapfel joint third.

The competition did not attempt to impose a new procurement method on the university or state but merely added the very significant additional process of the competition itself. For the work involved in this the four finalists were given an honorarium of $40,000 each.

Note
1. All quotes in this essay are from its original publication in *Competitions*, Volume 10, No. 4, Winter 2000.

Finalist
Leers Weinzapfel Associates
(Boston, MA, US)

Competition board with
night perspective, floor plans
and elevations

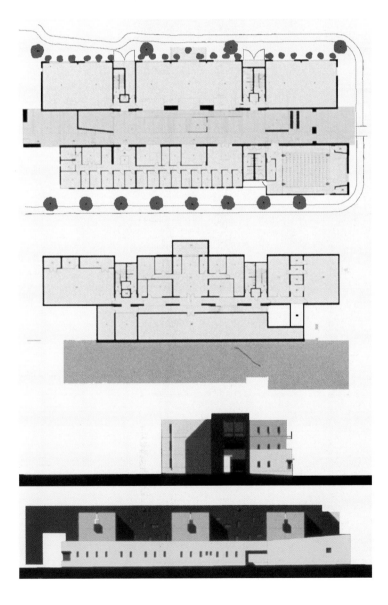

Roger L Schluntz FAIA

Public Libraries

Snøhetta (Oslo, Norway)
Alexandria Library,
Alexandria, Egypt
Competition 1989
Completion 2001

Ever since the advent of the 'information age', libraries have been in the business of implementing recent technology, to become more user-friendly. To go with this, they have decided that image is all important, and that the old picture of a rather stuffy environment should be avoided at all costs.

Around the turn of the 20th century, the Carnegie Endowment not only provided funds for building public libraries in the United States, but sponsored a number of competitions for their design. Thus, libraries in cities such as Milwaukee, Indianapolis and San Francisco were the result of competitions; and most Americans may not even realise that their country's best known library, the inestimable and incomparable Library of Congress in Washington DC, was a product of a competition held in 1873.

For a variety of reasons, the number of design competitions greatly diminished in the US from the late 1920s and they were infrequently employed for public works during the building boom following the end of World War II. Recently, however, and unlike other and earlier postwar public works efforts in the US, one now finds a resurgence in architectural design competitions, and particularly for the design and architect selection for new library facilities.

A sizeable number of library projects have been initiated since 1980. The need for these new facilities is not surprising, and follows the demands necessitated by both the relative explosion in the amount and number publications and other print material along with the increasing population growth in many metropolitan areas. And with these expanding demographic numbers come growing user needs, as well as an expanding tax base capable of supporting new public works projects.

Beyond size, other changes are readily apparent in the basic characteristics of today's public library. These transformations range from the accommodation of new types of information resources – including multimedia and, quite significantly, digital files and internet access – to enhancements in the human experience within the confines of the library buildings. Interest in energy conservation, 'green' building and natural lighting are now heavily vested in the public library project, as well as a widespread desire to establish a memorable civic presence in the urban fabric while regaining the historical tradition of the public library as a notable cultural icon.

Perhaps taking a lesson from the successes of booksellers Borders and Barnes & Noble in consumer attraction and customer satisfaction, libraries

now compete to become more user-friendly – with considerable attention given to the user's well-being and physiological needs. The conspicuously indulgent children's area has demonstrated, perhaps, embedded strategies for making the adult environment more inviting and enjoyable. For example, the design of reading areas and lounges is more attentive to casual use, seating comfort and natural daylight, while the traditionally strict separation of collections and reference materials from food and beverage has diminished. All of these trends have contributed to both larger and more complex facilities.

One might speculate that any client group for a civic project, which typically includes strong representation of the end users, is extremely interested in having the opportunity to review alternative approaches to what are frequently very complex programmes (the formidable programme 'brief' for the Chicago Public Library ran to 1,000 pages) before committing to either a design approach or to the engagement of the lead designer. In this regard, the deliberative and comparative approach of a design competition can be quite compelling. In developing programmatic requirements and reaching consensus on their specific needs, the librarian as a client is typically engaged in the process. Having frequently worked in facilities that were woefully inadequate and outdated, it should come as no surprise that librarians are appropriately apprehensive.

Two ventures that gained considerable attention among the architectural profession stand clearly at the forefront: the limited design competition held in 1981 for the relatively small, 10,000 square foot San Juan Capistrano Public Library and the highly controversial design/build

competition format for the massive, 500,000 square feet of assignable space, $140 million Chicago Public Library conducted a few years later in 1988. Because of the significance of the respective locations and the international prominence of the competing architects, both of these competitions were widely publicised in the press and closely scrutinised by the design profession.

Additionally, the competition process for what later became officially known as the Harold Washington Library Center in Chicago was immortalised in a 1989 PBS televised NOVA documentary, 'Design Wars', featuring all five participants: Arthur Erickson; Helmut Jahn; Mexico City's Ricardo Legorreta with Adrian Smith of Chicago's Skidmore Owings Merrill; Dirk Lohan, Lohan Associates; and the winner, Tom Beeby, also of Chicago. Because of the need to guarantee the construction cost by each of the respective builders who entered the competition and the elaborate expectations and models, it was estimated that the competitor teams would spend up to a million dollars to compete.

Following a request for proposals and interviews of five of the 47 respondents, the far more modest design competition for the San Juan Capistrano Public Library consisted of three finalists. The winning scheme was authored by the then emerging, but highly publicised, Michael Graves of Princeton, New Jersey. (Graves would later successfully capture the design for the landmark Denver Downtown Library through another design competition held a decade later.) The other invited competitors included Robert Stern (who later won three additional prominent library design competitions – Nashville, Tennessee in1998, and Jacksonville, Florida in 2001, as well as a smaller public library located in Miami Beach in 1998); and Moore Ruble Yudell of Los Angeles, the architecture firm founded by the legendary and peripatetic Charles Moore.

Unquestionably, the positive assessments of the new San Juan Capistrano facility and the visibility, if not notoriety, of Chicago's competition process and resulting new library encouraged and contributed to a wave of similar initiatives throughout the US. While it is difficult to demonstrate a cause and effect scenario, additional inspiration and incentive were undoubtedly provided by the highly publicised, blockbuster design competitions for major libraries around the world. Recent projects include the monumental national libraries designed and constructed in Alexandria, Copenhagen, Paris and London, as well as the Kansai-Kan National Diet Library for the National Government of Japan, an open competition with nearly 500 submissions which was won by Fumio Toki in 1996. A more recent design competition for the 330,000 square foot new public library in Montreal, won by the three firm team of Patkau/Croft-Pelletier/Gilles Guite, took place in 2000.

Regardless of the *raison d'être*, the line-up of public libraries in the US that unfolded in the 1990s reflects an unprecedented and impressive number of design competitions. In addition to those previously mentioned, these include now completed libraries located in the downtowns of Cleveland (Hardy Holzman Pfeiffer, Architects), San Antonio (designed by Ricardo Legorreta) and Las Vegas (a mixed use facility designed by Antoine Predock that also included the Las Vegas Children's Museum). A design charrette competition was held in 2000 for Seattle's new public library, resulting in the selection of Rem Koolhaas as the design architect, and, more recently, Mexico City's Enrique Norten (TEN Arquitectos) won an invited competition conducted for Brooklyn Public Library's Visual and Performing Arts Library, a $75 million facility.

Four other design competitions for major, downtown public libraries – projects that were served by this author as the Professional Adviser – were conducted for the City and County of Denver, Nashville, Salt Lake City, and Jacksonville, Florida. In each instance, the new library facility was also intended to act as a primary catalyst for the rejuvenation of the central downtown area. As with San Juan Capistrano, all of these competitions included a process that restricted the number of competitors for the actual design phase of the competition to three or four finalists.

In this type of a limited design competition, the process usually begins with an open solicitation (the Request for Qualifications or 'RfQ') that requires architects/firms to submit credentials, examples of previous work and responses to a variety of open-ended questions. In this, the initial phase of the competition process, the protocol normally replicates the standard procedures codified in a governmental agency's obligatory procurement regulations and ordinances. The empowered authority then reviews these applicants and selects the top-ranked applicants. For large or complicated projects, an additional step (or phase) is frequently added to the process that requires formal interviews of the top ranked respondents before determining the finalists for the actual design competition. With or without the formal interviews, in reaching the last stage of the process the field has now become exceedingly limited, typically three to six design competitors in number, with four perhaps the most common.

Because of the expense involved in participating, and the desire of the competition sponsor to provide a compelling reason for a firm to submit qualifications, a fairly substantial honorarium is provided to each of the final phase competitors in order to offset some, if not most, of the expense involved. The conclusion of the process is normally the formal presentation of each scheme by the architects to the selection committee, i.e. 'the Jury' (or more precisely, given that many governing authorities cannot delegate their decision-making responsibility for awarding public works contracts, 'the Jury of Recommendation').

Some exceptions to the 'limited' format were the design competitions conducted in 1990–1 for the envisioned 110,000 square foot public library in downtown Evanston, Illinois and the smaller library for the Chicago suburb of Matteson. In the former, the Library indicated that the decision to conduct a competition was based on three considerations: one, the triangular site and continued use of the existing facility during the phased construction were seen as highly problematic; two, a vast number of possible design alternatives and approaches seemed plausible; and, three, there was a need to generate public interest and support for the project, including an impending bond issue election. Funded in part by the National Endowment for the Arts, this was one of a relatively few library design competitions that was open to all qualified architects. In the 'open' competition format, the number of entries sometimes exceeds 100 serious submittals; for the Evanston Public Library, over 1,250 persons registered to receive the competition materials, and an astonishing 378 completed entries were received by the sponsor. In this case, a young, unknown architect from Philadelphia, Joseph Powell, won the competition. Subsequently, he teamed with a local Chicago firm, Nagle Hartray Associates, to see the project through development and construction.

Obviously, if the purpose of a competition is to encourage a broad range of creative approaches, the open competition format – the traditional method of design competitions – would seem to be preferable. Moreover, the open competition allows those without extensive previous experience in library design to demonstrate their abilities and insight in addressing the project at hand. Such competitions provide emerging talent in the design profession with substantially increased access to opportunities for significant projects, and are welcomed by most of those considered to be younger, emerging architects and firms.

Why, then, is the open competition so seldom employed for major projects, and, specifically, for new library facilities undertaken in the US? Perhaps the sponsor is concerned that the architect selected from an open competition will be a person or firm that lacks the knowledge that is deemed critical to the task at hand or experience with library design; or perhaps the client is concerned that the winner will be someone with whom they will not be able to develop a compatible working relationship. Conceivably, librarians as a class might be considered to be 'risk averse' by nature; sensing that the scheme selected will be entirely misdirected and/or that the architect will be unreservedly out of their control. Advancing the future of the architecture profession is simply not one of the primary considerations of either the municipality or the library director. But with the limited competition, the selected finalists – each usually highly regarded in the profession and possessing a strong track record with library design or buildings of similar size and complexity – can be formally vetted before the beginning of the design activity.

However, probably the greatest single obstacle to the deployment of the open competition in the US is the perceived inflexibility of the procurement regulations governing the selection of professional services for public works in most governmental agencies and major municipalities. Unless an agency's regulations specifically include a provision for a design competition as a method for selection of an architect, the standard procurement process – beginning with a RfQ and concluding with formal interviews – can be extremely difficult and time consuming to circumvent. The limited design competition, however, can be incorporated into the customary format and statutory requirements simply by requiring the design phase of the competition to be an additional step to the legislated process, rather than a new or substituted process for the obligatory selection procedures.

There is also the realisation by competition sponsors that many of the foremost and best-known architects simply will not bother with open competitions – the odds of winning are perceived as too long, and there are easier and more reliable means of securing new work in these offices, particularly during times of economic growth. To attract the nation's elite architects in an invited (or limited) competition, substantial honoraria are typically provided to each of the finalists in an attempt to offset at least part of the direct cost involved in the competition effort. Even then, many of the more prominent architects are not persuaded that the investment is worth the risk from a business viewpoint. One prominent and highly successful architecture firm estimates that the cost of engaging in a design competition will easily run at $10,000 per week for the duration of the design phase of the competition. For complicated projects with fairly elaborate requirements for submissions, the cost will frequently exceed $100,000 for each of the participating firms.

The design and construction of any major facility constitute an extremely complicated undertaking. Even with the most laudable intentions, a realistic budget, and the good-faith efforts of all parties and stakeholders involved, nothing can ensure the design excellence of the completed project. There is growing evidence, however, supported by the recent public library projects in the United States and elsewhere, that a carefully organised and orchestrated design competition can substantially increase the probability of achieving desired outcomes and a successful design.

Salt Lake City Library (2000)

Roger L Schluntz FAIA

From the very outset, the director of the Salt Lake City Library insisted that the competitive process employed to select the architect for its new downtown facility was not to be considered a design competition. Those seeking the commission were expected to understand that the interactive engagement with the invited architects was to be viewed as a means for the library better to understand each competitor's method and approach to problem solving, rather than defining the end solution for the envisioned project. Based loosely on the strategy employed by New York's Museum of Modern Art (MOMA) for selecting an architect for its expansion, fully developed schemes and elaborate presentation submissions were actively discouraged in the original brief.

The initial solicitation to prospective architects, the first phase of the selection process and the subsequent interviews of the six highest ranked respondents were similar to the process employed in Denver and Nashville. Four applicant teams were selected to compete in the final phase: Moshe Safdie/Valentiner Crane; Moore Ruble Yudell with Gruen Associates and Eaton Mahoney; William Bruder Architect with Thomas Petersen Hammond Architects; and Gwathmey Siegel Architects in association with Prescott Muir Architects. Each team was paid $50,000 to partially offset their expenses.

Representatives of these firms were convened in February 1999 in Salt Lake City to review, with the library staff, the programme for the new library and the site, tour the existing facility, and discuss the expectations and requirements for the competition phase. For this interactive process, the architects were given a series of specific questions and issues to address. Workshops with the end-user group, comprised primarily of key library staff, were scheduled at about three week intervals.

In April each team returned to Salt Lake City to make its final presentation relative to the initial 'issues to be addressed'. In order to be able to deliver specific responses to this formal list of questions and considerations, each of the four competitors did, in fact, develop fairly comprehensive concept design schemes.

Remarkably, and perhaps to everyone's surprise, the actual project that was developed and constructed followed very closely the competition scheme that Moshe Safdie had presented to conclude the two-month long 'interview' process. The $78 million, 225,000 square feet Main Public Library, civic plaza, and below-grade parking structure opened in February 2003, 'on time, on budget', and has been deemed an overwhelming success by the library, the city, and, most importantly, the enthusiastic public.

Winning Entry
Moshe Safdie & Associates
(Somerville, MA, US)

Night view of completed
building

**Winning Entry
Moshe Safdie & Associates
(Somerville, MA, US)**

Left Interior concourse
of completed building
Bottom
Competition model

The completed structure bore
a remarkable resemblance
in every aspect to the original
competition proposal

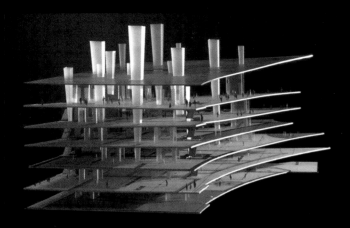

Finalist
William P Bruder Architect
Ltd/Thomas Petersen
Hammond Architects
(Phoenix, AZ, US/
Salt Lake City, UT, US)

Left Model with light
shaft detail
Below Model of site plan

Right
Finalist
**Gwathmey Siegel &
Associates/Prescott
Muir Architects
(New York/Salt Lake City,
UT, US)**

Perspective of computerised
model

Bottom
Finalist
**Moore Ruble Yudell/Gruen
Associates/Eaton Mahoney
Architects (Santa Monica,
CA/Los Angeles, CA/Salt
Lake City, UT, US)**

Aerial view of library facing
plaza

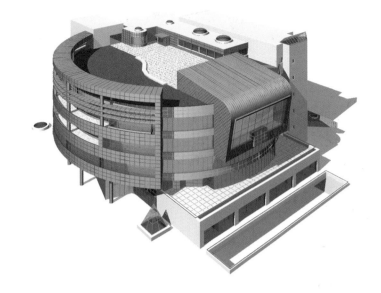

Kansai-Kan National Diet Library (1996)

Tony Coscia

That a significant addition to the Japanese National Diet Library was built in far-off Kansai Science City, and not in Tokyo proper, is a sure sign that the new information age is upon us in full force. To draw a parallel in the US, it would be rather like locating an extension of Washington's Library of Congress in the Research Triangle outside of Raleigh-Durham in North Carolina. Alas, storage of books and documents can now take place anywhere because they are virtually accessible!

Whereas the client – the national government of Japan – was clear as to the building programme (the space requirements and the advanced technology which would go into it), they were seeking an innovative structure which would be in keeping with the spirit of the age. The outside should reflect what was going on inside the building: 'The Kansai-Kan will be an advanced national library that looks ahead toward the 21st century ... a facility that symbolises culture, science and research ... a depository of all books ... and using the latest technology window of information ... transmitting from Japan to the world'.[1] Simultaneously, the library was also to function as a new centrepiece of the Kansai Science City. Not surprisingly, to find an innovative design for the library, the Japanese issued a call for an international, one-stage, open competition.

The choice of Kansai Science City in the Seika-Nishikizu District near Osaka as the site of the new library was no doubt determined by its location to the south of Tokyo, placing it almost equidistant to the capital and the population centres to the south on the island of Honshu. The project site itself was on the edge of suburbia, but contrary to the winding configuration of the streets in the residential areas, was located on a grid – Seika Main Street. There was some water adjacent to the site and rolling hills at its southern edge. It was surrounded by a growing number of buildings housing high-tech operations, the most notable of these being the Advanced Telecommunications Research Institute International and Keihanna Plaza. Down the road, and to the east, was the Kansai Science City Commemorative Park with attractive landscaping and architectural features. Almost all of the existing structures were of recent vintage and were relatively block-like in form.

For the purpose of judging this competition, an eight-person, blue-ribbon jury was assembled, five of whom were architects, including Fumihiko Maki and Arthur Erickson. The deadline for entries was 5 July 1996 and jury results were announced on 23 August. Of the 100 million yen prize money, 50 million went to the winner, Fumio Toki of Japan, and the remaining 50 million was shared equally among five second-place winners.

Out of the 493 works submitted, including 219 (44 percent) from foreign countries, 15 finalists were selected, 13 of which were Japanese. Juror Erickson noted that they were quite surprised when it was revealed that the Japanese were so heavily represented in the final round. Of five second prizes, one went to Kjetil Thorsen of Norway – praised as unique and dynamic, but too rigid and cubical in elevation. The only other foreign entry to crack the select circle of finalists with an honourable mention was S Hadid Mirmiran of Iran in collaboration with Bahram Shirdel – a finalist in the Nara Convention Hall Competition. Their entry resembled the two

**Winning Entry
Fumio Toki
(Tokyo, Japan)**

The winning scheme takes advantage of the site, boldly locating most spaces including the stacks and the general reference reading room below ground. A large sunken garden and a multistorey space are provided (a glass bar building at the rear of the site). The approach through a sawtooth skylight roof garden endows the work with a ritual quality. It was quietly distinctive in contrast to the many works with highly assertive forms. There was a view in the jury that it did not offer a clear 'vision' for the Kansai-Kan

minimal forms of the Finnish Pavilion at the 1992 Seville Worlds Fair by Arkkitehtuuritoimisto92 and the Tokyo Opera House Competition entry by Jean Nouvel with Philippe Starck.

If one goes on imagery alone, it would appear that the selected winning projects didn't live up to the 'visionary' stipulations of the sponsors nor to the level of design achieved by the winners of the last large-scale Japanese competition, the Nara Convention Centre. Most of the premiated designs did not reveal a significant departure from the box-like structures so common to the rest of 'Science City'. Furthermore, in dealing with the warehousing function of large-scale storage, the most common solution for the placement of the stacks was to bury them below ground due to their size and allowable buildable area within the site. The articulation of the other separate parts was only addressed in one of the honourable mention schemes, which was reminiscent of Rafael Viñoly's winning project for the Tokyo Forum competition in 1989.

For the most part the 15 finalists produced a minimum of dialogue between built form and surrounding landscape. In at least nine cases – two-thirds of the finalists chosen – there was no integration of the site with the interior spaces proposed, nor was there any exterior space created. All of the projects can be summed up as either a simple monolithic bar building or a large, closed glass warehouse box, or a combination of both, with varying amounts of buried programme. In fact, two projects bury the entire programme. One of these, the first runner-up with its light shaft towers and sunken courtyard, recalls Dominique Perrault's winning competition entry for the French National Library Competition of 1989.

It is apparent that this project has fallen victim to the same problem as the Japanese Science City itself, where box-style warehousing has become the rule. James Dearing points out in his writings about Scuba Science City that although the city is to be a catalyst for collaborations and new radical breakthroughs for the next century, it is mostly just the placement of large labs next to each other. According to the jury, many schemes were discarded as being too abstract. Juror Erickson stated that two entries which attracted a lot of interest were disqualified because they violated the site boundaries – in this case the setback. One of the disqualified entries elicited such a positive response form the panelists that they even made a serious attempt to fit it into the site without violating the rules – without success. Upon its disqualification, the entry's author was revealed to be a high profile Japanese architect. Although it is regrettable that this scheme did not play a role in the final selection, the process by which it was eliminated speaks volumes for the integrity of this competition.

Note 1. All quotes in this essay are from its original publication in *Competitions*, Volume 7, No. 1, Spring 1997.

Opposite
Winning entry
Fumio Toki

Top Entrance Cube
Bottom Aerial view of
completed project after
construction in 2002

Below
Second Prize
Yoshio Sakata
(Tokyo, Japan)
Elevation and aerial views

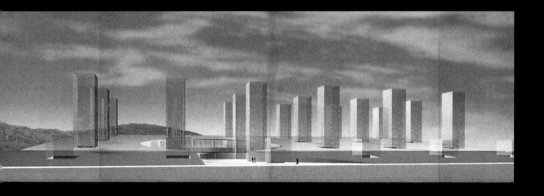

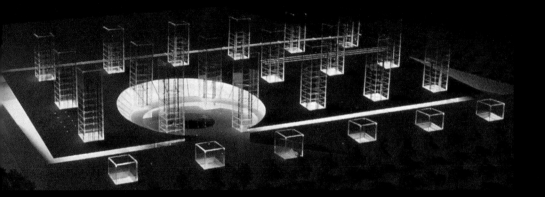

Left
Second Prize
Kjetil T Thorsen, Snøhetta
(Oslo, Norway)

Aerial view of model

Bottom
Second Prize
Kazuhiko Namba
(Osaka, Japan)

Aerial view and elevation

Competing Globally in Architecture Competitions

Top left + right
Second Prize
Yasushi Ikeda
(Tokyo, Japan)

Exterior and interior
perspectives

Bottom
Second Prize
Hiroshi Miyakawa
(Tokyo, Japan)

Aerial view of model

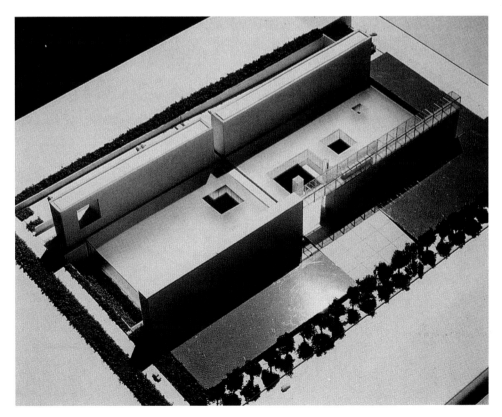

Brooklyn Public Library (2002)

Michael Berk

Since 1998, a team of prominent architects has quietly been drawing up a masterplan for the redevelopment of a section of downtown Brooklyn's Fort Greene neighbourhood as a cultural district, offering a wide variety of visual and performing arts experiences to the public, along with live-work spaces and support services and resources for artists. That masterplan, the brainchild of former Brooklyn Academy of Music (BAM) director Harvey Lichtenstein, calls for the renovation of several existing buildings in the area, and the construction of a variety of new structures, ranging from retail to live-work to mixed-use, on a collection of parcels of land currently home to four parking lots.

Initially, the BAM Lower Development Corporation (LDC) had commissioned a planning study from Skidmore, Owings & Merrill, but as BAM LDC president Jeanne Lutfy said, as she and her colleagues began to think on a larger scale they, 'wanted to bring on a team that could sort of take it to another level from a creative standpoint, who could really explore with us how – not only from a conceptual standpoint, but also from a physical and massing standpoint – to create a cultural district'.[1] By 2000 Rem Koolhaas and Diller + Scofidio had been brought on board, and they've been working to develop a masterplan ever since. All the while the LDC has been attempting to bring in tenants so that construction projects could begin.

In 2002, BAM LDC found an anchor tenant, and in spring 3002 that anchor tenant found an architect to design its new home, with a scheme that should satisfy the conceptual demands of the masterplan. Enrique Norten, of TEN Arquitectos of Mexico City, won the invited competition to design the Brooklyn Public Library's Visual and Performing Arts Library (VPA), a 150,000 square foot structure, budgeted at a projected $75 million, which is intended to become a central destination in the BAM cultural district.

Having completed renovation projects on several of the library's branch locations, along with a very successful privately funded renovation of the Central Library's Youth Wing in 2000, director Elizabeth Martin began drawing up a complex programme for the potential new space. Martin envisioned something that would be more than a conventional library, including extensive network infrastructure and support for new media facilities.

Since both the library and BAM LDC were concerned with making a significant architectural statement (on its proposed site the building would function as a gateway for the BAM cultural district as a whole), and the project would eventually be funded with a mix of private and public money, Martin began looking for ways to run a competition. She subsequently applied for the National Endowment for the Art's New Public Works grant, and in 2001 won a $50,000 award to fund the process.

A number of major firms were invited to enter the competition; in the end, four – TEN Arquitectos, Architectures Jean Nouvel, of Paris; Rafael Viñoly Architects, of New York City; and Huff + Gooden, of Charleston, South Carolina – agreed to submit schemes.

Though it was understood that this competition was taking place very early in the process, at a conceptual stage, Elizabeth Martin presented the competitors with a well-developed programme, clearly outlining the library's spatial needs and objectives. In

Winning Entry
TEN Arquitectos
(Mexico City, Mexico/
New York, US)

order to keep the proceedings as fair as possible (and to level the playing field between smaller firms and those with access to greater financial and personnel resources) she kept the submission requirements reasonable. Each competitor was required to submit five boards and a single scale model, built on a template provided by the library that – in the interest of clear comparisons – fitted into a corresponding scale model of the BAM cultural district as a whole. Martin said:

> We gave them volumes of information expressing our performance goals for the building, but the programme was designed as a descriptive programme rather than a prescriptive programme … absolutely it was meant to encourage creativity and vision from the architects. We talked about our vision, and suggested adjacencies that we thought would work, but we didn't mandate them, and in the end, everyone blocked and stacked the building differently.

While the programme set out space requirements for the VPA's traditional and new media collections, offices, research facilities and so forth, it also made some atypical demands. The architects were required to include a black-box theatre, extensive public space within the building, network infrastructure throughout the building, and provisions for a multimedia lounge/cyber café space to be open to the public 24 hours a day, seven days a week. Given its projected function as a resource centre for the BAM cultural district and the local community of artists, Martin and her colleagues envisioned a building that was more than a library, a building without clear precedent, at least locally.

However, as Terence Riley has pointed out, the VPA does fit into a developing building type. Several examples of this sort of multi-use building, combining research library, gallery and museum spaces, and workspaces for art practice under one large markable roof, have been built in Europe and Japan since the early 1970s; but this building type – known generally as a 'mediathèque' – has not yet found wide acceptance in the US. The paradigmatic mediathèque is Richard Rogers and Renzo Piano's 1971 Pompidou Centre in Paris (which as a very large-scale structure, encompassing a wider variety of functions than is currently typical of the form), while the most visible recent examples are Norman Foster's 1993 Carre d'Art in Nimes, France, and Toyo Ito's 2000 Mediathèque in Sendai, Japan.

The site itself – an elongated, triangular plot of land, currently home to a nursery and a parking lot – made it clear that the basic shape of any building that could satisfy the programme's square-footage requirements would approximate the shape of the site, giving it something of a built-in identity. And since the VPA building will eventually share its site with a theatre to be constructed directly to the north, the programme called for the architects to envision the space between the two structures as a public plaza. Even given these demands, the four competitors managed to come up with four highly divergent schemes, which made for an animated two-day discussion.

The jurors met in a two-day session; the first day each firm delivered a one-hour presentation to the assembled panel, after which there was an initial discussion of the schemes. The jury reconvened the following day. The fact that the jury included both architects and non-architects was not to be a problem: 'The discussion never got so effete that it wasn't inclusive of the entire group', said Helfand. 'The architecture itself was speaking to so many issues that we could just talk about those issues'.

Terence Riley felt that the librarians were particularly well equipped to discuss architecture:

> I think librarians are well aware, not just of space and functional needs, but of the ambience that makes a library great. They know that just solving problems functionally doesn't necessarily mean a building will be a great library … It was one of those very difficult competitions, where all of the contestants had very different positions. It was a very robust discussion … no two projects were similar enough that one cancelled out the other, and none of the positions taken were done so in a less than convincing way.

'It's not often that you invite four architects, and you get four schemes where you would love to build any one of them', said Martin. 'They're all different, and they're all extraordinary'.

Enrique Norten's winning scheme, according to Thomas Hanrahan, was 'probably the most sophisticated urbanistically … a really interesting series of indoor and outdoor spaces that engaged the other buildings, and Flatbush Avenue, and really best engaged the planned building to the north'.

Norten was very successful in integrating the site's exterior public spaces with the building's interior public spaces. His building provides public access from both the southern apex and the northern plaza, bringing a sculptural structure down to human scale at street level. Norten situated many building services (including the collections) below-grade, reducing the building's bulk and opening up the plan for gallery spaces, reading and multi-use use rooms, the 24/7 café, and the theatre.

Now that the library and BAM have selected a designer, they are busy working to solidify funding for the project. Meanwhile, Norten and TEN Arquitectos have been hired to continue the design process. Construction is projected to begin in 2005, which should provide an adequate amount of development time given the currently difficult fundraising climate.

Note 1. All quotes in this essay are from its original publication in *Competitions*, Volume 12, No. 4, Winter 2004

Winning Entry
TEN Arquitectos
(Mexico City, Mexico/New York, US)

Right Model
Bottom Section

The jurors felt that Enrique Norten's scheme most skillfully handled the vpa's relationships with neighbouring structures, and his treatment of the plaza to the north, partially enclosed within the skewed 'V' shape of the structure, did a great job of defining an exterior public space to match the elegant playfulness of his building's interior spaces. His plaza, which includes access to the vpa via a staircase that doubles as outdoor amphitheatre seating, makes a dramatic sculptural gesture, but at the same time, according to Margaret Helfand, 'isn't overly intentional in appearance'

Below
Finalist
Atelier Jean Nouvel
(Paris, France)

Aerial view of model

Jean Nouvel's entry opened much of the building's street level to a pass-through public space, usable as an open-air gallery, which he described as an 'urban hall'. Facing Flatbush Avenue, the building's facade would be defined by a glittering brise-soleil of mirrored panels, behind which art pieces, messages, or advertisements for events could be hung. Thomas Hanrahan remarked that Nouvel had treated the

library 'almost as the programme of an art museum', bringing to the project an extremely elegant handling of light. Terence Riley pointed out that of all the entries, Nouvel's 'had by far the most legible kind of appearance'

Opposite
Finalist
Huff + Gooden
(Charleston, SC, US)

Partial competition boards, with aerial view of model (above) and elevation and section

Elisabeth Martin had asked that the architects consider the building's virtual presence as

well as its physical structure, and of all the competitors, Huff + Gooden went the furthest in incorporating the virtual, using a 'digital core' of network and new media services as an organising principle of equal weight to the 'archival core' of traditional collections. The South Carolina firm's scheme addressed the building's theoretical concerns very clearly – Thomas Hanrahan felt that their scheme had 'the most dynamic and intricate web of spaces of all...with a really dynamic circulation among the spaces, almost as if their scheme was making the complexity of the web really visible'

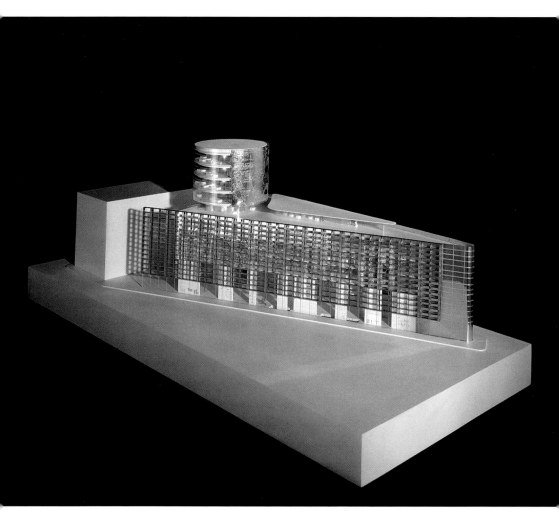

Competing Globally in Architecture Competitions

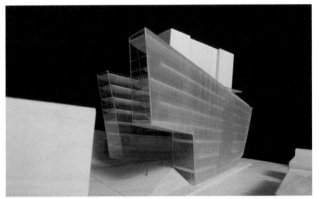

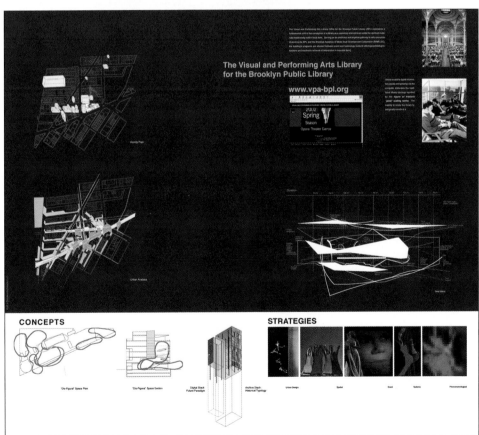

Finalist
Rafael Viñoly Architect
(New York, US)

Opposite, left Perspective
Opposite, right Aerial view
of model
Below Section

This scheme, a dramatic wedge that arcs up from grade at the southern apex of the site, sweeps up in an arc over the plaza to overhang the theatre building to the north, culminating in a top-floor reading room offering dramatic views of Manhattan. Viñoly's relocation of the public spaces to the upper floors did pose potential security issues.

Also, although all the jurors were impressed by the arcing building's aesthetic engagement with the surrounding buildings, the fact that the reading rooms actually vaulted over the plaza and neighbouring building to the north was seen by some as less effective in establishing a working spatial relationship with the neighbourhood

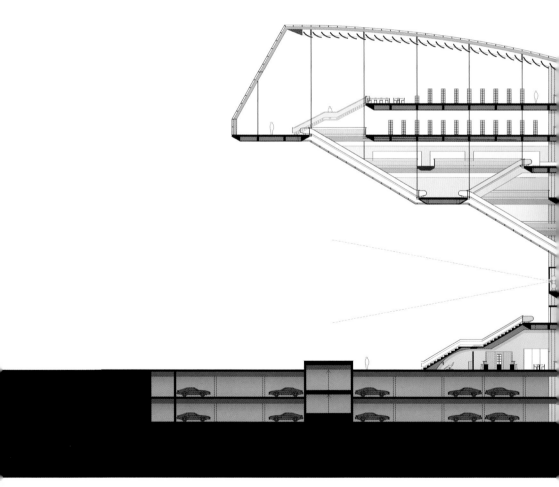

Competing Globally in Architecture Competitions

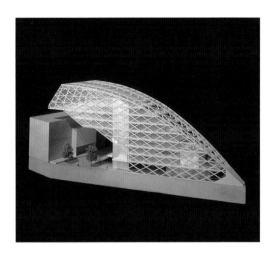

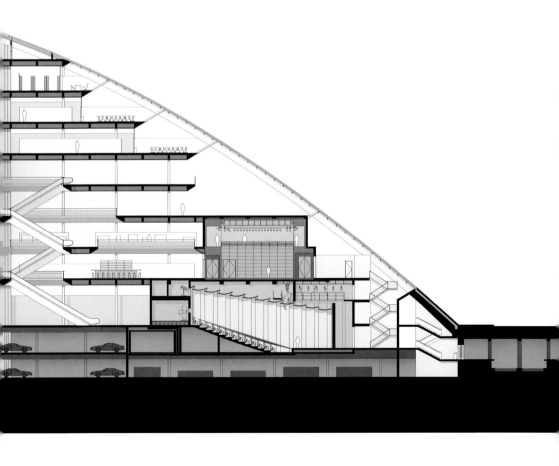

Québec Library, Montréal (2000)

William Morgan

Montréal is the world's second largest francophone city. But with the occasional exception of work such as Moshe Safdie's Habitat for Expo '67 or Peter Rose's Canadian Centre for Architecture, Montréal never makes the list of architecturally exciting places. A competition for the design of a major new library in Montréal, La Grande bibliothèque du Québec (GBQ), signalled a new approach. One hoped-for result – the creation of a positive climate for more competitions in French Canada – may have been realised in that a more recent international competition held there for a music hall attracted worldwide publicity.

The government agreed to a competition for the GBQ, hoping to garner international prestige. Furthermore, the library programme was so complicated that a competition was thought the best way to discover and unravel 'the largest number of enigmas' and have 'the capacity to solve new ones over time'.[1] Even so, the ideal solution might prove elusive, as the GBQ will be a cultural centre as well as a repository for Québec culture. In addition, backers expect it to revive Montréal's tired Latin Quarter.

The heavy symbolic baggage of the library ('offering a democratic access to culture and knowledge') comes with formidable requirements. The five-storey GBQ will house one million books, four times as many documents, plus numerous public spaces including a café, garden, gallery and theatre; of course, there is to be a children's library, but there will also be second-hand bookstores, a 24-hour library, and an entrance to the Montréal Métro. This super-library will occupy approximately 330,000 square feet, filling an entire city block.

All competitions are fraught with risk, but the Montréal library had some unusual circumstances. Supporters were afraid that the modest construction budget ($58 million Canadian) would be too small to attract notable foreign competitors. Also, Québec architects have limited experience with joint ventures, not to mention possible resentment at having to share the stage with non-Québeckers, much less Americans. Nationalistic, xenophobic Québec also imposed a language requirement.

The international call for proposals was fairly straightforward; it was a 'request for qualifications' rather than an open competition. For the first stage, architects had to submit portfolios of previous work, information on their practice and a conceptual response to the project requirements. Additionally, all entrants had to be registered Québec architects or associated with one. Furthermore, French was the only language of the competition – all documents to and from the committee were en français. If this were not discouraging enough, of the five candidates selected to go on to the second stage, two firms had to be from outside Canada, while two had to be based in Québec.

The first stage attracted 37 supplicants from Denmark, France, Germany, Israel, Spain, Switzerland and Uruguay, as well as the United States. Although the GBQ will not release the identities of the unsuccessful firms, the fact that 40 percent of the finalists had to be from Québec was, in the words of one juror, 'an enormous constraint'.

Despite having to select two 'international' and two Québec firms, the jury came up with a curious, but remarkable group of finalists. The jury was directed by Phyllis Lambert of the Canadian Centre

Winning Entry
Patkau Architects/Croft-Pelletier, architectes/Gilles Guité, architecte (Vancouver, Canada)

Top Elevations
Middle Night perspective
Below Model view

The design was clearly the most appropriate in terms of the library's needs – the one that best resolved the questions of the building's service and cultural functions. The solution of placing the cloistered, contemplative spaces of the collections on the upper levels, while having the café, theatre, bookstores and circulating library close to the street, neighbourhood and Métro is the most carefully considered

for Architecture, and she was joined by Columbia University's Bernard Tschumi, Georges Adamcyzk, director of the University of Montréal's school of architecture, architect Ruth Cawker from Nice, and Mary Jane Long, a principal of the firm which designed the British Library. In addition, René Laperrière, a city planner, and three representatives of the library, Irene Whittome, Lise Bissonnette, and Yvon-André Lacroix took part in the deliberations.

The discipline inspired by the site's long and narrow block resulted in a certain similarity in the finalists' designs – a kind of Modernist rectilinearity. But there was also considerable variety, and even the local Québécois architects stood up moderately well against better known competitors.

The long, joint venture names will ensure that these firms will never become household names. FABG/GDL/NOMADE/Yann Kersalé/Ruedi Baur, for example, produced a slick glass box with an

emphasis on lots of light. This earned notice from the jury for 'playing on a nearly absolute transparency', while respecting the neighbourhood's vernacular streetscape.

Saucier + Perrotte/Menkès Shooner Dagenais, architectes/Desvignes & Dalnoky, paysagistes/Go Multimedia offered the weakest of the five final designs. The jury diplomatically cited the design for 'great subtlety in the nuances of the topography of the site'. The presentation is marred by computer-generated renderings (whatever happened to the very French notion of drawings?) in which the perspective is skewed for no apparent reason other than cleverness; the plans are confusing and the elevations are busy.

Far more intriguing is the submission by Christian de Portzamparc (or rather, Atelier Christian de Portzamparc/Jean-Marc Venne/Birts Bastien/Bélanger Beauchemin Gallienee Moisan Plante/ Élizabeth de

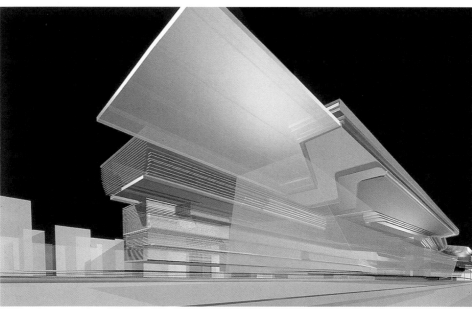

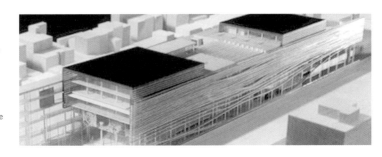

Opposite
Honourable Mention
Zaha Hadid/Patrick
Schumacher/Boutin Ramoisy
Tremblay, architectes
(London, UK/
Montréal, Canada)

Top Detail
Bottom Pedestrian perspective

This page
Finalist
Saucier + Perrotte/
Menkès Shooner Dagenais,
architectes/Desvignes &
Dalnoky, paysagistes/
Go Multimedia
(Montréal, Canada)

Top Aerial view of model
Middle Section
Bottom Pedestrian perspective

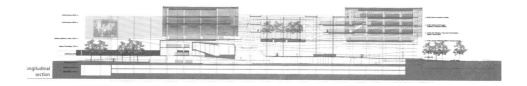

Portzamparc). Here the computer graphics far better explained how the various wedge-shaped, boatlike areas fit together. Some of the collections are suspended from the roof, giving the entire library a space-exploration quality. The design represents a maturation of the young Pritzker Prize winner's work as the GBQ is more thoughtful and purposefully monumental than his Cité de la Musique.

Perhaps a Parisian would have been palatable to Montréalers, but one can only guess that the Portzamparc design appeared a bit over the top for the province's first international competition. But the thought-provoking response and boldness are what one hopes the competition crucible will inspire. Zaha Hadid, in association with Boutin Ramoisy Tremblay, architectes, won an honourable mention. If the Portzamparc plan seems mind-bending, the fluid Zaha Hadid scheme stretches credulity – it is about graphics and metaphor, and only coincidentally about a workable building. It is understandable that the GBQ jury would pick Hadid as the runner-up (described as 'New concepts of public libraries that translate into a voyage of adventure and discovery of new spaces'): this design would never have flown in Québec, but by singling it out, the jury garnered avant-garde credentials.

It is perhaps predictable that Bernard Tschumi might lean towards another Paris-based, fellow la Villette architect; that Phyllis Lambert would glide along Zaha Hadid's cutting edge; and that Ruth Cawker might lean toward the Patkau, about whose work she has written. Perhaps, too, it may be assumed that the winner, if not a Québecker, was at least going to be Canadian. Nevertheless, the winning design by Patkau Architects/Croft-Pelletier, architectes/Gilles Guité, architecte is not a compromise. Rather, it is just right. It deserved to triumph.

Some critics see the Patkau team project as the most conservative, yet it was clearly the most appropriate in terms of the library's needs – the one that best resolved the questions of the building's service and cultural functions. The solution of placing the cloistered, contemplative spaces of the collections on the upper levels, while having the café, theatre, bookstores and circulating library close to the street, neighbourhood and Métro is the most carefully considered. The librarians cited the Patkau design for its capacity to evolve, yet the architects stand 'in favour of books, at a time when many think books are on their way out, and when many think of repositories of knowledge in terms of media centres' is quite refreshing.

The heart of the library's symbolic persona is the Québec Collection, and Lise Bissonnette, head of the GBQ, singled out the architects' placing of this and the Montréal Central Library Collection in two different wooden boxes, which are themselves contained in a large copper box. The space between these 'rooms' is part of an architectural promenade that begins at the entrance and climbs through the library on ramps and stepped reading terraces.

The use of copper, wood and granite – all Québec materials – is in keeping with the Vancouver firm's reputation for regional works that evoke a rich sense of place. These materials also evoke the aesthetic of that other quiet northern country, Finland. The spirit of Alvar Aalto, instead of Frank Gehry, seems very much the right choice for the Grande bibliothéque du Québec. And, despite any difficulties caused by issues of language and provincial pride, the competition's intention of providing a starting point for something architecturally memorable in Québec seems to have succeeded.

Notes

1. All quotes in this essay are from its original publication in *Competitions*, Volume 10, No. 4, Winter 2000.

Opposite
Finalist
FABG/GDL/NOMADE/Yann
Kersalé/Ruedi Baur
Montréal, Canada

Night view of library

This page
Finalist
Atelier Christian de
Portzamparc/Jean-Marc
Venne/Birts Bastien/ Bélanger
Beauchemin Gallienee
Moisan Plante/Élizabeth de
Portzamparc, (Paris, France)

Top Pedestrian perspectives
Bottom Structure detail

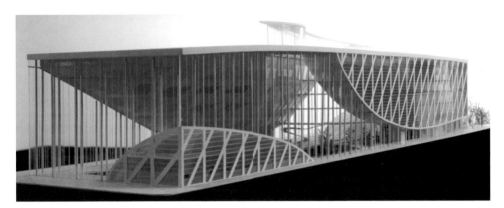

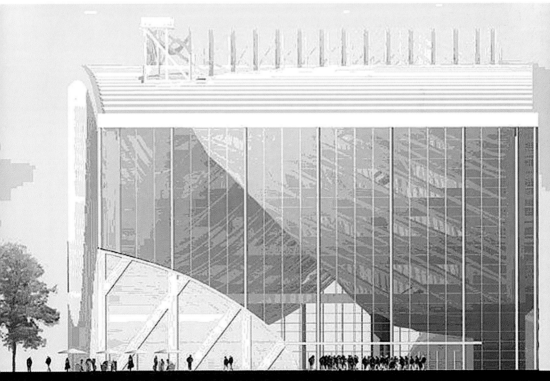

Museums

The Buchan Group
(Sydney, Australia/
Christchurch, New Zealand)
Christchurch Art Gallery,
Christchurch, New Zealand
Competition 1998
Completion 2003
Gallery at dusk

This art gallery was the result
of a 1998 national
competition with 97 entries.
It was won by the Buchan
Group, a large firm with
offices in several cities in
New Zealand and Australia.
The Gallery was dedicated
in May, 2003

Partially because many of the new museum projects are not state-sponsored and require fundraising, we find competitions being used for that very purpose. Moreover, in an age where museums need to produce revenue, it is helpful if the result is a signature building which is highlighted in the international press and brings in visitors from far and wide.

Seldom does a competition grab the attention of the world architectural community as did the recent Egyptian Museum Competition, co-sponsored by the International Union of Architects (UIA) and supported by the government of Egypt. Much as we speak of 'blockbuster' art exhibitions, this event had every characteristic of those 'blockbuster' shows. Everyone wanted to be part of it. Architects from large offices in numerous countries, who normally would not enter an open competition, sheepishly admitted that they were going to spend time outside of their corporate workday drawing up a scheme for that programme. In the end, the winners, Roisin Heneghan and Shi-Fu Peng, were a young firm based in Ireland. But, among the 1,557 entries, Coop Himmelblau from Austria was runner-up, a certain indication that there was participation from high profile firms. Although one cannot predict the future of the winners with any certainty, it would come as no surprise should they follow in the footsteps of other architects who have won blockbuster competitions i.e. Aalto, both Saarinens, Piano and Rogers, Foster, Viñoly, Snøhetta, Perrault and Carlos Ott, to name just a few.

A competition from the past decade which surely would have deserved the status of 'blockbuster' had it been open, and not invited, was for the redesign of New York's Museum of Modern Art (MOMA). In that competition, a Japanese architect whom many in the US would have considered a 'wild card' beat a small field of invitees from around the world. In the final analysis, Shin Takamatsu's very Modernist, rational approach won out over a more far-reaching scheme by Herzog & de Meuron of Switzerland, architects for the Tate Modern. In this confined urban setting, it was again a question of how to stack galleries in such a manner that circulation did not result in total chaos. Two other notable museum projects – one a competition – which were forced to deal with tight urban footprints were Cincinnati's recently completed Contemporary Arts Center by Zaha Hadid and the present renovation of Edward Durrell Stone's existing building on New York City's Columbus Circle into a new facility, the Museum of Art and Design. The latter project, by another

Right and below left
Steven Holl
(New York, US)
Kiasma, Contemporary Art
Museum, Helsinki, Finland
Competition 1992
Completion 1998

Right Museum entrance
Below, left Ramp to
upper levels

Below, right
Zaha Hadid
(London, UK)
Contemporary Arts Center
Cincinnati, Ohio, US
Competition 1998
Completion 2003

Stairs from grade level
to second floor

Ever since Frank Lloyd
Wright's Guggenheim Museum
in New York, the journey
through the building has
become as important to
museum design as the exterior
appearance of the building.
Zaha Hadid and Steven Holl
both pay homage to this idea

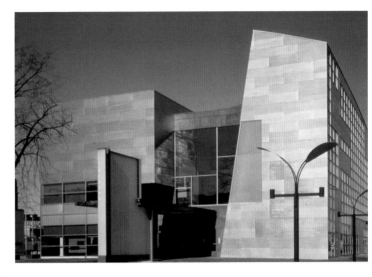

Daniel Libeskind
(Berlin, Germany)
Jewish Museum,
Berlin, Germany
Competition 1989
Completion 1999

Perspective with landscape
design in foreground

young firm from Portland, Allied Works Architecture, uses a scheme similar to that of Hadid to guide the spectator from the upper levels downwards. This is, of course a tradition in New York, ever since Frank Lloyd Wright and Marcel Breuer designed their masterpieces, the Guggenheim and the Whitney. Brad Cloepfil of Allied Works points out that this is hardly an anomaly, since there will continue to be a demand for additional museum space in confined urban settings.

Of all building commissions, museums rank high on the priority list of many architects – mainly because of the number of people (and potential clients) who are exposed to its architecture in the most intimate of circumstances. Moreover, an art museum has become more than an exhibition venue for paintings, sculpture and various kinds of installations; as a 'signature' building, a museum can become one of the most important destinations in a city – for locals as well as visitors. It may well appear as a logo on brochures which are circulated throughout the world. To best illustrate this, one only need think of the Eiffel Tower, one of the most famous competitions to take place in France. To assume that such a structure can place its imprint on the image of a city, such as has been the case with Frank Gehry's Guggenheim Museum in Bilbao, and simultaneously serve as an engine to stimulate the economy, is every architect's dream.

Finally, it can not have escaped the attention of the architectural community that museum clients often have deep pockets, and are willing to raise the money needed to cover cost overruns if the added frills can be justified in their minds. One of the more extreme cases, though not a competition, is Calatrava's addition to Milwaukee's Museum of Modern Art, where the budget, which started out at $10 million, ended up somewhere in the neighbourhood of $130 million. On the other hand, the more recent Museum of Contemporary Art in St Louis by Allied Works Architects was realised for close to $100 a square foot.

An Urban Generator with Star Format

New museum projects have become part and parcel of plans to renew entire sections of cities. Aside from Bilbao, the Tate Modern on the South Bank of the Thames in London is a prime example of a museum project which has raised property values and encouraged investment in a neglected urban area. On the other hand, Barcelona's new Modern Art Museum by Richard Meier, also conceived as part of a grand renewal scheme, has only been moderately successful in this regard. Where other infrastructure elements have been added to the mix – London's Millennium Bridge and the Jubilee underground line is the best example – the chances for a successful outcome are more favourable.

Because of the success of Bilbao, more and more communities – especially in the US – are seeking out architects who can provide them with a 'signature' building. Thus, museum competitions, more often than not, are invited, rather than open, to ensure that the client is going to get a 'star' architect instead of an unknown entity. When fundraising is in the forefront, it is easier to attract big donors when name designers are on the shortlist. And even if the competition is open, it will often be held in two stages, so that the clients may gain firsthand knowledge of the finalist competitors.

State-sponsored competitions in Europe and even Japan have resorted to the 'star' format – as witnessed by the German-sponsored competitions for the redesign of the Museuminsel complex in Berlin. In Helsinki and Nara, Japan, another variation of the competition format occurred, combining an open event in the first stage with the finalists competing in the second stage against a selected list of paid participants. In the case of Helsinki's Kiasma Museum of Contemporary Art (won by Steven Holl) and the Nara Centennial Hall (Arata Isozaki), both winners turned out to be from the invited list. Local reaction to these results was mixed. The Kiasma result did not sit well with Finnish architects, who resented the special treatment accorded a foreign architect. In Japan, the reaction was

Machado and Silvetti
Associates
(Boston, MA, US)
University of Utah Art
Museum, Salt Lake City,
US Competition, 1998
Completion 2000

quite different, where the local architectural community could hardly complain about one of their own winning.

The list of urban regeneration projects undertaken in the past decade which include museums is impressive: besides the Tate Modern, there is Manchester's Imperial War Museum by Daniel Libeskind, a new Science Museum in Columbus, Ohio by Arata Isozaki, San Francisco's Museum of Modern Art by Mario Botta, the Pulitzer Museum by Tadao Ando and neighbouring Museum of Contemporary Art in St Louis. Usually at the edge of viable urban activity, these are viewed as building blocks which can infuse energy into a troubled neighbourhood.

Destination as 'World Class' City

Museums now rank right up there with sports facilities, aquariums and national monuments as prime tourist destinations. Even mid-sized cities are finding ways to fund the construction of impressive structures to house art collections. Often, the underlying motivation for acquiring a signature building is the promotion of the architecture as much as the collection itself. And once an impressive building is in place, it may become easier to approach donors about expanding the collection (San Francisco comes to mind), especially if it makes the national headlines.

The European boom in museum construction in the 1960s and 1970s has been followed by one in America which has intensified during the past decade. Whereas the Europeans have built their postwar museums to house modern art collections (some elements of which could not be shown during the period up to and including World War II, partially because of cultural restrictions imposed by the Nazis), the move to expand museum space in the US did not take place at the same pace, notwithstanding such major additions as the East Wing of the National Gallery by IM Pei, Louis Kahn's Kimbell, Wright's Guggenheim, and the Whitney. Gordon Bunshaft's remarkable postwar addition to the Knox Museum in Buffalo had to be one of the exceptions in the mid-sized city market.

Creating new exhibition space for modern art collections is not the only factor in motivating communities to build new museums. There is also that ever-present competition between cities and states in the US to attract major corporations to their front door. A city must have a major museum, theatre and performing arts groups, as well as professional athletic teams as part of their sales package. In the same way that Washington, DC, as the US capital, had to have a major modern art museum to take its place within the international community, each state has a major city which leads the cultural charge for its region. Likewise, the rather provincial city of Bonn would not have aspired to establish a major art museum – the result of a competition won by Axel Schultes – had it not been the German capital.

Among those cities in the US which chose to utilise competitions in the 1990s as a means to select a design and architect were Kansas City, Denver, Fort Worth, Fresno and Palos Verdes, California, as well as Cincinnati. Of those only Fresno and Palos Verdes were open competitions. To date, only Tadao Ando's Modern Art Museum of Fort

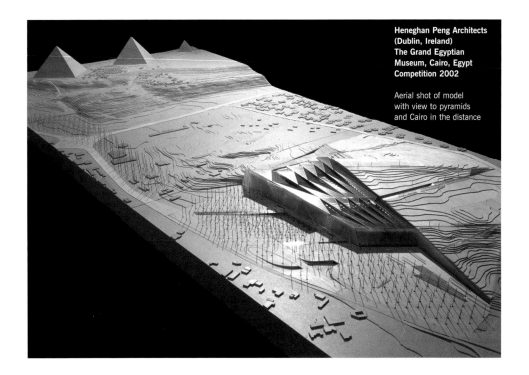

Heneghan Peng Architects
(Dublin, Ireland)
The Grand Egyptian
Museum, Cairo, Egypt
Competition 2002

Aerial shot of model
with view to pyramids
and Cairo in the distance

Worth and Zaha Hadid's CAC in Cincinnati have been completed. Steven Holl's design for the Nelson-Atkins Art Museum addition in Kansas City has encountered some budget problems – and value engineering. Daniel Libeskind's Denver Art Museum addition has begun construction and should be completed some time in 2005. The Palos Verdes Arts Center, although not to be built on the anticipated site, is still in the development stage, using the same competition-winning architect, Andrea Ponsi, from Italy.

Two universities, the University of Utah and San Jose State University, also held competitions for their department galleries. The Utah competition, won by Machado and Silvetti of Boston, was invited with five participants, and the building was completed in 1999. The competition for the expansion of the San Jose State University galleries was decided in 2003. The winner, WW of Cambridge, Massachusetts, which prevailed over more than 160 entries from around the world, relied heavily on new materials to make a compelling design statement.

Besides the Kiasma Museum competition in Helsinki, the only large museum competition of note in Europe during the 1990s was for an extension of the Prado in Spain. Daniel Libeskind's Jewish Museum in Berlin, a competition which took place in 1989, was completed in the mid-1990s. The same architect's Victoria and Albert expansion in London and the Museum of Modern Art in Stockholm by Moneo in 1991 were both by invitation. The first Berlin Museum Island competition in 1993 ran into difficulty after the winner later resigned. David Chipperfield won the second round in 1997. The Prado results became meaningless with a change in the Spanish regime, and the V&A extension, after long delays and much lobbying for the Libeskind design, appears finally to be on track.

One of the most extraordinary designs resulting from an open, national competition was the recently completed Christchurch Art Gallery in Christchurch, New Zealand. Staged as a national competition in 1998, it had 97 entries and was won by the Buchan Group, a multinational firm based mainly in Australia, but having offices in New Zealand – hence their eligibility to participate in the competition. The long, glazed sculptural wall which graces the front facade of the museum is the overriding design feature which distinguishes the structure and sets it apart from its neighbours.

A competition which on the surface seemed to be quite promising was for a Korean Cultural Center in Los Angeles. Staged in 1993, the existence of a first-class jury attracted worldwide attention to the event. The only problem was that the suggested site was not owned by the competition sponsor: posted signs indicated that it was to be the location of a future shopping mall. Although it turned out to be nothing more than an ideas competition, it did produce a plethora of interesting designs, and the winners could enhance their portfolios due to the high profile jury. Still, although this was not by any means the only competition which was not realised, its very freelance nature spelled trouble from the outset and illustrates the problems which can occur in the US where regulatory standards are lacking.

Due to the demands of major donors who support the new museums and seek the participation of 'star' architects, it is highly probable that such competitions in the future will be primarily of the invited variety. Still, the format under which these competitions take place is sometimes due to the processes with which the competition advisers running the competitions are most familiar. Since the UIA has not been asked to sponsor a competition in the US in recent history, it is highly unlikely that an event such as the Egyptian Museum Competition or the more recently completed Nam June Paik Museum competition in Korea will occur there.

Modern Art Museum of Fort Worth (1997)

George Wright

When, in 1996, the Trustees of the Modern Art Museum of Fort Worth announced that a competition would be held to select an architect for a new building, a tradition of great museum architecture in Texas was already well established. Through patrons such as the de Menils, the Kimbells and the Nashers, post World War II Texas has not only become a collector of important works of art; it has been in the forefront of elegant museum design: Louis Kahn for the Kimbell (1972); Philip Johnson for the Amon Carter (1962); and Renzo Piano for the de Menil Collection (1987) – the former two museums in Fort Worth and the latter in Houston.

Significantly, the new Modern is sited in the great green park that is on a gently sloping hill looking back to the heart of the city. To be located across the street from the Kimbell, it joins that museum together with the Carter to form a great triad of impressive buildings dedicated to the arts. Although this competition was held at about the same time as the MOMA competition in New York, it did manage to attract some of the biggest names in architecture, from the US as well as from abroad.

The competition process itself was somewhat of a departure from the ordinary. First, it was announced that the jury, named to select the architect, would consist of the Executive Committee of the museum's Board of Trustees of the Fort Worth Art Association, the governing entity of the museum. There were to be qualified advisers reporting to the group, but they would be without a vote. Compounding this situation, the Building Committee, as it was called, was seemingly of a conservative bent not given to risk-taking or setting the courageous directions one might

expect to be reflected in the design of a 21st century museum for contemporary art. The new building would not be a mirror of the work of a Frank Gehry, a Rem Koolhaas, or their like. Rather, one anticipated a more traditional style suited to the presumed preferences of the Committee members who would make the selection. Before the shortlist was named, the spectre of an 1870s' style contemporary art museum seemed a distinct possibility to some concerned observers, especially since a number of the more recently designed public buildings in the city were throwbacks to architectural styles of years past. Many critics were wont to recall the competition for the design of the Sainsbury Wing of the National Gallery in London as a possible model for a catastrophe. Fortunately for all, these fears eventually turned out to be groundless.

In fairness to all involved, much of this nervousness about the composition of the jury was excessive and almost paranoid. It was the 'track record' of several of the architects who were invited to compete several months after the competition was announced that raised concern among the doubters. Roger Shattuck, writing in the *New York Times*, made the astute and to-the-point riposte (while discussing another matter) that 'Business acumen and wealth are perfectly compatible with artistic discrimination'. Actually the jury was well qualified to serve as experts, especially as the four advisers, chosen later, were of the highest order.

As for being situated right across from the Kimbell, it was assumed that the new museum should neither mimic the Kimbell nor dispute its primacy. The alternative choices for the architect-to-

Winning Entry
Tadao Ando
(Osaka, Japan)

Night view of completed
museum

Finalist
Richard Gluckman
(New York, US)

Left Interior courtyard view
Below, top Aerial view of model
Below, bottom Elevations

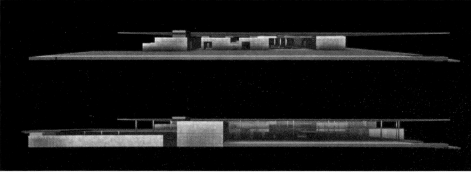

be appeared to include relating their design to the Kimbell in some respectful manner, or placing the new Modern in such a way as to be as remote from the Kimbell as the new site would permit, thus avoiding a comparison, or lack of respect, as much as possible.

On 21 and 22 April, six architects – whittled down from an original list of over 50 – presented their projects to the Trustees, the Building Committee and a few invited guests. They were Tadao Ando, Richard Gluckman, Arata Isozaki, Carlos Jimenez, Ricardo Legorreta and David Schwarz. Each was to receive an honorarium of $25,000 for fulfilling the programme requirements. Presentation took place in alphabetical order, with Tadao Ando the first to speak. Each contestant was allowed one hour to speak with 30 minutes added time for questions. The two-day schedule provided for three presentations each day.

Of the six entries, Ando's design clearly showed the most spirit and conceptual energy. The jury was intrigued by the Zen-like atmosphere it conveyed. The

others seemed to pale in comparison – ranging from the 'adobe hacienda' of Ricardo Legorreta to Gluckman's tightly knit formalism. The museum staff was reported to be happy with the diversity of approaches to the project. The participants produced solid work without pushing the design envelope in the manner of Gehry, Rogers or Steven Holl. Some might hasten to explain that the six contestants represented a good fit with the presumed conservatism of the jury. At least three of the designs were worthy of selection: those of Ando, Gluckman and Jimenez, and roughly in that order.

Within less than a month the Building Committee was called upon to meet and discuss their preferences prior to a final vote on the winner. It was anticipated that this would be a lengthy procedure, possibly lasting over a period of several weeks. To everyone's surprise, the decision fell in Ando's favour in a session lasting little more than one hour. At the very least, the competition proved that, in Texas, Modernism was alive and well.

Finalist
Arata Isozaki
(Tokyo, Japan)

Top Museum organisation
Middle Model perspective
Bottom Gallery perspective

Left
Finalist
David Schwarz
(Dallas, TX, US)

One of three submitted plans

Finalist
Carlos Jimenez
(Houston, TX, US)

Middle Aerial view of model
Bottom Entrance perspective

Competing Globally in Architecture Competitions

Finalist
Ricardo Legorreta
(Mexico City, Mexico)

Top Aerial view of model
Bottom Plan

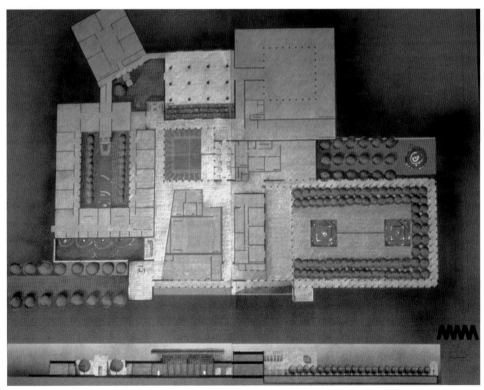

Palos Verdes Art Center (2000)

Larry Gordon

Peter Phinney expected a respectable response to the design competition he arranged for a renovation and expansion of a community art centre on southern California's lush and hilly Palos Verdes Peninsula. After all, Phinney, an architect who was volunteering his time, felt certain that the cachet of a visual arts-related project in the Los Angeles area would draw some interest. And he hoped his extremely detailed and inviting prospectus – placed on the internet with a video tour, easy links and discussion postings – would be accessible to architects and students around the United States and the world. The total of $10,000 in prize money for six winners might snag some entries too, he thought. None of that, however, prepared him for the response.

It was like a tidal wave coming from the Pacific Ocean just over the ridge from the Palos Verdes Art Center campus. More than 650 individuals or teams from 44 countries registered, each paying $50 for the right to compete. 'It exceeded our expectations literally tenfold', recalled Phinney, whose wife Gail is the programme director for the art centre. 'It was very gratifying'.[1] That astonishment held true by July's deadline, when 254 sets of boards – and scores of intricate and expensive models – arrived from as far away as Hong Kong, Germany and Boston in a parade of delivery trucks.

Los Angeles area architect Mark Mack, one of the seven jurors, suggested that the response was so large because this was one of 'the first truly internet competitions, and it was very well organised, conceived and executed'. Plus, he pointed to the relatively low fee, the lack of prequalifying restrictions and the sense that the sponsors actually wanted to

build something. That is unlike so many other competitions which, Mack complained, are 'just vehicles to raise money and consciousness about a project'.

The non-governmental, non-profit art centre in Rancho Palos Verdes, founded in 1931, had grown into its present hillside campus from the 1970s and 1980s into an awkward hodgepodge of studios, classrooms, galleries, offices, reception areas and a gift shop among several structures. While its 1,500 loyal members and many visiting students produce a steady stream of paintings, sculpture, fashion and photography, conditions are cramped. The layout does not take advantage of the site's stunning views of the Los Angeles basin and its own prominence at a major intersection. One recent visitor dismissed the centre as looking like a garden supply outlet or a funky nursery school.

The centre's leaders want to double its size, to about 20,000 square feet, add underground parking and gain a sense of architectural identity without offending the affluent neighbourhood or potential donors. Also, the competition programme insisted that any design should take 'full advantage of our glorious southern California climate'.

'I wanted as many ideas as possible. I really wanted something that would be a visual icon,' explained Scott Ward, the centre's executive director who was one of the jurors. He went into it looking not for a complete design, but at least part of one or 'a first draft'.

The jury convened for one day in August. It also included landscape architect Todd Bennitt, artist Philippa Blair, architectural critic Michael Webb,

Winning Entry
Andrea Ponsi
(Florence, Italy)

This page
Winning Entry
Andrea Ponsi
(Florence, Italy)

Left Entrance
Middle Elevation
Bottom Aerial views of model

Ponsi's project proposes a set of four boxy but delicate pavilions stepping down the hillside, all with multiple horizontal bands of wood and ribbon glass. It is International Style in form, but feels Craftsman in style and warmth. The campus is linked to the parking garage with a banded trellis and walkway, and through the centre of the buildings runs a water element, sometimes fountain, sometimes stream, that brings a sense of nature into the artistic environment

Opposite
Second Place
Johnston, Marklee &
Associates
(Los Angeles, CA, US)

Aerial view of model

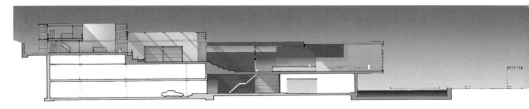

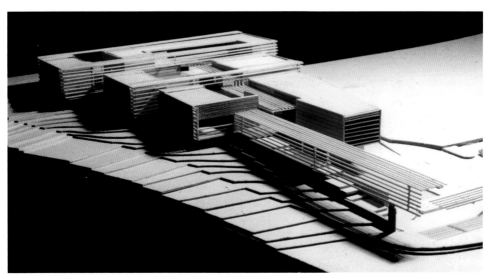

architect Eric Lloyd Wright (grandson of you know who), all from the Los Angeles region, and New Zealand architect Phillip Max Cheshire. They worked intensively to narrow down the possibilities, first to 75, then to 35, then to 10. Some jurors said they wished they had more time. But the pressure was on, because an exhibit and reception were scheduled for that evening, and the guests were expecting to see the winning designs.

Some submissions, of course, were outrageous and probably unbuildable. For example, a Japanese team suggested two skyscraper garages that would move cars via elevators. A group from France created a very beautiful, if kitschy model, of a giant Airstream trailer that would be the centre's front edifice and offices, a sort of European homage to California road culture. Some seemed more in love with their computer graphics skills than the working needs of artists and students.

However, nearly all 254 entries showed enthusiasm, expense and effort, said Phinney, adding that many were 'buildable, pragmatic and beautiful'. According to Mack, about 100 were quite good, 'showed quality, had substance and dealt with the issue at hand'. A fellow juror, Blair, said she was exhilarated by the judging process, even with the tough deadline. She was very pleased that the contest was arranged to 'give people in outlying places a chance to show their work' and to allow 'for a freedom that wouldn't necessarily be allowed in a normal, everyday, practical venture'.

By the end, there was little disagreement over the first place, $5,000 prize: it went to Andrea Ponsi, an architect from Florence, Italy who had worked in California but not visited the Palos Verdes Art Center.

Ponsi, who earned a master's degree from the University of Pennsylvania, said that much of his professional practice had been restoration, interior design and mixed-use residential-commercial projects. He had stayed away from competitions in recent years but was drawn by the California location and by the 'efficiency and enthusiasm' evident in Phinney's internet posting. He also 'liked the idea that the art centre had a hilly terrain and could combine various architectural typologies: private villa, factory warehouse, and museum'.

He worked alone for three weekends and then, with assistants, spent two weeks on drawings and models. 'I was convinced that I had a very good scheme. However I was greatly surprised to discover that my project did not get lost among 250 entries, many of them probably executed with much more spectacular presentation techniques than mine'.

Wright said he was impressed by 'the strong simplicity of it, and how it seemed to fit very nicely into the site'. Fellow juror Mack said Ponsi's plan 'had a grace and simplicity about it. It was not overwrought. It was kind of pragmatic and poetic too'. Center executive director Ward praised Ponsi's design as 'clean, elegant and modern, not a sharp stick. We live in a community where a sharp stick might not be accepted'.

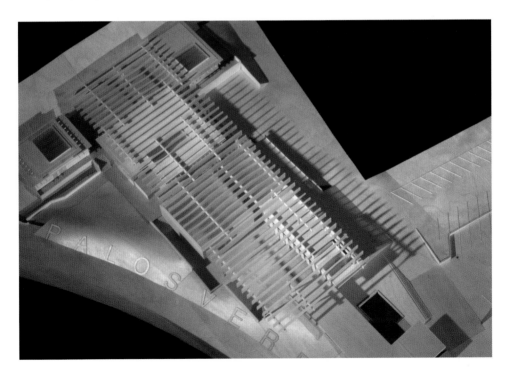

Top
Honourable Mention
Robert Courser
Syracuse, New York

Aerial view of model

Bottom
Third Place
Jenny Wu/Dwayne Oyler
(Cambridge, MA, US)

Model elevation perspective

Second place ($2,000) went to Sharon Johnston of Lee, Johnston, Marklee & Associates of Los Angeles, and the third place ($1,000) winner was Jenny Wu and fellow Harvard student Dwayne Oyler. Chad KL Zane of University of Hawaii, at Manoa, was given the student award ($1,000). Two honourable mentions ($500 each) went to Robert Corser, assistant professor of architecture at Syracuse University, and to Heimo Schimek of Austria.

Third place winner Oyler said he and his partner Wu were drawn to the website's inviting flavour even though they were discouraged by the apparent number of rival contenders. They went ahead, working eight hours a day for more than a month, in what was their first competition. Their design was most notable for its large movable canopy that would both identify and cover the front of the art campus. 'I believe that the overwhelming majority of participants in a competition such as this enter primarily for the sake of fulfilling their own desire to create architecture. Being recognised by others is obviously a great honour, but it is only a bonus,' Oyler said.

Another contestant Jeffrey O'Brien, whose Minneapolis firm is called Archigenesis, said he was as pleased with the competition as a losing entrant can be. After first spotting the Palos Verdes prospectus on the web, he decided to compete because it seemed to invite 'open dialogue, which is rare in the professional competition settings I have been involved with, competing against large architectural firms for multi-million dollar commissions'. And while his design took time away from growing his business, it also 'provided me with a free outlet, and also a chance to express myself without the restraints I am used to'.

Meanwhile, competition organiser Phinney is pleased with the process and the outcome. (The competition broke even financially, with all the entry fees paying for such expenses as jurors' honoraria.) In his regular, full-time practice, Phinney specialises in retail projects and commercial interiors for the Torrance firm of Bryant, Palmer, Soto. He now is so intrigued with the possibilities of competitions that he is interested in devoting more time to their administration.

'It allows me to do what I enjoy most in architecture, the real true design of it, the intellectual aspects of it, without getting bogged down with the pragmatics of budgets', he explained. 'It's refreshing. And it ultimately leads to buildings.'

Note 1. All quotes in this essay are from its original publication in *Competitions*, Volume 10, No. 4, Winter 2000.

Nam June Paik Museum (2003)

G Stanley Collyer

If there ever was a museum of discovery, this could well be it. The winning competition design for a new museum honouring the works of Korean artist Nam June Paik is all about approaching culture with a large dose of adventure added. Dubbed 'Matrix' by the author, the design seeks to enable museum visitors to create their own programme. Although there are plenty of hints, one can pick and choose – and then come back for more. The winning design by the young German architect, Kirsten Schemel, in contrast to the runners-up, is more about integrating the museum into the hilly landscape, rather than simply using it as a contributing factor in which to park the various components.

The competition, approved by the International Union of Architects (UIA) and supported by the Kyonggi Cultural Foundation in Korea, drew 439 entries from around the world. The sponsors had allotted five days for the adjudication process, but the jury was able to reach a decision after only three days. This was facilitated by the method in which the jury went about selecting the finalists. Instead of each juror indicating preferences, then discussing each one in detail, they were asked to eliminate those entries from the very start which they deemed inadequate. As a result, all but 70 entries were eliminated on the first day; and by the end of the second day, the jury had tossed all but 17 submissions. When the field was narrowed to the final six, then three, the discussion focused more and more on the finer details – for instance, to what extent each of the submissions were appropriate for the work of the artist.

The jury was part Korean, part international, and very professional. It was presided over jointly by Odile Decq (France, representing the UIA) and Jong Soung Kimm, an architect from Korea and President of the Federation of Institutes of Korean Architects. The other voting members were: Jin-Kyoon Kim (Korea), Ki Soo Oh (Korea), Axel Schultes (Germany), Roberto Simon (Brazil) and John Hanhardt (US). Hanhardt, an expert on the works of Nam June Paik, replaced American architect Ricardo Scofidio, who was unable to attend for health reasons, and Simon replaced Arata Isozaki, who was unable to attend the first day's deliberations.

Although the jury had narrowed down the finalists to three after only three days of deliberations, the final choice did not come easy. For an extended period there was a deadlock, with what turned out to be three votes for Schemel and three for the second place winner. The seventh juror didn't budge from his preference, the Japanese third-place entry, for some time. When Simon finally joined the group that supported the Schemel entry, the die was cast. It was four to three. When the envelopes were opened, Schultes surmised that the winner was probably from France or the UK. To everyone's surprise, it was the young German architect, Schemel, who although practising in Berlin, was completely unknown to Schultes (and other Berlin architects I talked to, as well), who also calls that city home. Second place went to a young Korean architect presently residing in the US, Kyu Sung Woo. As coincidence would have it, the three Korean judges had supported his entry, without definitely knowing that its author was a Korean. But because some of the features of the design might be considered typically Korean, some of the jurors thought it could well be the case.

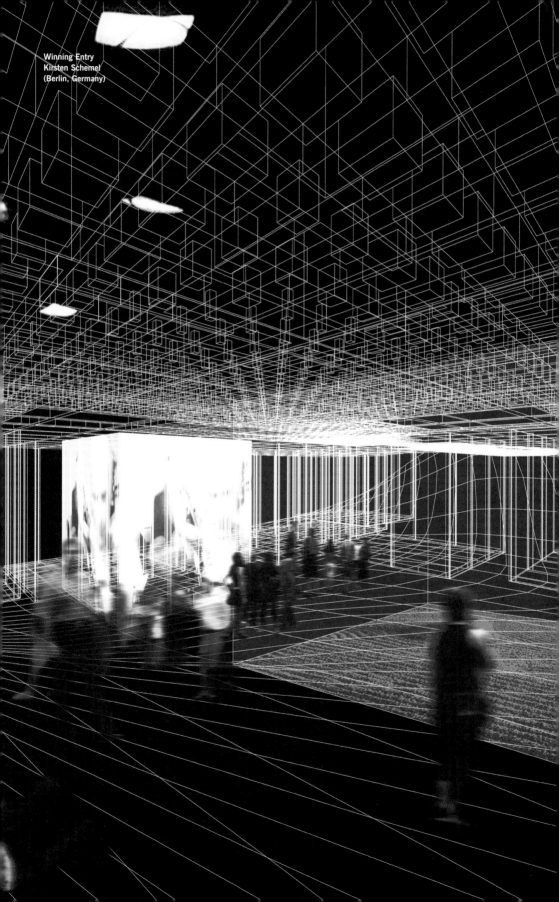

Winning Entry
Kirsten Schemel
(Berlin, Germany)

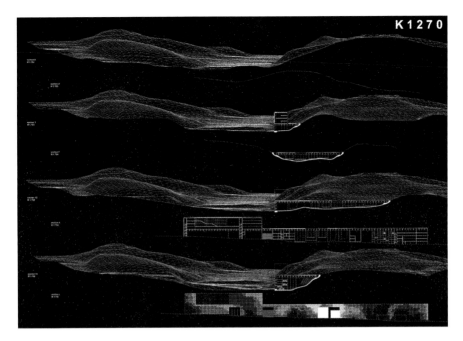

K 1 2 7 0

The Winning Entries

Schultes said that the appeal of the Schemel scheme was based to a great extent on its flexibility. It suggested anything but rigidity, and in essence represented a 'shell', rather than a finished, highly defined space. According to Schemel, 'We don't want a kind of hierarchical linear space, we imagine a matrix with spatial complexity. That structure is the search for a form of the pleasure of an art experience'.[1] She visualises this structure as a continuation of the landscape – tucked into a depression between two hills. The use of interior gardens reinforces this impression, and she looks to landscapes such as Central Park, Skeppsholmen, Stockholm, or Berlin's Tiergarten/Forum, all of which are totally enclosed, but have numerous programmes within their perimeters.

Although the roof consists of a large, continuous plane, the interior is broken up both visually and physically by the topographical descent created by the landscape. Thus, moving from level to level, rather than room to room, is the main organisational factor while wandering through the museum. Creating different levels also can break up the interior so that it does not resemble a giant convention hall. Visually, one is somehow reminded of Mies's National Gallery in Berlin, but instead of being situated on a platform, it is inserted into a landscape in a more fragmentary manner.

The scheme of the runner-up, Kyu Sung Woo, was more typically Korean in that it was a single building with two platforms (the jury interpreted this as two buildings) embedded in the landscape. A sculpture garden was to be located on the side away from the

road. Thus we have the so-called 'experimental boxes', which were not intended to 'emulate the work of the artist', but serve as a platform for Nam June Paik's work.

Third place went to the Japanese architect, Noriaki Okabe, who used a bridge to bring attention to the work of the artist. Here we have the exhibition areas suspended over the valley, a reasonable assumption, but not totally convincing to the jury. As this project, eventually covering an area of 9,000 square metres, is to be built in phases, one might wonder how a bridge as a flexible building platform would work in light of this programme.

Honourable mentions were awarded to Karlheinz Sendelbach, Schneider + Sendelbach Architekten, Germany; Diego Suarez, OAV, UK; and Hannelore Deubzer, Deubzer König Architekten, Germany.

When the jury tried to get in touch with the winner, it took them some time to track her down, as she was away from her office on vacation. This was the second open competition she had entered – the other was for the Egyptian Museum – after working on several residential projects and an invited competition for a building in Hamburg, for which she received a 'Purchase'. Now that Kirsten Schemel has stepped into the limelight, one may be sure that this is not the last we will be hearing from her.

Although it is assumed that the project will go forward, there has been some disagreement as to the small budget allotted for the square footage which the museum now requires. If the Koreans remain inflexible in that respect, the project will no doubt be chopped up into more phases – assuming they want the entire project completed as programmed.

Note 1. All quotes in this essay are from its original publication in *Competitions*, Volume 13, No. 4, Winter 2003.

**Winning Entry
Kirsten Schemel
(Berlin, Germany)**

Opposite Interior perspective
Right Floor plan and
organisation
Bottom View across
rooftop into the meadow

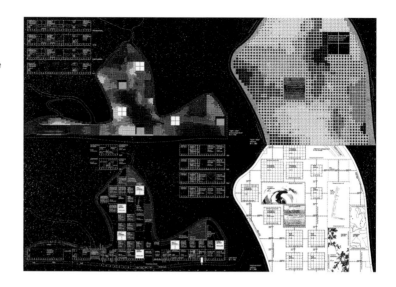

lake

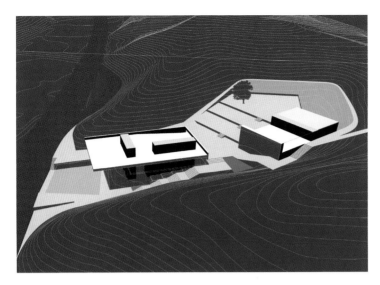

Second Place
Kyu Sung Woo
(Cambridge, MA, US)

Top Aerial view of
computerised model
Bottom Site plan

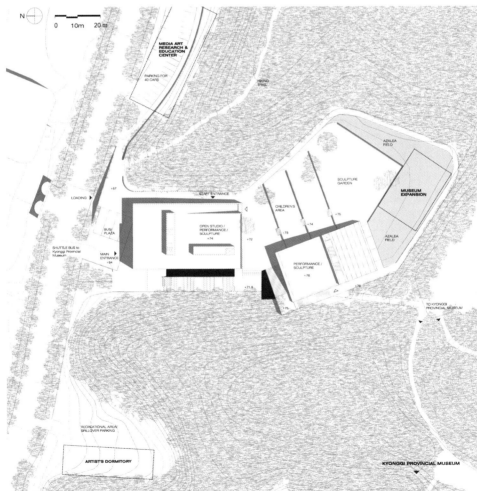

MEDIA ART
RESEARCH &
EDUCATION
CENTER

PARKING FOR
40 CARS

MUSEUM
EXPANSION

AZALEA
FIELD

SCULPTURE
GARDEN

AZALEA
FIELD

STAFF ENTRANCE

CHILDREN'S
AREA

LOADING

BUS/
PLAZA

OPEN STUDIO /
PERFORMANCE /
SCULPTURE

PERFORMANCE /
SCULPTURE

SHUTTLE BUS to
Kyonggi Provincial
Museum

MAIN
ENTRANCE

TO KYONGGI
PROVINCIAL MUSEUM

RECREATIONAL AREA/
SPILLOVER PARKING

ARTIST'S DORMITORY

KYONGGI PROVINCIAL MUSEUM

Competing Globally in Architecture Competitions

**Third place
Noriaki Okabe
(Tokyo, Japan)**

Top Perspective
Middle Aerial view
of site with model
Bottom Axonometric
view of model

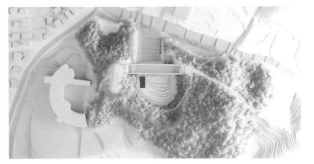

Robert G Shibley AIA, AICP

Housing

Valerio Associates
Cotton Palms Senior
Apartments
Two-stage competition 1988
Project completion 1991
This development proposal
competition was sponsored by
the City of Colton, California,
east of Los Angeles. Overall,
the organization is based on a
nine square; each square is a
three story cluster of nine to
twelve apartments, with the
center square removed for a
green. Opposite the Beaux
Arts composition of Fleming
Park, laid out in the thirties, is
the palm court.

Beset by government budget cuts and conservative governments which look to the private sector for housing solutions, competitions have managed to address many of the issues which have not been fully investigated by government bureaucracies, at the same time raising the bar in architectural expression.

Housing in Europe has traditionally been highly subsidised, and even innovative, going back to projects undertaken by architects in the 1920s. Complexes such as the 1927 Weissenhof Siedlung in Stuttgart, where architects like Peter Behrens, Gropius, Mies van der Rohe, Oud and Le Corbusier participated, or Bruno Taut's Horseshoe housing (Berlin-Britz, 1925) and affordable housing for workers (Argentinische Allee) in Berlin were the best examples of a contemporary approach to housing in their time. In postwar Europe, the Berlin Bauaustellung conceived for the most part to alleviate the intermittent vacant parcel condition near the Wall as a result of the wartime Allied bombing, produced a number of interesting infill solutions by a large number of name architects – from Charles Moore to Peter Cook and Aldo Rossi. With the advent of the European Union regulations in 1993, European-wide competitions have moved to the forefront. Of these, Europan, which stipulates housing solutions for various sites throughout the region, has gained the most attention.

Unfortunately, over the past two decades public housing construction has been in decline. This is due to several factors, not least of which is the presence of conservative governments – Reagan and Thatcher in the US and UK – which have traditionally looked to the private sector for solutions. Furthermore, just when immigration has increased demand for low-cost housing, budget problems, and then inflation in the housing sector have prevented governments and non-profit making organisations from meeting demand. During the 1990s in California, for instance, the price of housing construction increased from $65 per square foot at the beginning of the decade to $125 per square foot in the year 2000. This was enough to frighten off even most non-profits, who had been carrying some of the burden. Also, there has been a tendency to bring suburban architecture to the inner city in the US, where 'New Urbanism' has gained favour with many planners.

Against this background, competitions have provided a ray of light in a sector beset with economic ills. Not only the aforementioned Europan, but various competitions staged at the local level have helped to raise the aesthetic bar worldwide. In the US, one of the more ambitious non-profits

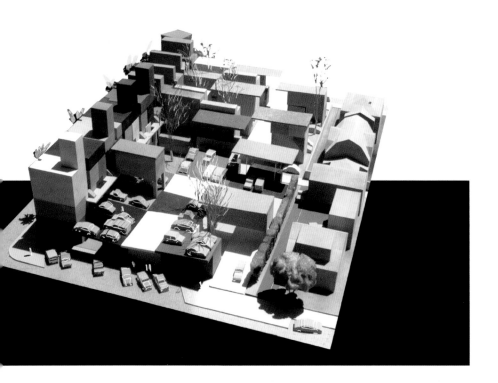

Above and right
Winning Entry
McCormick, Smith & Others
in collaboration with Lloyd
Russell, AIA Livable Places
community development
masterplan, Los Angeles,
California, US Competition
2003

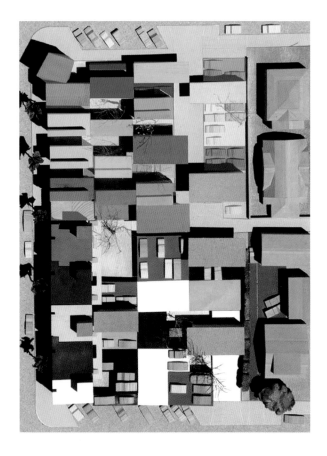

experiencing success with this approach is 'Livable Places', based in Los Angeles. Several of their projects have been completed and received international acclaim.

For the most part, housing competitions in the US since 1991 reveal a preoccupation with low cost and special purpose housing. Jackie Leavitt and Eric Lee suggest that, 'Affordable housing competitions provide a rich forum for extending ideas about the built form to discussions about policy and equity'.[1] Out of this experimentation came some important design variations testing traditional housing assumptions. For example, the competition results add depth and further substance to the earlier New American House Competition of 1984 and the New York City Infill Competition of 1985. Both of these efforts, and the material since, address new styles of living, offering 'granny flats', rooms off the kitchen and other approaches to the changing demographics of the American family.

The last two decades of housing competition also provided new insights into specialty housing, working with people living with AIDS and the mentally impaired. In the area of specialty housing, the competitions actually lend still more credibility to the idea that what is good for specialty markets in architecture is often also good for the general populations to be served.

The competitions of the 1980s, 1990s and into this decade also deal with a broad range of other concerns, if not by the requirements of the competition programme, then by the commentary of those who review the efforts. They address expanding the role of the competition jury, working with mundane or extraordinary contexts, acquiring community support for

Right
New York City Infill
Competition (1985)
The winning design by Michael Pyatok (above) shows the rear yard view. The street-front apartments are one unit deep and recieve light and air on opposite sites. Corner location of back-to-back courtyard units provides exposure on adjacent sides.
The courtyard schemes combine no more than thirty to forty families per shared entry and courtyard. This is intended to encourage the ability of people to territorialize the space in small groups as key to establishing long-term, built-in security.

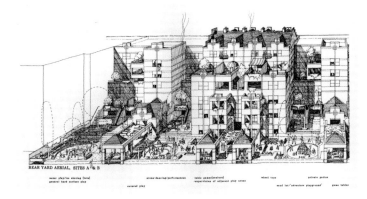

Competing Globally in Architecture Competitions

Right
New Urban Housing (1992)
Pittsburgh, Pennsylvania
Winning Entry
Peter Fillat/Randy Sovitch
Studio Wanda
Baltimore, Maryland.

low-cost housing development, establishing physical connections to the community, educating the broader public and working with the concept of compact neighbourhoods when the existing context is scattered. All of this is about competitions servicing the broader social agenda established by programme sponsors.

Consider, for example, Jill Watson's report of the New Urban Housing Competition, where she identifies a very proactive jury in setting the direction of the competition and in the implementation of the results. The jury is a consulting and educating body, and not just the judge. Consider also the work of winning submissions in the Chicago Westside Affordable Housing Competition (1998) or the Low Cost Housing Competition in South Central Los Angeles in 1994, both of which put a great deal of emphasis on context sensitive infill as well as the acquisition of community support through the competition process. The same is also true of the Salt Lake City competition (1994) that looked at low-income infill housing while questioning the role of context when the existing context is weak. Several of these same competitions also involved spending a great deal of time in building community consensus through the process, as seen most notably in the work of the San Diego Affordable Housing Competition won by Michael Pyatok in 1993.

Still more complex social programme issues were addressed when Baltimore attempted to sort out the implications of a significant loss of population by creatively rethinking the patterns of density in 1999. This, taken together with competitions like one in Channahon, Illinois (1998), look at the economic, social and ecological costs of sprawl. Even with all of this, the potential promise of a paradigm shift in housing typology has been illusive. For example, in spring 2003 the explorations of the ideas

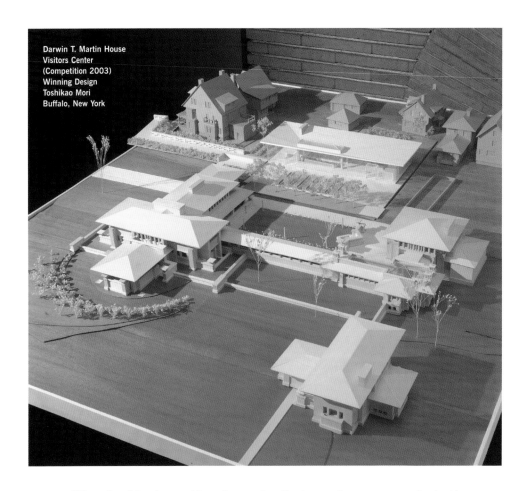

Darwin T. Martin House
Visitors Center
(Competition 2003)
Winning Design
Toshikao Mori
Buffalo, New York

competition for Monterey Housing actually to seek responses to both existing and new typologies did not return a winning submission in the paradigm shift category.

A subtext of the reports on housing competitions in *Competitions* magazine is a consistent call for quality design. Juries did not always find the submissions convincing, but awards were made, ideas were advanced and some projects were built. In general, however, there is a refrain of missed opportunity. A critique by a 'cranky' Mike Brill, applicable not just to housing competitions but to much of our experience of competition results, spoke of his concerns about the capricious use of 'automatic centres, interior streets, imagery, and the pastiche drawn from architecture magazines'. He further asserted that the landscapes of many of our competition winners are 'unexamined'. Brill decried the casual assertion of symbol, protesting that just 'saying something is a symbol doesn't make it so'.

In the history of architecture the 'home' has been a traditional place to explore architectural ideas that are, of course, about the social and economic agenda embedded in a programme. But it is also a place to explore architecture *per se*. Issues of typology, formal organisation, building site relationship, material and cultural expression, structure and technology are not subordinate to the social programmes. They are, rather, the inventive way in which such programmes are realised.

If our competitions are to find approaches to contemporary problems and advance the field of architecture, then the solutions must be free to simultaneously embrace site context and create a contemporary if not visionary dialogue with it. A recent competition for the visitor centre of Frank Lloyd Wright's Darwin T Martin House in Buffalo is an excellent example. Toshikao Mori's winning submission sets up a dialogue with the historic home built in a Frederick Law Olmsted 'parkside' community laid out in the 1870s. In effect we have a 21st century interpretation of an early 20th century home in a 19th century landscape. Professor Mori has interpreted without mimicry, and has been respectful and aggressive in formal expression without once repeating Wright's effort to deconstruct the corners to build a stronger relation to site. The result is an extremely visionary interpretation of Wright's largest and, some argue, best prairie home. It is transparent where Wright is opaque or translucent. Both the visitor centre and the Martin House are the best of their time in technology and design: both are experimental with light, form and building site relationship. Yet they sit comfortably together and with their Olmsted neighbourhood host. They are complementary in their landscape treatment, and are true to the organic ideals of Wright's architecture.

Note 1. All quotes in this essay are from its original publication in *Competitions*, Volume 1, No. 2, Summer 1991.

Chicago Housing Authority (2001)

Rosemarie Buchanan

The Chicago Housing Authority's competition for a mixed-income housing redevelopment began and concluded, as many competitions do, with brazen optimism tempered by a shot of reality. It's clear that Brian Healy Architects, Boston, won; but the realisation of the project is in question.

The competition's seven competing architects, four chosen outright and three plucked from 118 contestants, were given a heady proposition: design one square block of housing for a vacant square block of an aging public housing development on Chicago's west side that will accommodate three income levels – market value, affordable and low-income housing; craft it so those three constituencies are indistinguishable from the outside; distribute all three types evenly across the development, providing one-third for each group; and ensure that every unit should be solely accessible from the outside like a single-family house— in other words, there should be no common entrance. The 'redevelopment requires that … public housing no longer is visually stigmatised as the poor man's house',[1] states the competition's original grant proposal to the National Endowment for the Arts (NEA).

The four chosen architects included Shim-Sutcliffe Architects, Toronto; Doug Garofalo, Chicago; Coleman Coker, Memphis; and Stanley Saitowitz of San Francisco. The three selected from the open competition were Brian Healy of Boston; 3D Design Studios, Chicago; and the Chicago-based team of Wheeler Kearns Architects with Roberta Feldman and Xavier Vendrell. The jury judged all seven teams' entries anonymously and each one received a $20,000 honorarium plus travel expenses. Healy

received the $15,000 First Place Award and the possibility of negotiating with a developer to have his design constructed – although there are doubts whether that will happen, according to Lee Bey, deputy chief of staff for the mayor's office.

The competition's square-block site borders the wide and speedy Roosevelt Road, the University of Illinois at Chicago (UIC), and a rapidly gentrifying patch of town. Lofts and condos go for between $300,000 and $500,000 nearby. With two HOPE IV grants totalling $59 million awarded to ABLA in 1996 and 1998, as well as HUD (Federal Housing and Urban Development Agency) funds, the city's department of planning appropriates $140,000 to construct each affordable unit and $106,000 for each Chicago Housing Authority (CHA) unit. The market's construction cost for masonry homes in the area market hovers around $200,000 or more. So, the available funding and market construction costs are two ends that don't meet. The competition brief brought this problem to the table and asked the architects to solve it, but in the end a developer will be hired to find a solution.

All the competitors' designs are long and narrow to accommodate the shape of the site, 220 by 600 feet –more narrow than the typical Chicago city block due to the widening of the bordering Roosevelt Road in the 1960s. The competition brief stipulated that single family townhouses and two-flats be incorporated in the designs. Total hard construction costs should not exceed $115 per square foot. A quarter of all units should be 700 square feet with one bedroom; half of the units require two bedrooms at 900 square feet; 15 percent of the units should

Winning Entry
Brian Healy Architects
(Boston, MA, US)

Top Front view of unit
Bottom Rear view of unit

have three bedrooms at 1,200 square feet; and 10 percent with four bedrooms at 1,500 square feet.

The words 'backdrop', 'field', 'potential' and 'scaffold' highlighted the entrants' statements of purpose, as if each was allowing the occupants to make of the design what they would as opposed to the architect dictating how they should live. Each skated a line between blurring and dignifying the residents' identities. While those patterns have been jostled by 20th century commercial and institutional development, each also negotiated between embracing the area's 19th century urban residential patterns, and rejecting them.

Shim-Sutcliffe's design divided the site into a linear two-third/one-third proportion with a corridor stretching down the middle. Clusters comprised of various arrangements of differently sized apartments and a courtyard repeated to create an overall pattern. Sometimes apartments wrapped and interlocked around one another in an effort to mask where one ended and another began – and hence blur the ability to potentially discern one income level from another. Their brick clusters formed a line of defence against Roosevelt Road – a common feature among many of the entrants' designs – and in some places rose to four stories, topped with a ramp-like roof.

Doug Garofalo's design wove apartments into ribbed, undulating, barge-like clusters of concrete, brick and glass en pilotis and incorporated the potential for home businesses and modest commercial retail development. Green space penetrated the site and extended between the development and a nearby school. Garofalo's accompanying statement said that he counterbalanced the dualism between the 'individual nature of domesticity' and the 'standardised, repetitive building practices' in his proposal. The jury awarded him an honourable mention – a last-minute award, jurist Howard Decker said, that was conceived as a nod to Garofalo's ingenuity just an hour and a half before the winners' announcement.

Coker's creation subsumed parking under his clusters, which connected in a linear fashion down the length of the site. Entrances were planned for level two and living space for levels three and four. The exterior surface treatment vaguely resembles Karl Ehn's Karl Marx Hof in Vienna.

Stanley Saitowitz's more insular urban village sprang from a grid and set out to value 'simplicity and regularity over complexity'. Saitowitz used two corridors to divide the rectangular-shaped block into equal thirds. Glass diminished the distinction between the clean-lined domestic space and outside, semi-private courtyards. He referred to the design as a 'scaffold', signalling once again a space for residents' potential.

Wheeler Kearns with Feldman and Vendell encircled the perimeter of the square block with apartment clusters and based their development's plan on the street and alley system. Balconies stretched and overlapped units to encourage neighbourly interaction. This team interprets their designs as being respectful of 'Chicago's urban pattern yet resists the insularity of the private lot'.

3D Design Studios' submission was the only one to bisect the square block laterally. Each individual cluster resembled an extenuated townhouse, tall and narrow. Their stated mission: 'to disintegrate the superblock'.

Lastly, winner Brian Healy's design is based on a 'typical Chicago block'. Perhaps 'everyday' could describe Healy's characterisation of the design. He cites the 19th century pattern of the streetscape and alley system as the infrastructure. Parking runs underneath blocky, 25-foot modular units – which Healy attributes to the proportion of Chicago's existing city blocks. The design takes Modernist principles, such as arise from a grid, and teams them with a Charles Moore-ish stylistic vocabulary. Stating that an 'overreliance on symbolism is a bad thing', Healy decries the label 'modern' to describe his proposal, preferring to describe the language of his project as a warehouse – something that avoids pastiche. Juror Lamarr Reid of Perkins & Will said Healy's design was by far the most buildable and feasible. 'We're confident this [design] can be followed through', he said. 'And it engages the street.'

The competition site is only 8 acres amid ABLA's whopping 95 acres. ABLA, a conglomeration of four separate public housing developments erected between 1937 and 1962, and one of Chicago's oldest and most decrepit public housing developments, is in its entirety the subject of an overall masterplan now being reviewed by HUD. Once HUD gives it a stamp of approval, the city will publish a request for proposal for developers to take on the entire site for redevelopment.

Ultimately, the chosen developer will determine whether Healy's design or that of another architect will be built. Developers attending the award ceremony diplomatically lauded the competition for its wealth of ideas, but then levied some criticism: 'How are you going to pick up the garbage in that?' said Peter Lavari, senior vice president of Brinshore Development in Chicago and a developer for two other CHA housing developments in the city. He said the architects didn't have to design around the zoning and other rules imposed upon developers and their teams. 'This isn't reality and we also don't want a city that's pretty; we want it to be functional.'

Bruce F Klein AIA, an architect from Chicago's Sonoc Architects which helped to design the ABLA masterplan along with several consultants including Peter Calthorpe, says the designs themselves might draw interest, but ultimately, 'regardless of design competitions, public housing residents want what they perceive as what everyone else has – brass doorknobs ... the more traditional. This stuff is more

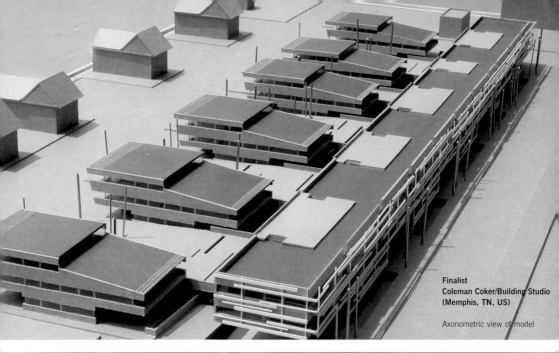

**Finalist
Coleman Coker/Building Studio
(Memphis, TN, US)**

Axonometric view of model

Instead of reducing potential residents to their perceived least common denominator, we propose a 'weave' of housing that composes a diverse field from which individual lives may be played out. Landscape and materiality unfold to form a backdrop for community relations, mirroring the complexity and richness that a successful mixed-income development offers its residents.

VIEW ALONG ROAD

LOOKING WEST ON ROOSEVELT ROAD

ENTRY COURT LOOKING TOWARD SITE INTERIOR

BIRD'S-EYE VIEW OF UNITS AND COMM

Left
Finalist
Stanley Saitowitz
(San Francisco, CA, US)
Interior street scene

for interest and innovation.' Developers attending the award ceremony announcing Healy's win expressed sour grapes at the architects' offerings.

The 'stuff' to which Klein refers comprises the seven entries themselves – models of the site plan and sections of one unit, as well as renderings – displayed anonymously at the city's Harold Washington Library over the summer. No one but competition director, Denise Arnold AIA, programme director for the Mayor's Office for People with Disabilities, knew for sure which architect designed which entry until the winner was announced. 'The intent of this competition was to choose an architect, not a scheme,' Arnold said.

The CHA's Timothy Veenstra, development manager for ABLA, also undercuts the importance of this particular design, speaking of the winner more as a design consultant for future development than an executor of the winning design. However, the city's interpretation is different: this is a small piece of a bigger pie. Ideas may be folded in, but when it comes to execution, the developer will have his or her way. Nonetheless, jury members say that regardless of whether it will be built, the designs will definitely have impact. The city agrees: 'This could be built or we could use it in other parts of ABLA or in another housing project altogether. It could be repeated on a much larger scale – not just on this particular square block,' said an employee with the Mayor's office. While that may sound promising, the site-specific

architecture created by Healy and his six colleagues would be objectified if uprooted and placed *ad infinitum* at ABLA and elsewhere.

The CHA's protocol for this competition stood its usual procedure on its head. Typically, the authority solicits requests for qualifications and then proposals from developers to initiate a capital improvements project. Then, the developers put together a team of which architects are only a part. Denise Arnold says that the developers cast for CHA developments are associated with the same architects time after time.

This time, the CHA started with architecture. Why? 'To show that we're giving architects a chance to say something,' says Timothy Veenstra, ACHA development manager for the ABLA Homes. Bey, speaking for Mayor Richard Daley's office, said the competition is a chance to ameliorate the past – a 'second chance for public housing'.

During the spring of 2000, Arnold, then a Chicago department of housing employee, applied for funds from the NEA's New Public Works Grant Program. To her bemusement, the grant application landed the city of Chicago $50,000 to solicit innovative designs for a square block of the ABLA homes, located on the near west side. The problem was that Arnold had to drum up support and pad the NEA money with private funds to make a competition feasible. In six months, she had to figure out how to make the money work, or lose it.

Arnold lobbied the city and the CHA to garner

monies and services from the MacArthur Foundation, the Driehaus Foundation, UIC, the Chicago Community Trust, the Fannie Mae Foundation and others. Over a year later, on 27 August 2001, Arnold and the CHA announced that architect Brian Healy of Boston had won the CHA's competition for the new mixed-income housing.

The means and order of the competition entrants' display should be noted. Numbered one through seven, four renderings, a site model and a unit model comprised each entrant's display. Because it was an anonymous competition, the identity of each 'number' was not revealed until the night the winner was announced. It could be said that, loosely, the proposals became more contextually minded as you proceeded from numbers one through seven. Number one, as it turned out, was by 3D Design and number two by Garofalo. Numbers six and seven both mentioned taking impetus from the existing patterns of the city while numbers one and two did not. Number seven, the last entrant displayed, was in fact the winner, Healy.

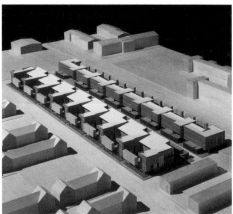

Note 1. All quotes in this essay are from its original publication in *Competitions*, Volume 11, No. 4, Winter 2001.

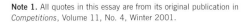

Europan (1993)

Lucy Bullivant

Europan's Brussels headquarters, Europan-Europe, defines the mission of this prestigious biannual housing design competition for architects up to the age of 40 years old as one which 'creates ideas, solutions, approaches, designs and contributes to the debate on architecture and urban design at a local, national and international level'.[1]

Founded in 1989, Europan is a competition that is run in parallel by member offices in 20 European countries, each of them staging the event to a common theme. Each time an event is held, they arrange the sites and liaise with the collaborating municipal bodies that are prepared to develop the winning schemes. It would be realistic to assume that a high level of the Dutch awards, for instance, have over the years been realised as built schemes, as a result of the advanced level of partnership between local councils and housing associations in the Netherlands. However, just surveying a few of the case histories indicates obstacles common to all the parallel competitions, and which mirror those in the wider world of urban planning: the availability and condition of the site; the views of the clients; and whether funding can be partly or fully secured. The obligations that the awards carry for the bodies participating with Europan are extensive, and they also have to carry the limitations to which any live project is subjected.

One fascinating aspect of Europan is the shift that took place in the 1990s in the definition of the assignments set, paralleling wider cultural shifts in the way city planning and the contexts of sites were viewed. As part of this, Europan's criteria concerning location impacted on a growing awareness of the site

in relation to the housing scheme. This was clearly due to the overall success of some of the competition winners in realising their schemes. As with all competitions or commissions, a smooth development stage could not be predetermined, even if the commitment of the network of municipalities supporting the process was impressive.

From the first, entrants were free to pick sites from not just their own country but others, and indeed to elect a specified or a free location. Among the realisations for Europan 1 awarded in 1989 was a design submitted to the Netherlands competition which won a prize in a category called 'free location'. This was exceptional, and Europan has published the fact that the option for a free choice of location was abandoned by the time of the second European competition 'because the chances of realisation were very small due to the absence of potential municipal support'.

The scheme of the French team of Daridan, Marzelle, Manescau and Steeg, however, was not realised either in the Netherlands or at the architects' originally intended location. The design consisted of variable container-like housing elements for a variety of new, non-regulated categories of occupants such as refugees and asylum-seekers. The team made a prototype and began negotiating with a Dutch firm specialising in the making of prefabricated building elements. However, a site was finally found for the project in Bordeaux where local council clients wanted to house immigrant pensioners. The container homes were first put in use in 1994, five years after the award was made.

Further analysis of the evolution of the Dutch

Winning Entry
S333 Studio for Architecture
and Urbanism – Jonathan
Woodroofe, Chris Moller
and Dominic Papa
(Rotterdam,
Netherlands/Auckland,
New Zealand) Europan,
Groningen, Netherlands

Below Axonometric perspective
Right Site model

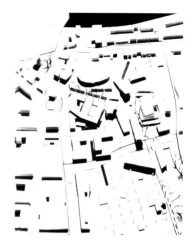

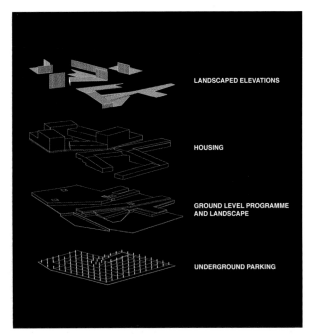

LANDSCAPED ELEVATIONS

HOUSING

GROUND LEVEL PROGRAMME
AND LANDSCAPE

UNDERGROUND PARKING

competition is provided by the example of another Europan 1 award, made to local architects Köther and Salman for a designated site at City Blocks in Arnhem. However, as the soil on the site turned out to be highly contaminated, the municipality offered the team an alternative assignment: 35 low rent social housing units in the Spijker district in the same city. A new design was commissioned, and the quality of the original competition design was retained in the construction, which was also completed five years after the award.

Another hazard to the development stage of Europan is financial cut backs. An honourable mention was made in the Dutch competition for Europan 1 to Austrians Dietmar Prietl and Gerhard Sacher for their design for the Caritas site in Amsterdam North. Under the terms of the competition, the municipality was under no obligation to carry out a plan that had received an honourable mention rather than an outright award. However, it was enthusiastic about the design. The architects, adapting the plans to the clients' minimum space requirements, designed housing blocks with a narrower gap between them, and one block was left out to let sufficient sunlight through. Despite financial cutbacks, because of their ingenuity the experimental elements of the plan – the buildings' design and their unusual floor plans – were retained when they were built, in a time span very similar to the other two.

Occasionally the Europan jury has made an award to a team, only for the municipality in question to find its plan unfeasible. This happened with the Dutch team of Linnemann, Bannenberg and Klaasse (Kamiel Klaasse went on to found the highly regarded

practice, NL Architects). While the jury admired the fact that their scheme fitted well into the transitional area between the city and the suburbs, and discovered an unorthodox location that reinvented the suburban home, the municipality was not convinced and found them an alternative location.

One of the most professionally celebrated Dutch Europan wins was the Circus site in Groningen, awarded to the British-New Zealand team of Jonathan Woodroofe, Chris Moller and Dominic Papa under the name of S333 Studio for Architecture and Urbanism (the name this now well-established and reputable practice still retains) at Europan 3. The theme of the competition was 'At Home in the City – Urbanising Residential Neighbourhoods', and sought proposals that rethought the relationship between the city's public and private spaces, and the spatial scaling from domestic intimacy to urban collectivity.

This was a high level brief and, owing to the complexity of the area, the municipality predicted long delays in the development and realisation stages. This prompted them to offer an alternative site, which the architects declined. The municipality finally agreed that the architects would draw up a masterplan in cooperation with the city's Department of Urban Planning for the entire 14 hectare CiBoGa site, for 1,000 housing units, 1,000 parking spaces and 30,000 square metres of mixed use and recreational programme. This expanded remit gave S333 the opportunity to carry out intensive research in order to make a set of propositions.

Collaborating with city urbanists, they initiated studies, forums and typological research, working with other architects to explore contemporary living

Winning Entry
S333 Studio for Architecture
and Urbanism – Jonathan
Woodroofe, Chris Moller
and Dominic Papa
(Rotterdam, Netherlands/
Auckland, New Zealand)
Europan, Groningen,
Netherlands

Opposite page left Programme
Below Perspectives
of completed project

Winning Entry
S333 Studio for Architecture
and Urbanism – Jonathan
Woodroofe, Chris Moller
and Dominic Papa
(Rotterdam,
Netherlands/Auckland,
New Zealand)
Europan, Groningen,
Netherlands

Perspectives of completed
project

and working patterns, issues of time-share, security and privacy. On-site workshops led by Foreign Office Architects and members of the Architectural Association's Housing and Urbanism Unit mapped movement and spatial linkage. Research projects by environmental engineers, and workshops with developers and local business groups explored the potential conflicts of the new commercial programmes and leisure-based facilities on the adjacent urban fabric. S333 also worked with the city's urban ecologists and with landscape architects to examine how initiatives in ecological sustainability can direct the development of a critical mass of housing.

It is likely that no other Europan win has resulted in such an intense form of scrutiny of the city, based on a defined discourse about social change, that, according to S333, 'urban dwellers, in establishing new parameters for the appropriate use of public and private space, are promoting spatial usage that is more time-based, aligned to individual work/living patterns, mobility and their own personal choice'.

When Europan 5 was announced, a broader assignment was set, contrary to previous competition rounds in which the architectural design was central. Europan 5 asked for an examination of the area which encompasses the location. This meant that within the assignments, in addition to architectural components, urban and landscape components also came up for discussion. Programmed and logistic components also played a role. Europan's explanation in its website archive is as follows: 'the development of a planning area does, after all, have its own particular dynamics stemming from changes in

approach and schedules of requirements with the passing of time. Consequently it is important that a spatial concept is strong enough to stand on its own merit. The broadening of the assignment does have consequences for the material to be submitted, however. It means, among other things, that the entrants' view on the planning area will need to have a solid basis'.

This change meant that competitors needed to develop a closer relationship with the context of their chosen site or sites than was hitherto the case. Given the theme of Europan 5, 'New Housing Landscapes, Travel and Proximity', and the request to answer the question 'Can new forms of urban landscape be developed which avoid rigid, functionalist planning?', this was essential, and the new breadth was also reflected in the locations and briefs put forward by Europan. Moreover, by the time Europan 6 was launched, an internal reflection on the groundbreaking nature of S333's research and consultation strategy for CiBoGa had taken place (the first housing schemes were successfully completed in 2003). Interestingly, the theme of hybrid urban developments bringing together two areas with distinct identities, or two uses of a building twinned in some way, was chosen. Europan's credentials for innovative developmental and planning in European cities were coming of age, and the architects' plan for CiBoGa was cited as one of two examples 'of a conscious strategy to create a new hybridity in a border zone between two differing systems'.

Note 1. All quotes in this essay are from Europan competition announcements.

Sustainable Housing, Lystrup, Århus, Denmark (2003)

G Stanley Collyer

In one of the largest public housing competitions to be recently held in Europe, jurors were charged with looking for architecture of exceptional quality and sustainability – as well as financial and environmental viability – in selecting winners of the Ringgården housing competition in Århus, Denmark. The siting of 130 sustainable, affordable housing units in an open rural landscape of four hectares also represented a formidable challenge for the eight participating teams from Germany, the Netherlands and the home country, Denmark. In the words of the sponsor, 'The overriding purpose of the competition is to demonstrate the significant convergence between elements creating compelling, beautiful and well-functioning architecture and elements creating sustainable buildings and constructions that benefit the global environment, the quality of life of the occupants and the life-cycle costs'.

Towards the end of 2001, on the initiative of Dansk Centre for Urban Ecology, the Ringgården Housing Association entered into an agreement of cooperation with Italian, French and Portuguese housing organisations called SHE (Sustainable Housing in Europe). The goal of the collaboration is to construct a number of sustainable dwellings in all four countries. The project received approval from the European Union's 5th Framework Programme and will encompass the construction of sustainable demonstration projects totalling 50 housing units in each participating country. The motto of the projects is 'From the Extraordinary to the Ordinary', and the goal is to show that it is possible to build in a far more sustainable way than is done today.

The programme set forth by the Ringgården Housing Association differed in that it set out to build

sustainable dwellings on a larger scale than the SHE project allows. The idea was developed to supplement a Danish contribution to the SHE project of an additional 80 housing units, bringing the total to 130 housing units, after hosting an international design competition. Thus, the project 'Architecture and Sustainability' was born. In October 2002, the project received approval from the Fonden Realdania foundation for the financial support of 'an international design competition for the construction of 130 public housing units combining high architectural quality with sustainability considerations'. The competition was held in compliance with Council Directive 92/50/EEC as amended by Council Directive 97/52/EC.

The Office for Official Publications of the European Communities was informed of the competition on 28 February 2003, and the following eight multidisciplinary teams were invited to participate in the competition:
• Architectuurstudio Herman Hertzberger, Amsterdam, The Netherlands
• Herzog + Partner, Munich, Germany
• Joachim Eble Architektur, Tübingen, Germany
• AA Arkitekter A/S, Århus, Denmark with Plus + Bauplanung GmbH, Transsolar Energietechnik GmbH, Cowi A/S, Schønherr Landskab and Hanne Lehrskov
• Arkitema, Århus, Denmark, with Niras A/S
• Schmidt Hammer & Lassen, Århus, Denmark with Birch & Krogboe A/S and Arup Group Ltd
• Tegnestuen Vandkunsten, Copenhagen, Denmark with Dominia A/S and Viggo Madsen A/S
• Vilhelm Lauritzen A/S, Copenhagen, Denmark, with Prisme Arkitekter, Peter Holst Landskabs-arkitekter Oluf Jørgensen A/S and Cenergia Aps

Winning Entry
Dwellings A + B
Schmidt Hammer & Lassen
(Århus, Denmark)

View of Dwellings A
showing roof towers

bebyggelse c : 40 boliger

bebyggelse a : 40 boliger

bebyggelse b : 50 boliger

NORD
PLAN 1 : 500

Opposite
Final Site Plan
Schmidt Hammer & Lassen
(Århus, Denmark)
Herzog + Partner
(Munich, Germany)

SHL's Dwellings A + C are
in white. The Herzog grouping
of Dwellings B are to the
left in yellow. The one-storey
Senior Dwellings are at the
upper right of the site

This page
Winning Entry
Dwellings A + C
Schmidt Hammer & Lassen
(Århus, Denmark)

Right One-storey senior
housing is distinguished by
the wooden decks which
give the impression that
the structures are "floating".

Below SHL perspectives

Winning Entry
Dwellings B
Herzog + Partner
(Munich, Germany)

Below Plans and sections
Opposite Exterior perspective

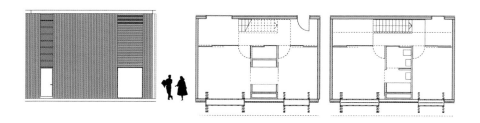

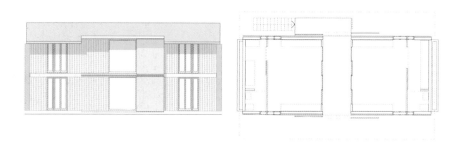

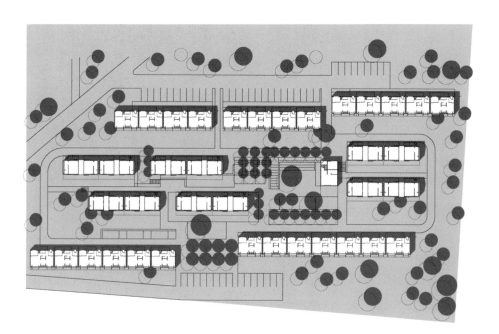

Competing Globally in Architecture Competitions

The first three teams were invited in advance to participate, while the other five were selected after a pre-qualification phase in compliance with the aforementioned directive. On 7 July 2003, all the selected firms' submitted proposals were accepted for assessment by the jury. The competition proposals were assessed according to the following three, equally weighted criteria:

• Architectural and functional objectives
• Environmental objectives and sustainability: fulfilment of environmental objectives, the environmental profile of the building, eco-index, etc.
• Financial aspects: to what degree the project is kept within the financial framework, and assessment of its overall cost effectiveness

Jury Proceedings

The jury was chaired by Anne Erichsen of the Ringgården Housing Association and included architects, engineers and ecologists. In compliance with the competition brief, winning projects were to be selected for Dwelling Group B (50 housing units) and Dwelling Groups A and C (a total of 80 housing units), while allowing for the possibility of the two winning projects being selected from the same competition entry.

To facilitate the evaluation process of the jury, a number of technical and financial assessments of the proposals were carried out. These were performed by the By og Byg (these included the calculation of environmental profiles, eco-indexes and energy requirements), Carl Bro architcts (indoor climate assessment, development costs and life-cycle analysis) and the Danish Centre for Urban Ecology (overall sustainability assessment). The results of these studies appeared in the jury's individual comments to the entrants.

Jury assessment commenced on 12 August 2003. The jury held four meetings and, during the final assessment on 26 August 2003, it unanimously selected the entries of Schmidt Hammer & Lassen (SHL) as the best solution for Dwelling Groups A and C and Herzog + Partner for Dwelling Group B.

The Winning Entries

According to the jury report, Schmidt Hammer & Lassen's entry suggested the 'best overall solution for the site'. The concept of a distinctive, shared and beautifully shaped green entrance and parking area, providing equal access to all three dwelling groups'

Winning Entry
Dwellings B
Herzog + Partner
(Munich, Germany)

Below
Interior view
Opposite
Exterior perspective

This interior view shows the "buffer zone" which is intended as an energy conservation measure, one of the features which the jury embraced enthusiastically.

The jury also liked the flexibility inherent in the Herzog design, making it adaptable to diverse uses for a diverse population

Competing Globally in Architecture Competitions

diverse entrance areas, emerged as a powerful, informal space for the overriding social environment. There was also a compelling interplay created architecturally between the clarity and precise geometric simplicity of the buildings and the gentle undulating landscape.

The strong iconic feature of the SHL entry was the use of 'roof towers' which could function either as 'a sunlight entry or serve as access to the units and roof terraces'. The jury found in these dwellings a reference to the Danish functionalist tradition typical of architects such as Arne Jakobsen and Mogens Lassen. However, the SHL scheme exhibits a greater degree of flexibility than those of its forerunners.

The SHL proposal for Dwelling Group C's 40 senior residences featured one-storey, white terrace houses with one-sided roofs sloping towards the south. By surrounding them with wooden decks, the buildings give the impression of floating above the landscape along the edge of the woods. Light is optimally integrated in the dwelling through the roof slope of the buildings, and a sunlight entry is located in the high back of the building facing north, 'creating intriguing combinations of direct and indirect sunlight'.

All of the SHL dwellings perform far more efficiently than the targeted levels of heating consumption, and the solar collectors cover over 50 percent of the consumption of Group C, fulfiling the energy objectives. On the downside, SHL's competition proposals exceeded the development budget because of the choice of brick, plastered outer walls and the interior brick walls. Also, extensive use of the striking roof towers increased costs. In Dwelling Group A, the freestanding masonry

walls in the outdoor areas particularly put a strain of the development budget. Still, the relatively simple and compact dwelling types and the great effect of repetition are all factors that reduce project costs, and the choice of materials and technical systems also provide annual budget savings.

The jury's choice for Dwelling Group B, Herzog + Partner, stood out because of its interplay with the landscape. The buildings were 'laid out carefully and simply in conformity and harmony with the topography of the landscape'. The overriding landscape interpretation took precedence over the consideration of general landscaping between the dwelling groups. The shape of the buildings was determined to a great extent by the orientation of the solar power system, good daylight conditions and minimal heat loss.

To conserve energy, a buffer zone – a gradual transition between outdoor and indoor climate – has been incorporated in all dwelling types. This buffer area uses toplighting as a main light source, and it is the best lit and ventilated room in the building. The dwellings embody a functionally, ecologically and architecturally compelling response to a flexible home, irrespective of the model selected. They can accommodate many diverse lifestyles and thus diverse user groups.

Aside from the very commendable results which this competition produced, it was significant for its exhaustive jury report which, at 33 pages, revealed the minute detail with which each entry was examined. For a jury to spend four days discussing eight proposals says volumes about the thoroughness and fairness of the process. The jury report has also been posted on the sponsor's website: www.dcue.dk

COMPETITIONS BY COUNTRY

Australia

A continent-sized nation, with vast, empty deserts and hinterlands, Australia is also one of the most urbanised nations, with a very high percentage of its population living in urban centres (almost exclusively along the coastal fringe). This paradoxical nature of Australia is reaffirmed in its legacy of architectural competitions. As it is a very large geographical nation made up of a relatively small population, opportunities for public, institutional or civic buildings (and competitions to commission them) remain limited. Given the small size of the population (currently 20 million), Australia only seems able to support a major institutional or cultural building through the competition process once every five years or so.

Within Australia, a number of the most important modern or contemporary buildings have been the result of architectural competitions, but, as with many other countries, the vast majority of building works are not awarded by this process. Significantly, and seemingly particular to Australia, there has been an uncomfortable recognition that many of these important competitions have been adversely affected by political interference and public rejection (if only at an early stage). Under an impression that competitions are always problematic, there is little public or institutional support for them.

Nonetheless, it would be unfair to say that Australia, or at least the two major centres of Sydney and Melbourne, have not used architectural competitions in the commissioning of major projects, particularly during the 20th century. Yet there does not exist, either nationally or locally, any consistent, structured mechanism to determine whether a project should to be initiated as a competition. In the last ten years the Royal Australian Institute of Architects has established criteria for the management and propriety of competitions, but it has no official position on the necessity or efficacy of architectural design competitions. Local, state and the national governments have been ambiguous at best in their support for competitions as a commissioning mechanism. The tradition is patchy and inconsistent.

Part of this lack of support may derive from the troubled history of several major competitions. In the 20th century, one can identify at least four major projects, with important architectural legacies, that were awarded on the basis of international design competitions but proved problematic in their commissioning and execution. The master planning scheme of Walter Burley Griffin for the new national of capital of Canberra, in the early part of the century, was subjected to continuous political manipulation and interference during development and implementation. The saga of the Sydney Opera House by Jørn Utzon is an even more widely known drama of resignations and ill-conceived political impositions onto what nonetheless remains the most iconic architectural symbol of the nation. Although less a history of interference and manipulation, the new national parliament building in Canberra by Romaldo Giurgola underwent protracted development and resolution, and the uncertainty over its symbolic and institutional relevance produced lingering debates over the efficacy of competitions for important public institutions. Most recently, the Federation Square project in Melbourne by Lab architecture studio, rekindled debate on the role of government commissioning (this time at the level of the state). This debate was made even more acute when the

controlling political party changed after a state election, and the new government initiated interference to the winning design based on ill-defined political motives rather than design criteria.

In another context, the Sydney Olympics was seen as a successful sporting event, but less so as an architectural result. The antecedent of Barcelona was most often invoked in the aspirations of young Australian architects hoping for new opportunities when Sydney was awarded the 2000 Olympics. In practice, almost all works in the Olympic precinct went to very established, corporate offices, determined by limited, and constrained commissioning protocols. The resultant buildings were mostly well-received, but seldom identified as significant architectural statements.

Perhaps more relevant, are the series of cultural and civic infrastructure projects initiated by the state government in Victoria under the premiership of Jeff Kennett in the 1990's. Primarily in Melbourne, but also in a few regional centres, projects included the Melbourne Museum, the Aquatic Centre, the Australian Centre for Contemporary Art, the Immigration Museum, the Bendigo Regional Art Gallery Annex, the redevelopment of the National Gallery of Victoria, and the Federation Square project, itself an amalgam of numerous cultural institutions, public spaces and commercial facilities.

This use of competitions as a means of introducing either young or adventurous architectural practices was uneven, but nonetheless resulted in several successful projects. However, it was not seen as establishing a continuing government policy and is currently dormant. Ultimately, this is consistent with the prevailing attitude in Australia, defined by an ad hoc implementation of competitions, which are seen as being problematic at the best of times. **Donald I Bates**

Canada

From the date of the earliest recorded architectural competition in Canada (for the new Public Gaol in Montréal in 1825) to the present day, the history of the competition process in this country is one of impressive success and discouraging failure. Indeed the record of projects actually implemented after a public call for entries is only about 50 percent. Exhaustive research conducted during the past decade into the subject of Canadian architectural competitions in both the 19th and 20th centuries has uncovered numerous examples of political meddling, client interference, public contempt and outright abandonment of projects.

Notable successes can be seen in the results of the international competitions for the federal Parliament Buildings in Ottawa (20 entrants; won by Fuller & Jones, 1859) and, in the last century, for the Toronto City Hall (520 entrants, won by Viljo Revell of Finland, 1958). Two more recent and successful open competitions include the Mississauga City Hall (240 entrants, won by Jones & Kirkland, 1982), and the Kitchener City Hall (153 entrants, won by Kuwabara Payne McKenna Blumberg, 1989).

However, the continuing trend in this new century for architectural competitions in Canada is not a promising one. Instead of open, democratic calls for designs based on merit, a disturbing tendency is towards the use of the pre-selected entrants who, among other requirements, are being asked to submit proof of financial solvency as an essential precondition to competing against their peers. Design ability takes on a secondary role, and the built results often show it.

Similarly, in more recent examples of government or institutional competitions, there is evidence of public sector clients purposely seeking out a winning entry submitted by a culturally balanced (i.e. 'politically correct') bilingual team that is supposedly geographically representative of the various constituencies that battle for a share of the pie and a piece of the action.

Even more disturbing is the recent practice of institutional clients (like the Royal Ontario Museum in Toronto, 2001) to invite leading world-renowned architects to submit ideas without offering any financial compensation of any kind. This is justified by the claim they must do so in order to determine if their proposals are aesthetically acceptable and will captivate the public imagination with the prerequisite 'Bilbao effect'. Of the 12 firms initially asked to describe their visions for this Toronto museum, four firms wisely elected to abstain from participating.

Some public agencies still strive to uphold the notion of the 'open and fair' competition process, and are to be commended for doing so (like the Montréal Symphony Orchestra Hall, 2003), but the results can backfire. The recently announced winning entry, submitted by the Amsterdam firm Architekten Cie, has now been roundly condemned in all quarters as 'arrogant, hideous, and monumental' and is now 'presently under review' by the newly elected Liberal government who claim the $280 million cost is far too high for the province of Québec to afford.

Even the adverse effects of international terrorism and 9/11 can intrude on bold and provocative architectural visions. The winning scheme by Rem Koolhaas and Bruce Mau for the Downsview Park military base in Toronto (won in early 2001) has now, with the departure of Koolhaas, been shelved as the federal Department of National Defense rethinks its strategy of handing over its regional military headquarters and air base for recreational use.

The large amount of time and money needed to stage an open competition is discouraging many institutions from even thinking about this, hence the trend to 'preselected' design competitions, like Concordia University (five designs invited, won by Kuwabara Payne McKenna Blumberg, 2001), and Parliament Hill Bank Street Building competition (12 designs invited including KPMB; winner to be announced in December 2003).

Those very generous honoraria paid to teams in the US simply cannot be matched in Canada. The practice in Canada is for clients to offer 'honorarium' fees which barely cover costs. At KPMB, for example, the firm normally spends twice the amount of an honorarium when entering an 'invited' competition (for example, if offered $5,000, $10,000 is normally spent on drawings, models, staff time, etc.).

No wonder Canadians look with envy at current competition activity in France and Germany, where enthusiasm, bold determination and swift implementation result in the construction of innovative and striking landmarks. **Robert G Hill**

Denmark

Formal rules for the organisation of architectural competitions have been in use for nearly 100 years in Denmark. Before the rules were introduced, competitions took place under very different conditions, and in 1907 members of the Architects Association of Denmark (AA) - the organisation for all Danish architects educated in accordance with the European Union directive 85/385/EEC) thought the time had come to establish a clear framework for competitions. The result was the adoption of the AA Competition Rules, whose purpose is to ensure that architectural competitions are organised in a way that is satisfactory to all parties involved while at the same time giving the organiser the optimum response.

The number of competitions held each year has, of course, depended on economic trends. However, following the adoption of the Services Directive by the European Union (EU) in 1993 and rapid growth in the Danish economy, there was an almost explosive increase in the number of competitions organised. The Services Directive stipulates that architectural and engineering services supplied to government authorities for which the fee value exceeds 162,293 euros must be put to competitive tendering in all EU member states. The sum is 249,682 euros for projects initiated by local authorities and other public-sector contracting authorities.

Over the past 10 years the average number of competitions held each year has been 33. About 20 percent of these competitions have been open competitions, while the rest have been restricted competitions, the typical number of architects invited to participate being five or six. These figures relate to competitions organised in accordance with the AA Competitions Rules. In addition, about 15 other, non-registered competitions have been held each year for the design of minor projects. The competition conditions applying to these competitions have been somewhat unclear. These statistics do not include design-and-build competitions, which are not considered to be architectural design competitions since they are aimed at developers who appoint architects as subconsultants.

Denmark has a population of 5.4 million people, of whom about 7,000 are qualified architects. Almost all major buildings in Denmark and many major urban development projects have been realised following an architectural competition. This is true of the new Orestad urban district in Copenhagen and a very large proportion of the buildings that are currently being constructed in the district, including the future head office of the Danish Broadcasting Corporation (DR).

The AA Competition Secretariat participates in the majority of architectural competitions in Denmark. The Secretariat offers advice and assistance to public- and private-sector clients about matters relating to competition procedures throughout the competition period – from the first initial planning and the formulation of the competition brief to the jury's assessment of the entries submitted. The AA also appoints architects – usually two or three – to sit on the jury. The actual number depends on whether it is an open or a restricted competition and on the scope and complexity of the competition assignment. As opposed to general practice in several other European countries, the AA has made it a strict rule that the client's representatives must have the majority of seats in the competition jury.

It used to be an invariable rule in Danish architectural competitions that entries should be submitted anonymously, but in recent years various deviations from this rule have applied in some restricted competitions. Concurrent with an increase in the number of consultancy assignments, and the development of new approaches to collaboration in the building sector, it has proved expedient – particularly for clients – to open up a dialogue between competition entrants and jury members to ensure that the building design will take place on the best possible basis. Consequently the AA has waived the rule of anonymity on certain conditions, one being that competitions must always aim to ensure equal treatment of entrants as well as good architectural quality.

New types of competitions are developed and tested on an ongoing basis, for example, competitions with several winning entries and subsequent negotiation with the winning entrants; restricted competitions with 12–15 entrants and the award of prizes rather than fixed fees; interactive, internet-based competitions; or conceptual competitions in which the focus is on the overall architectural concept.

However, the typical approach remains a restricted competition with five participating teams. In many such competitions the entrants are requested to submit a fee tender as well. The last sentence is a bit long and confusing. I suggest: 'Almost all competitions are for total consulting services, which requires a consultant, or a group of independent consultants in a single joint agreement, to perform all, or the most important parts, of a project's architectural, engineering and landscape design consultation.

In most countries, including Denmark, it is difficult for newly started architectural practices to obtain design contracts through restricted competitions, since the number of entrants invited is generally limited to five or six, and the focus is often on teams that can supply total consulting services.

The AA always suggests that the client invites a wide circle of architectural practices to submit entries in a competition, including young and talented architects. If requested by the client, the AA appoints one or two independent advisers to assist the client in selecting entrants for a specific competition. It should be noted, however, that the AA in no way interferes in the actual selection of entrants. These initiatives have had a certain positive effect but it is still difficult for young practicing architects to obtain invitations for participation in restricted design competitions. Instead, they have to gain a reputation in open competitions. The AA is continuously working to increase the number of open design competitions but there is, of course, a limit to the number of open competitions that can be held if a sufficient number of entries is to be achieved in each individual competition.

Architectural competitions are held because many years' experience shows that they ensure greater architectural quality for clients and contribute to innovation and development in the architectural profession. To this should be added that most architectural practices in Denmark have been established on the basis of a first prize won in an architectural competition that subsequently led to an actual design and planning assignment. In other words, architectural competitions are a precondition for the generation of 'growth layers' in the architectural profession

in Denmark and consequently for the continued development of Danish architecture. **Jesper Kock**

France

The history of the architectural commissions, starting with the kings of France (the Royal commissions) and ending with the state (or the president of the Republic), is clearly an old tradition in France. Even if young French architects are not as fortunate as their Dutch counterparts to construct cities and millions of square metres immediately after graduation, they do have the possibility of competing for recognition through the competition system.

However, in the first decades after World War II, the best commissions always went to offices of a few established architects. Two events helped to change this: the Revolution of 1968, led by young students, and the international competition for the Centre Georges Pompidou in 1970, won by Richard Rogers and Renzo Piano. The success of the completed Pompidou Centre lent validation to the competition system, and in 1977 the first Law on Architecture was passed, declaring 'Architecture to be in the public interest'. Moreover, pubic agencies were set up in the regional Departments to sensitise the public to the need for good architecture. Simultaneously, a decentralisation of authority took place in the design and construction of public buildings in France. This encouraged local mayors to become involved in the process – and stage competitions for their own local projects. To this end the MIQCP (Mission interministérielle pour la qualité de construction publics) was established in 1978. Its purpose was to prod the national government and its ministries to construct better buildings. To this end, it encouraged the use of the competition process.

In 1980 the competition process was embedded in the national law code, whereby any edifice over and beyond 170 square meters (1,700 square feet) should be designed by an architect and any public building, social housing or public edifice (over 135,000 euros) should be commissioned through competition. In 1986, the process underwent a revision: all competitions for government buildings were subject to a requirement whereby all participants were invited – and duly compensated for their work. There were still some open ideas competitions which young architects could enter to promote their careers. But aside from a small number of large projects, such as the French National Library, the selection process for the design of government buildings was limited.

The competition system did bring a vast array of young architects to the world stage. Architects such as Portzamparc, Nouvel, Castro, Perrault and many other French architects are the result of the system. PAN (Programme Architecture Nouvelle) was the original format of the competition system for the young French architects to enter the practicing realm. This was soon transformed to Europan (enlarging its territory to Europe) allowing young designers to build their first commissions. Though the French competition system is being criticised and is encountering many problems, it still is – and should remain – the most encouraging manner in which architecture should be promoted.

Since there are virtually no private schools, universities, museums, theatres, etc. in France (with very few exceptions), most of the commissions are hence subject to competition and related to the state or the local administrative bodies.

There are two main categories of competitions in France:
1. Open competitions. These are mainly ideas competitions open to all for projects concerning programmes with national interests. These are unpaid and extremely rare.
2. Competitions with pre-selection based on presentation of portfolio of works. This is the most common type of competition and the selected architects are paid up to a maximum of 80 percent of the sketch design phase of the contract.
2a. Competitions with pre-selection based on a portfolio of works and a first phase proposal of ideas. This system allows for the client to choose amongst many proposals, often choosing ones closest to his aesthetic preference. This type of competition often typecasts architects in categories such as: name architects; those experienced in the domain; young architects; and female architects.
2b. Competions with pre-selection based on an interview.
2c. Commission-only, through selection based on a portfolio of similar works. This procedure assumes that an architect can only build if he has built before and reduces the knowledge of the architect to that of a specific type.

Pre-selection competitions, the most common form, tend to select architects based on experience in a specific type of building. Under this system Charles Garnier would have never won the Paris Opera House, since his only experience when he won the competition was a small and ordinary housing block in Paris.

The competition system in France has become restrictive; it now requires an architect to have at least one built project similar to that for which he is competing, or to have built a project of the same type, and have had a healthy practice of at least two million euros income.

In the last 20 years, France, through its competition system, has proved its interest for multicultural relationships as well as proving that architecture is still closely related to power, politics and politicians. The 'Grands Projets' of Mitterrand and the Museum of Art and Civilisation – under construction by Jean Nouvel – launched by Chirac in his first year of presidency, are amongst the last vestiges of architecture as a form of politics.
Nasrine Seraji

Germany

Germany after World War II might have been the last place one might have expected design competitions to flourish. But the need to rebuild the country and the rapid economic recovery, together with democratic reforms which took hold with the establishment of the West German Federal Republic, paved the way for the spread of another form of democracy – the anonymous design competition. By the time the Germans held the Olympic Games in Munich in 1972, design competitions had become firmly institutionalised – as witnessed by projects such as the Olympic Stadium by Freie Otto and Günther Behnisch which were won by way of this process.

It was under the leadership of architects such as Behnisch shortly after World War II that the leaders of the German state governments endorsed the idea, and went along with the National Association of German Architects (Bund der Deutschen Architekten), to stage numerous competitions for municipal projects. Many large projects became the subject of open competitions, run under the supervision of the regional associations and according to the rules laid down in the Principals and Guidelines for Competitions (Grundsätze und Richtlinien für Wettbewerbe).This included many schools, libraries, airports, hospitals and almost any building with a high enough price tag to automatically place it in a category which would trigger the process. Although any one of the state associations had the right to withdraw from the system if they so desired (and some did), they invariably came back into the fold.

Riding the crest of a robust German economy, this system resulted in hundreds of design competitions for several decades. It enabled many young architects such as Meinhard von Gerkan (Von Gerkan, Marg & Partner) and Axel Schultes to make their mark much as had an older generation led by Gottfried Böhm, Egon Eiermann and Hans Scharoun. By the mid-1980s, the culture of competitions underwent some subtle changes which were to have lasting effects. The Internationale Bauausstellung Berlin, or IBA as it was commonly known, saw architects from around the world invited to design a number of projects, mainly housing. Almost none of these were open competitions; several were invited. But it did serve to usher in the idea of 'star' architects automatically involved by invitation in limited competitions on quite a large scale.

In the meantime the European Union (EU) was drawing closer together, not only economically but also institutionally. This impacted the German system in that it opened many up to European-wide participation – with more limitations placed on entering. Today many German competitions for large projects, when not limited by region, almost always have a shortlist of invited participants who will compete in a final stage with winners from an open, first stage. Moreover, in many cases the Germans have even resorted to a lottery system to determine what non-invited competitors might be invited to participate. Although there are still a few open competitions, they are few and far between. And when they do occur, there are so many entries that chances of winning are slim to none. Such was the case with the Leipzig Library competition in the mid-1990s, when over 700 entries were submitted. The situation has been exacerbated even more by the downturn in the German economy and the results of overbuilding – especially in Berlin – after the reunification of the two Germanys. Moreover, to prove their democratic credentials, the Germans have advertised their EU-wide competitions very openly so that they were there for all to see. This transparency is not necessarily always common to other countries in the Common Market.

German competitions are listed (in German) at: www.wettbewerbe-aktuell.de

Other information on announcements as well as results can be found in the following German publications: Wettbewerbe Aktuelle (announcements and results) and Architektur + Wettbewerbe (contains only results in both German and English).
G Stanley Collyer

Japan

Competitions were not yet institutionalized in postwar Japan, as evidenced by two major contests shortly after World War II, one for the World Peace Memorial Cathedral in Hiroshima (1948) and other for the Hiroshima Peace Centre (1949). The jury for the former declined to award first prize – one of the jurors was eventually tapped to design the building, intensifying the controversy – and the sponsor of the latter gave the job of designing an auditorium originally included in the program to a local architect rather than the winner, Kenzo Tange. In the 1950s gradual economic recovery led to the reconstruction of local government buildings, often through limited competitions. Tange won the contest for Tokyo's city hall, further burnishing a reputation first established in wartime competitions.

Competitions remained controversial. Purses were small, architects were not always in the majority on juries, and as in the National Diet Library competition (1954) organizers sometimes reserved the right to change or reject the winning scheme. In the period of intensive economic growth in the 1960s, competitions held for a number of high-profile projects, such as the National Theatre and the martial-arts venue for the Tokyo Olympics, were criticized for not only the quality of the winning designs but the closed processes of deliberation. In the case of local government projects, many limited competitions in that period were suspected of being rigged.

The 1986 competition for the Shonandai Cultural Centre (in which Arata Isozaki and Fumihiko Maki were among the jurors) was a turning point in Japanese architecture. Innovative young architects with small practices (such as the winner Itsuko Hasegawa) beat larger, more conventional offices as well as architects affiliated with construction companies.

From around that period the process of deliberation in competitions gradually became more transparent; competitions began to be held for more diverse building types. However, organisers were not yet prepared for foreign participation. An English translation of the brief was only belatedly distributed for the Second National Theatre competition (1986); nevertheless, several well-known architects entered and placed. The construction boom fueled by Japan's bubble economy in the late 1980s led to increasingly vocal demands for foreign access to large-scale public projects. Under US government pressure, Japan at last made the Kansai International Airport Passenger Terminal Building the subject of a limited competition (1988), which was eventually won by the Renzo Piano Building Workshop. The Tokyo Metropolitan Government in turn went to great lengths to assure that the Tokyo International Forum competition (1989) would be Japan's first UIA-approved contest. The enormous cost (estimated at about $1.5 billion), time and effort involved in that project have had repercussions for subsequent public projects in Japan.

Since the bubble burst, plunging Japan into a prolonged recession, authorities have been wary of following Tokyo's precedent. Anxious to cut costs, many local governments now prefer competitive bidding (i.e. price-based selection) for architectural services to genuine competitions. The tight schedules common to Japanese projects also weigh against the holding of competitions. Japanese agencies reportedly even go so far as to manipulate budgets to circumvent World Trade Organisation rules requiring the holding of international competitions for public projects of a certain scope. Despite this negative atmosphere, ambitious local governments still turn to international competitions for certain projects, as in the 1995 contest won by Foreign Office Architects of London for the Yokohama International Passenger Terminal.

Information on competitions is available (mostly in Japanese) at the Japan Institute of Architects website(www.jia.or.jp). Shinkenchiku, the Japanese-language architectural magazine of record, is another source; it also sponsors its own annual residential-theme competition. **Hiroshi Watanabe**

Latin America

Architecture competitions in Latin America must be understood in a context quite different from that which prevails in Europe. The enormous distances and exuberant geographical features peculiar to this continent have somehow acted as obstacles for the integration of Latin American professionals in competitions. Generally, we can say that there are some common characteristics to most countries that are worth mentioning.

Latin American competitions have been, with a few exceptions, of national character and usually sponsored and administered with more or less strict guidelines. All the national associations belong to the International Union of Architects (UIA) and also under the aegis of the Pan American Federation of Architects Association, founded in 1930.

Private competitions, which were more common before World War II, have always generated a certain scepticism among participants because of the general lack of guarantees. For that reason, they have had very limited reach and little resonance during the last half of the 20th century. Nevertheless, two of them, the Lloyds Bank (SEPRA with Clorindo Testa, Buenos Aires, c 1959) and the skyscraper for the Telefonica de Chile (Mario Paredes Associates, Santiago, Chile, c 1994), have produced two important signature buildings that are exceptions to this trend.

Since the end of World War II, international competitions, mostly developed with UIA assistance, were few, but of great importance. Among them are the Monument to the Discovery of America (Santo Domingo, 1948) with jury members such as Frank Lloyd Wright, the Masterplan for Novacap Brasilia (circa 1955), the Peugeot skyscraper (Buenos Aires, 1959), Santiago de Chile's Civic Center (1962), Mass Housing (Lima, 1965), and, more recently, the Museum of Latin American Art/MALBA (Buenos Aires, 1998).

That said, it is necessary to emphasise that competitions run by the respective national associations have been very efficient instruments in many of those countries. In Argentina, there have been two good examples, not only for the continuity of the policies governing competitions, but also for the positive effect the competitions had in the quality of the designs and the ultimate realisation of the projects. These competitions have not only facilitated the elevation of young architects to another level – Rafael Viñoly and Pedro Paulo Mendez da Rocha are prime examples – they have also been powerful antidotes to the commissioning of important public buildings to connected architects and, more important, to the frequent practice of assigning the design task to the architecture offices of the different state ministries – often resulting in mediocre buildings.

The Argentine rules and guidelines for competitions are an immaculate legal instrument where not even the slightest detail is left to chance. Offering extraordinary guarantees to sponsors as well as participating architects, once the contract is signed between the sponsor and the architect's association, it is the Society of Architects that takes care of all the details, from the selection of the juries, publicity to the payment of the prize money, and oversees the contractual details between the winning architect and client. This is so 'above discussion' that more than 40 such competitions have resulted in buildings which have been brought to fruition without any substantial conflict. Among these are the National Library, the Juan P Garrahan Hospital (the largest pediatric hospital in the world), the Tower of the Industrial Union, the Complex of Government of Pampas (Argentina), and a multitude of banks, housing complexes, hospitals, and so on. This pragmatic attitude also is prevalent in Brazil.

There is no systematic listing of competitions for all of Latin American, either in Spanish or Portuguese publications. News of competitions restricted to the countries is usually disseminated by the association to their members by way of direct communication through various media. **Carlos Casuscelli**

Norway

Architectural design competitions have been used in Norway since the end of the 19th century, primarily for the solution of large public building assignments, and the need to regulate competitions has been a main concern for the Norwegian Association since its instigation in 1911. The problems at the beginning of the 20th century were largely the same as they are today: making sure the first prize winner gets the commission to build; quality control of the programme; ensuring the adequate representation of architects in the jury; anonymity; adequate prizes or fees; and so on.

Norway is a country with a small population, some 4.5 million people, but with a relatively high number of architects, about 4,000 practicing members of the profession. Of these, however, only relatively few are employed by larger offices of say 20-30 people, a fact which usually limits the number of potential participants in open competitions to around 100, as few of the smaller practices can carry the strain on manpower and finances of producing regular competition entries.

Competitions have traditionally offered young architects an opportunity to gain commissions, and this is still a possibility in open competitions. The open national competitions in recent years have almost exclusively been held by Statsbygg, the Directorate of Public Construction and Property, or local municipalities, at the rate of three or four per year. During 2003 there has been a significant rise to 13-14 open competitions, but it is too early to say whether this represents a steady trend. Other public projects are often occasions for limited competitions, where there is a tendency to choose the final four to six participants from among the same group of experienced practices. Whist this of course narrows the possibilities for young architects, it also has the effect of preventing local protectionism.

The Scandinavian countries have a history of collaboration in many fields, and before the European Union the professional governing bodies of the various countries held regular meetings which were significant in regulating local practice, but which also paved the way for inter-Scandinavian competitions. This practice has now effectively ground to a halt, as each of the Nordic countries has their hands full protecting their own internal job markets. Not that there is no longer anything to discuss: the Scandinavian countries could, for example, still gain from presenting a common front to Brussels on many issues, but the formal collaborative practice is no longer a priority. Contrary to expectations, EU membership has not increased international participation in Norwegian open competitions. Usually you will get a few Danish entries, perhaps as collaborations with Norwegian practices, and a token Italian or Portuguese. The requirements for use of Norwegian language, knowledge of local building regulations and so on also limits the winning chances of foreign practices. Also the projects themselves are small. More than anything, the effect of opening the competition market has been to regulate and standardise domestic competition practices.

The current regulations governing public commissions in Norway are aimed at protecting public funds by ensuring that the building bodies get value for money. In some cases, this focus has led the client after a competition to want to negotiate not only with the first prize winner but also with second and thirrd prize, in order to introduce a degree of competition in the contracting process and the fee bids. Many architects, to their credit, eschew this practice and have refused to negotiate at the expense of the winner. Nonetheless, the main challenge currently facing the architectural profession is to convince their clients that efficiency is not necessarily guaranteed by choosing the lowest fee bids, but also by initiating processes that ensure the quality, flexibility and integrity of the project itself.
Ingerid Helsing Almaas

Sweden

The impact competitions have had on the architectural profession in Sweden began to significantly make its mark sometime between the mid-19th century and the early 20th century. During this time architectural competitions shifted from individual experiments to a regular method for selection. Decisions on the appointment of architects for such projects were mostly handled by committees which were expected to act in an impartial, democratic way. Objectivity became important. However, the earliest competitions seldom generated any results that could be developed. The reason for this was mostly the client's lack of interest in the program.

Starting the building process with a schematic building programme became one of the most important results of the competitions and, thereby, one of the central prerequisites for functional architecture. Around the turn of the century, competitions gave rise to a critical architecture with an intent to present something new. Whatever ambition an organiser had for an individual competition, the system in itself gave rise to new ideas and spread them widely.

Two roots of the modern competition, the academic and the marketplace, resulted in two different kinds of architectural competitions. The academic type aimed for maximum quality with a reasonable price, while the marketplace type aimed at a reasonable quality with the lowest possible price – a pattern which still prevails.

However, during the 19th and early 20th centuries, the academies also had a role in setting the standard regarding taste. Thus, public competitions in the academic tradition were to establish a 'proper architecture' as defined by the most prominent representatives of the profession.

Sweden first opened its doors to international competitions around the time of the Paris Exhibition in 1925. The modernist movement had become very strong at this time and Le Corbusier's proposal for the Nedre Norrmalm area of Stockholm won high recognition. The nature of Sweden's postwar political climate, together with the generally weak position of architects in the country's building process, has for many years been a deterrent for high profile architectural competitions. Lately however, Sweden's membership in the European Union and a more international climate has paved way for larger scale competitions. The first major competition to be won by a foreign architect in recent times was Rafael Moneo's proposal for the Museum of Modern Art in Stockholm in 1991. Danish architects have in the past years seen Sweden as a potential marketplace, much due to their proximity and understanding of Scandinavian tastes, and are strongly represented in many of today's competitions.

Competitions in Sweden fall under one of two main categories - the traditional competition, open or by invitation, and the parallel commission.

Competitions are judged, as in most countries, by an expert panel, consisting of at least one member appointed by the Swedish Board of Architects (Sveriges Arkitekter). In open competitions, prize money is determined and dispersed accordingly at the discretion of the jury. In competitions by invitation, each participating firm is reimbursed equally. A program for the successful candidate's further collaboration is clearly outlined and compensation is generally guaranteed should the project never reach the drawing board.

Parallel commissions are staged when the goals usually associated with a competition less definite, such as creating a general interest in the project or finding an actual proposal to implement. The intent of a parallel commission is therefore to shed light on unclear or alternative conditions that may influence a project's development possibilities. There are usually no promises that the commission will go any further. The aim is not to choose a winner or a winning proposal though there is of course a competitive edge since the client may choose to go further with any one of the proposals. These commissions are usually given by institutions, larger building societies and local governments, and are a commonly used tool in the selection process of an architect today in Sweden.

More information on Swedish competitions and the rules governing them can be found at www.arkitekt.se/tavlingar
Peter Sjostrom

United States

In 1973, the American Institute of Architects (AIA) was in the process of moving toward regulation of design competitions much as had been the case in Europe after World War II. Having issued a 'Code' which outlined the conditions under which its members might enter 'approved' competitions, the AIA suddenly encountered a roadblock. The Federal Trade Commission took exception to the 'fee structure' which the AIA had also included in the document and declared that the rules set down by the organisation constituted a 'restraint of trade.' Subsequently, the AIA issued a Design Competition Handbook, which is not binding on competition sponsors, but often serves as a guide for professional advisers and consultants who are administering these events.

The effect of the Federal Trade Commission's decision was the total deregulation of the process, so that any municipality, government agency or private individual staging a competition could set their own rules, i.e. determine if the competition should be open or invited, establish the composition of the jury, level of submission requirements, etc. Thus, the history of competitions in the US has been determined not so much by a common set of rules, but by private contractors, chosen not just for their expertise in the field, but for their 'flexibility' in acquiescing to ever present political pressures surrounding such events. One of the more recent trends is the inclusion of more lay-persons on juries, so that the jury process is lengthened due to the lack of expertise on the part of that group.

One federal agency which has staged exemplary competitions is the General Services Administration (GSA), in Washington, DC. Although most of the GSA competitions from the early 1990s to the present have been for the design of federal courthouses, the results are compelling. Using the Request for Qualifications process, the GSA traditionally narrowed the shortlisted field to four offices before engaging them in a competition. This has resulted in some of the more remarkable civic design to be observed during the past decade. Although some of these courthouses are still in the development process, all indications point to the completion of most of them by the year 2009.

The lack of countrywide competition regulation has not deterred foreign architects from participating in those open competitions which do occur in the US. Most recently, European and Latin American architects have won some open competitions, and appeared as finalists in several others. Andrea Ponsi of Italy won the Palos Verdes Art Center Competition (2000) and Weston Williamson of London won the New England Biolabs Competition (2002), where half of the 300 entries originated outside the US and three of the five finalists were from abroad. Several foreign architects also won competitions either staged or administered by New York's Van Alen Institute. John Choi and Tai Ropila of Sydney, Australia won the Times Square Ticket Booth Competition (683 entries), and a German team headed up by Sebastian Knoor of Regensberg, Germany was one of the first place winners in the Pier 40 competition. A recent competition for the design of the Memphis, Tennessee waterfront produced three foreign finalists from 170 entries.

All of this indicates that there are not that many open competitions worldwide where young architects have a unique opportunity to vault to prominence. In those cases where open competitions have taken place in America, foreign participation has recently been very strong, a sure sign of a lack of such opportunities in their own countries.

Publications on competitions: *Competitions* magazine. Website: www.competitions.org **G Stanley Collyer**

United Kingdom

Acclaim and controversy continue to be associated with architectural competitions in the UK, and the debate about their merit continues unabated. Equal numbers support as oppose them. Those who advocate competitions see positive factors: choice for clients; a vehicle to showcase design quality; and providing the opportunity for younger practices to become better known.

Unlike other European countries, such as Germany, France, and the Netherlands, the UK does not operate a government-supported system where major projects of national significance are automatically put out to competition. Lack of direct Government endorsement has meant that far fewer competitions are held in the UK than across Europe, and their use is left to the discretion of commissioning clients. Very few projects of national significance are put out to competition and the few that are tend to be by invitation only. It is not a route by which an unknown architect can make his or her name.

The major force responsible for devising and implementing competition regulations in the UK has been the Royal Institute of British Architects (RIBA). For the past century the RIBA has been at the heart of the debate about the need to regulate competitions and in 1907 the first recommended rules became mandatory. Since then many changes have taken place with modifications and refinements being made along the way. Today the RIBA has a dedicated Competitions Office that is responsible for all competitions promoted under the RIBA banner. It is seen by many in the profession as the UK authority on the subject. Whilst independent competitions do take place, organised by clients directly with architects, the RIBA is the major promoter of the system throughout Britain.

Currently the RIBA Competitions Office is busier than at any time in the last 20 years. Clients include those from the private and public sectors, with many choosing to do repeat business. The reason for this increase in the number of competitions is most probably due to the fact that the RIBA has moved significantly away from the rigid competition rules associated with the system in the past. That is not to say that the system has become less efficient or rigorous. It simply offers more choice and flexibility to clients.

A fundamental review of the system took place in the mid 1990s when it was decided to offer a more client orientated service. It was decided, from discussions with clients, that their needs were not necessarily being met. Clients felt that competition options were restrictive and did not allow them to become as involved in the process as they desired. Clients felt they needed more input. It was agreed that competitions could and should be tailored to suit the requirements of each individual client and project. Six basic rules were established which had always to be met:
• Independent architectural assessors;
• Clearly defined rules;
• Clearly expressed, accurate briefing material;
• Payment for design work;
• Appropriate time to prepare for interview or make a submission;
• Quality.

Based on these fundamental principles, clients in discussion with the RIBA Competitions Office were able to tailor packages to meet their individual needs. Affording the clients this freedom resulted in a closer and more trusting relationship with the RIBA Competitions Office at the outset of the project.

Increasingly popular over the last decade has been the use of the Competitive Interview allowing a client to meet architects at the start of a project to discuss their past work and their approach to the project in hand. A hybrid variation of this option, combining interview with a small element of design work, has emerged as another very popular form. Clients appear to appreciate the dialogue which interviews allow. This combined with the submission of design work, prepared against a set brief, enables the client to additionally gauge the quality of design response.

This method of combining interviews with design allows the client, and also the competing architect, the opportunity of early contact at the onset of a project. Chemistry between architects and clients should not be underestimated. A practical advantage of the competitive interview, with or without added design, is that this form of competition is less time consuming and costly for both competitor and client alike.

A very positive trend that has been recorded over the last decade has been the increase in the number of competition winning schemes that have been built. Since 1995, 67 percent of the competitions that have been organised by the RIBA have either been built, are in the process of being built, or have secured funding. This is good news for all involved in the promotion of the system and hopefully augurs well for the future.

Louise Harrison

BIBLIOGRAPHY

Manuals

American Institute of Architects, *Handbook of architectural design competitions*, American Institute of Architects (Washington DC), 1988

Design Competition Manual, National Endowment for the Arts (Cambridge), 1980

Design Competition Manual II: On-site Charrette, National Endowment for the Arts (Cambridge), 1982

Grundsätze und Richtlinien für Wettbewerbe, Karl Krämer Verlag (Stuttgart), 1982

J Ollswang & L Witzling, *The Planning and Administration of Design Competitions*, Mldwest Intstitute for Design Research (Milwaukee), 1986

J Strong, *Winning by Design: Architectural Competitions*, Butterworth-Heinemann Architecture (London), 1996

Royal Institute of British Architects, *Architectural Competitions: RIBA Code of Practice*, (London) 1986

Monographs

Arbeitsgemeninschaft Wettbewerb Spreebogen, *The Spreebogen International Competition for Urban Design Ideas*, (Berlin), 1993

P Arnell & T Bickford (Eds), *A Tower for Louisville: The Humana Competition*, Rizzoli (New York), 1982

P Arnell & T Bickford (Eds), *Southwest Center: The Houston Competition*. Rizzoli (New York), 1983

P Arnell & T Bickford (Eds), *A Center for the Visual Arts: The Ohio State University Competition*, Rizzoli (New York), 1984

P Arnell & T Bickford (Eds), *Mississauga City Hall: A Canadian Competition*, Rizzoli (New York), 1984

Regina M Bellavia & Gregg Bleam, *Cultural Landscape Report: Jefferson National Expansion Memorial*, St. Louis, Missouri, National Park Service

Aaron Betsky, *1993 San Francisco Embarcadero Waterfront Competition: Winning and Selected Entries*, 2 AES (San Francisco), 1993

Michael S Cullen, *Der Reichstag: Die Geschichte eines Monumentes*. Parkland Verlag (Stuttgart), 1990

Nicholas Crickhowell, *Opera House Lottery, Zaha Hadid and the Cardiff Bay Project*, University of Wales Press (Cardiff), 1997

Larry Paul Fuller (Ed), *Sequicentennial Park: The Design Competition*, Central Houston Civic Improvement (Houston), 1987

General Services Administration, *An Urban Courthouse for the 21st Century: Design Competition for the Los Angeles Courthouse*, US General Services Administration (Washington DC), May 2001

S Gunn, *Eagle Ridge: An Architectural Design Competition from Inside the Jury Room*, Inner Images, Inc (Dallas), 1983

Judy Hart (Ed), *A Vision Realized: The Design Competition for the Women's Rights National Park*, K-Mar Press, Inc (New York),

Internationale Bauausstellung Project *Report: Berlin, Internationale Bauausstellung* (Berlin), 1987

Charles Jencks (Ed), *The Architecture of Democracy: The Phoenix Municipal Government Center Design Competition*, St. Martin's Press (New York), 1987

Jyväskylä Music and Arts Centre: *Jury Report for the Open International Design Competition*, ER-Paino

Meeting the Challenge: Designing a New Government Center in Leesburg's Historic District; Design Competition Catalogue, 1987

Detlef Mertins & Virginia Wright (Ed), *Competing Visions: The Kitchener City Hall Competition*. The Melting Press, 1990

Jack L Nasar, *Design by Competition*. Cambridge University Press (Cambridge), 1999

Michael John Pittas & Janet Marie Smith (Eds), *Urban Design International: Urban Design Competitions, USA*, Volume 5, No. 2, 1985

Richard Rogers & Mark Fisher, *A New London*, Penguin (London), 1992, pp 183–214

Robert G Shibley, *Buffalo, New York: Design Research on the Retail Core. The Buffalo Urban Retail Core Design Competition*, State University of New York at Buffalo (New York), 1988

S Frederick Starr (Ed), *The Oberlin Book of Bandstands*, Preservation Press (Washington DC), 1987

United States Department of Energy, *Sunwall Design Competition: National Solar Design Competition*, 2001

Charles Waldheim, *Constructed Ground: The Millennium Garden Design Competition*, University of Illinois (Urbana), 2001

Felix Zwock, *Central District Spreeinsel*, Birkhäuser Verlag (Berlin), 1994

References

H de Haan & I Haagsma, *Architects in Competitions – International Architectural Competitions of the last 200 years*, Thames and Hudson (London), 1988

Cees de Jong & Erik Mattie, *Architectural Competitions 1792–1949*, Benedikt Taschen (Cologne), 1994

Cees de Jong & Erik Mattie, *Architectural Competitions 1950–Today*, Benedikt Taschen (Cologne), 1994

James D Kornwolf (Ed), *Modernism in America 1937–1941: A Catalog and Exhibition of Four Architectural Competitions*, Joseph and Margaret Muscarelle Museum of Art, College of William and Mary (Williamsburg), 1985

Hélène Lipstadt (Ed), *The Experimental Tradition*, Princeton Architectural Press (New York), 1989

Paul D Spreiregen, *Design Competitions*, McGraw-Hill (New York), 1979

Elisabeth Tostrup, *Architecture and Rhetoric: Text and Design in Architectural Competitions*, Andreas Papadakis (London), 1999

GG Wynne (Ed), *Winning Designs: The Competitions Renaissance*, Transaction Books (New Brunswick), 1981

Periodicals

Architektur + Wettbewerbe

CC - Compe & Contest, nos 1–60, Tokyo (last issue, September 1998)

Competitions

Wettbewerbe Aktuell

PHOTO CREDITS

p 7 © Zugmann/Snøhetta; pp 9(b), 12, 29, 60, 63 (see below),149(t), 150 and 151 photos: © Stanley Collyer; p 9(t) © Daniel Herren AIA/FSA; p 10 photo: © Debbie Franke Photography, Inc; pp 14, 101 © Benisch, Benisch & Partner; pp 16, 133(t), 178, 185(br) © Zaha Hadid Architects; p 18(t) photo: © Benjamin F Brown; p 18(b): © Peter MacCallum; p 20(b) © Michael Dulin; p 20 (t+m) © Holt Hinshaw Architects; pp 23, 26 photos: © Stefan Müller, Berlin; p 25 photo: © Dr Christian Richters; p 28 photo: © Steven Evans; p 30 © James L Alcorn AIA; p 31(t) photo: © Taylor Sherrill; p 31(b) © MWM Architects – Oakland, CA; p 32 © Lee/Timchula Architects; pp 35–7 © US General Services Administration – Northwest/Arctic Region; p 38(t) © Koetter, Kim & Associates; p 38(m+b) © Thomas Hacker Architects Inc; pp 39, 141–2 © Antoine Predock Architect; p 41 photos © Michael Awad; pp 42–3 © KPMB Architects; pp 44, 179 courtesy of Saucier+Perotte Architects/Dunlop Farrow; p 45 © Dan Hanganu Architects; pp 47–9, 59 © Cannon Design Los Angeles; pp 50–1, 161(b) © Moore Ruble Yudell; p 52 HOK, Inc, Design Architect and Lockard Creative, Illustration; p 53 © Fentress Bradburn Architects; pp 55–6 computer renderings: © Advanced Media Design, Inc; pp 57, 174–5 © Rafael Viñoly Architects; p 58, 82 courtesy of Skidmore Owings & Merill LLP, computer renderings: © Douglas Jamieson; p 63(t) © Stanley Collyer; p 63(b) photo: © Armand Ostroff; pp 64–5, 195 © Arata Isozaki & Associates; pp 66, 92–3 © Arquitectonica; p 67(t) © Dominique Perrault Architects, Paris; p 67(b) photo: © Georges Fessy; pp 68, 166(t) © Snøhetta; p 70, 172 © Ateliers Jean Nouvel; p 73 © Nicholas Grimshaw & Partners; p 75 © David Brody Bond Architects/Leeser Architecture; p 76 © Morphosis; p 77 © Bernard Tschumi Architects; pp 79, 80–1 courtesy of Barton Myers Associates, Inc/Architekton; pp 83 © Van Dijk Westlake Reed Leskosky in association with Hargreaves Associates and Hodgetts & Fung; pp 85, 86(t) insert © Zita Cotti and Martina Hauser Architects; p 86(t) computer rendering: © Architron®; p 86(m+b) photos: © Jussi Tiainen; p 87 © Caruso St John Architects; p 89 photo: © Aker/Zvonkovic Photography LLP/PACF; pp 90-91 courtesy of Cesar Pelli Associates; p 94 photo: © John Caliste; p 95 © Office for Metropolitan Architecture; pp 97,109 (t,m) photos: © Tim Griffith; p 99(t) © Richard Dattner & Partners Architects PC; p 99(b) photo: © FUJITSUKA Mitsumasa; p 103 photo: © Simon Scott; p 105 photo © Peter Aaron/Esto; pp 107-108, 109(b) © Pfau Architecture; p 110 © Kennedy & Violich Architecture, Ltd; p 111 © William McDonough & Partners; p 112 © Leddy Maytum Stacy Architects; p 113 © Tolle Lundberg/Lundberg Design; p 115 © Marble Fairbanks Architects; p 116 © Ground Studio; pp 117, 126 © Mac Scogin Merrill Elam Architects; pp 118, 135–6, 137(b) © Smith-Miller & Hawkinson Architects; p 119(t+ml+mr) © Koning Eizenberg Architects; p 119(bl+br) courtesy of Ross Barney & Jankowski, Inc; p 120 © Jack L Gordon Architects; p 121 © Lubrano Ciavarra Design, LLC; pp 123–4 © Allied Works Architecture; pp 125, 196(m+b) © Carlos Jimenez Studio; pp 127, 137(t) © Charles Rose Architects, Inc; pp 129–30 photos: © Richard Barnes; p 131 © Office of Metropolitan Architecture; p 132(t) © Murphy/Jahn; p 133(b) courtesy of Eisenman Architects; pp 138, 145 © Leers Weinzapfel Associates Architects, Inc; p 139 © Julie Snow

Architects, Inc; p 143 photo: © Rob Quigley; p 144 © Barton Myers Associates, Inc and Architekton; pp 147, 149(b) © Zugmann/Snøhetta; pp 157-58, p 193, photo: © Timothy Hursley; p 159 courtesy of Moshe Safdie & Associates and VCBO Architecture; p 160 photos: © Bill Timmerman; p 161(t) © Gwathmey Siegel & Associates Architects LLC; pp 163–7 © Kansai Kan National Diet Library; pp 169 - 173 © Brooklyn Public Library; p 177 © Patkau/Croft Pelletier/Gilles Guité Architectes; p 180 © Gauthier Daoust Lestage architects and urban planners/Faucher Aubertin Brodeur Gauthier architects/NOMADE architecture/Drop others; p 181 © Christian de Portzamparc; pp 182–3 photo: © Murray Hedwig; p 185(t+bl) photos: © Paul Warchol; p 186 photo: © Jan Bitter; p 188 photo: © Michael Moran; p 190 photo: © Richard Davies; p 194(tr) photo: © Jock Pottle(?); p 194 (tl+b) © Gluckman Mayner Architects; p 196(t) © David M Schwarz/Architectural Services, Inc; p 197 © Ricardo Legoretta; pp 199–200 © Andrea Ponsi; p 201 © Johnston Marklee & Associates; p 202(b) © Dwane Oyler, Jenny Wu; p 202(t) © Robert Corser; p 203 © Heimo Schimek; pp 205–7 © Kirsten Schemel Architekten BDA, Berlin; p 208 © Kyu Sung Woo, FAIA; p 209 © Noriaki Okabe Architecture Network; p 211 photo: © Barbara Karant, Karant + Associates; p 213 © McCormack Smith + Others; p 214 © Pyatok Associates; p 215 © Studio Wanda; p 216 photo: © Biff Henrich; pp 219 © Brian Healy Architects; p 221 photo: © Coleman Coker/BuildingStudio (t); p 221 © Garofalo Architects (b); p 222 © Stanley Saitowitz/Natoma Architects Inc; p 223(m) © 3D Design Studio; p 223(t) © Wheeler Kearns/Xavier Vendrell Studio; p 223(b) photo: © John Howarth; p 225(tl) photo: © Jan Bitter; pp 225(b), 226–9 © S333 Architecture & Urbanism; pp 231–3 © Schmidt, Hammer & Lassen/Jørgen True/Søven Kuhn; pp 234–7 © Herzog & Partner, Munich.

ACKNOWLEDGEMENTS

In the 1960s I was fortunate enough to be living in Berlin, a centre of exceptional architectural activity where good design, and many of that city's great new buildings, were the result of state-sponsored design competitions. Not only did seasoned veterans, such as Hans Scharoun and Egon Eierman benefit from that system, but a whole new generation of young architects – such as Meinhard von Gerkan, Stephan Behnisch, and Axel Schultes – established themselves in the forefront of their profession by excelling in competitions sponsored under the umbrella of the German Architectural Federation (BdA). At the conclusion of these competitions, the models went on public display, and the discussions which ensued were always stimulating and informative. To Berlin architects Frederick Borck and Ivan Krusnik I owe a special debt for introducing me to the culture of competitions which prevailed in Germany (and in Europe) in that period.

When competitions began to pick up steam in the US in the early 1980s, a cadre of professional advisers were trained – with the support of the National Endowment for the Arts (NEA) – to administer and help in their organization and administration.

Among these were Paul Spreiregen, Jeffrey Ollswang, William Liskamm, Roger Schluntz, Don Stastny, Ken Paolini and Ted Liebman. The successful Vietnam Memorial Competition in 1981 gave new impetus to the process in the US, and it was followed by a number of competitions later in the decade.

When Competitions magazine was founded in 1990, it was undertaken with the purpose of tracking a phenomenon which was essentially under the radar in the US. Without the initial commitment and generous advice given by people such as Grady Clay, former editor of Landscape Architecture, and the above-mentioned professional advisers, Paul Spreiregen, Bill Liskamm and Jeffrey Ollswang in particular, the magazine would probably never have seen the light of day.

In the initial stages of development, the Competition Project also received support from Ball State University's School of Architecture and the University of Cincinnati's School of Design.

Finally, I wish to thank Helen Castle, my untiring editor at Wiley-Academy for her probing questions and support which have made this book possible.

CONTRIBUTORS

Main Contributors

Michael Berk, a musician and freelance writer living in New York, has written for Oculus, Competitions, and other publications. He is presently teaching a course dealing with the connection between architecture and music at Parsons School of Design.

Rosemarie Buchanan, a freelance writer living in Chicago, has been a contributor to the publications of the Chicago Chapter of the American Institute of Architects.

Lucy Bullivant is an architectural critic, author and curator of many exhibitions and symposia including 'Space Invaders: new UK architecture' (British Council, 2001) and '4dspace' (ICA, 2003). She contributes to a number of international publications including *Architectural Design*, *Architectural Record*, *Domus* and *Archis*.

Carlos Casuscelli, a Miami-based architect, has practiced architecture both in the US and Argentina. In recent years he has been the Director of Ball State University's Tropicalia programme in Miami, which was recently cited by the ACSA as the best off-campus student programme in architecture.

Anthony Coscia is a principal of Coscia Day Architects in Venice, California.

John Morris Dixon FAIA, former Editor-in Chief of *Progressive Architecture*, is currently writing a book on the modern movement in architecture.

Michael Dulin, an Assistant Editor at *Competitions* magazine, received a degree in landscape architecture from the Rhode Island School of Design.

Larry Gordon is a Los Angeles-based writer and frequent contributor to COMPETITIONS magazine.

Mark Gunderson, a practicing architect in Fort Worth, Texas, is past president of the Fort Worth AIA and a contributing author to a number of publications, including *Cite* and *Texas Architect*. He is also a contributing author of the book, *Buildings of Texas*, recently published by Oxford University Press for the Society of Architectural Historians.

William Morgan, former professor of Art History at the University of Louisville and a frequent contributor to numerous periodicals, lives in Rhode Island where he writes about architecture. He has authored a number of books on architecture, including the monograph, *Heikkinen + Komonen*. His most recent book is *American Country Churches*, to be published by Abrams in 2004.

Tom Reasoner AIA, University Architect at the University of South Dakota, was the Project Coordinator for the university's Business School competition.

Mark Tortorich, FAIA, a San Francisco-based architect, was the Project and Competition Manager for O'Brien Kreitzberg.

Roger Schluntz FAIA, Dean of the School of Architecture at the University of New Mexico, has served as the professional adviser for numerous competitions, including the Salt Lake City Library, Jacksonville Library, Rensselaer Polytechnic Arts and Media Centre and many others.

Brian Taggart, a freelance journalist living in Bloomington, Indiana, has been a contributing editor to *Competitions* magazine.

Susannah Temko is a freelance writer living in Oakland, California.

Robert Shibley, is Director of Urban Design at the School of Architecture and Planning, State University of New York at Buffalo.

George Wright FAIA, was former Dean of the School of Architecture at the University of Texas at Arlington.

Appendix Contributors

Donald I Bates lectured at the Architectural Association, London and worked for Daniel Libeskind before co-founding Lab architecture studio in 1994. The studio won Melbourne's Federation Square competition in 1997.

Ingerid Helsing Almaas is an architect and editor-in-chief of *Byggekunst*, the Norwegian Review of Architecture.

Louise Harrison is the manager of the RIBA's national Competitions Office based in Leeds and has worked for the RIBA since 1987. The office has steadily grown in size over the last 15 years and currently the team extends to 6 members of staff.

Robert G Hill is a registered architect and architectural historian who lives and works in Toronto, Canada.

Jesper Kock, architect MAA, heads the AA Competition Secretariat for the Architects Association of Denmark.

Nasrine Seraji AA dipl RIBA, is Professor of Architecture and Chair of the Department of Architecture at Cornell University, Ithaca, New York. She has participated in many competitions in France, and won the competition for the temporary American Cultural Centre in Paris.

Peter Sjöström Cand. Arch., MAA, SAR, studied architecture at the Royal Danish Academy of Fine Arts in Copenhagen and Oxford Brookes University. He has worked professionally in both Scandinavia and the United States and is presently with Moore Ruble Yudell in Santa Monica, California.

Hiroshi Watanabe is a writer and translator. Born in 1944 in Tokyo, he was educated at Princeton and Yale universities and is the author of *The Architecture of Tokyo* and the translator of *Space in Japanese Architecture*. In 1989 he was a consultant to the Tokyo Metropolitan Government during the Tokyo International Forum competition.

INDEX

References to illustrations are given in *italics*

3D Design Studios 218, 220, 223, *223*
AA Arkitekter 230
Aalto, Alvar 11, 84, 180
Abramson, Richard 87
Adamcyzk, Georges 178
Adams, Albert M 106, 108
Aida, Takefumi 33
AJ Diamond, Don Schmitt 42
Albuquerque 140, *141*, *142*, 143, *143*, *144*, *145*
Alexandria Library 71, *146–7*, *149*, 152
Allied Works Architecture
    Booker T Washington Arts Magnet School 122, *123*, 124, *124*
    Museum of Art and Design, New York City 184, 196
    Museum of Contemporary Art, St Louis 187
Allies and Morrison 21
Alsop, William 40
Alsop & Stormer 71
Amdersen, Amy 103
Amon Carter Museum, Fort Worth 192
Ando, Tadao 188, 189–90, *193*, 194
Andreu, Paul 68
Anshen and Allen Architects 102
Arab World Institute, Paris 66
Archigenesis 203
ARCHITEKTON 78, *79*
Argentina 30
Århus, Denmark 230, *231*, *232*, *233*, *234*, 235, *235*, *236*, 237, *237*
Arizona State University
    Fine Arts Center 69
    Visual & Performing Arts Center 78, *79*, 80, *80*, *81*, *82*, *83*
Arkitema 230
Arkkitehtuuritoimisto 92 164
Arnhem 226
Arnold, Denise 222-3
Arquitectonica 21, 65, *66*, 88, 91, *92*, *93*, *94*, 95
art galleries *see* museums
Arthur Golding & Associates 19
Asia 33
Atlanta 98, 101
Australia 26–7, 238

Balfour, Alan 72
Ball State University 102
Baltimore 215
Baniassad, Essy 42
Barcelona 187
Bastille Opera, Paris *63*, 65-6
Beeby, Tom 151
Behnisch, Günther 11, 26
Behnisch, Behnisch & Partner *14*, 17, *101*
Behrens, Peter 212
Beijing Opera House 68
Bennitt, Todd 198
Berkeley, California 102
Berkeley Public Safety Building 19, *20*, 21
Berlin
    Canadian Embassy 40, *41*, 42, *42*, *43*, *44*, 45, *45*
    German Chancellery Building *22–3*, 26, *26*
    housing 212
    Jewish Museum *186*
    museums 187, 190–1
    Philharmonic Hall *60–1*, 62

schools 101
universities 102
Beverly Hills Civic Center 27
Bibliothèque de France, Paris 65, 164
Bilbao 16, 39, 66, 186, 187
Bissonnette, Lise 178, 180
Blair, Philippa 198, 201
Bolullo, Mario 29, *29*
Bond, Max 74, *75*
Bonn 189
Booker T Washington Arts Magnet School, Dallas 122, *123*, 124, *124*, *125*, *126*, *127*
Bordeaux Courts Building 25, *25*
Botta, Mario 188
Boutin Ramoisy Tremblay *178*, 180
Brandt, Carol 122
Brasilia 30
Brazil 30
Breuer, Marcel 186, 189
Brickell Bridge, Miami 88
Brill, Mike 217
Bristol *14*, 17
British Library, London *150*
Brooklyn Public Library 152, 168, *169*, 170, *171*, *172*, *173*, *174–5*
Bruder, William P 80, 156, *160*
Buchan Group *182–3*, 191
Buffalo 189, 217
Building Studio *219*
Bunshaft, Gordon 189
Business and Professional People for the Public Interest (BPI) 100–1, 114

Cairo *190*
Calatrava, Santiago 187
Calgary, Alberta 29, 30
California 27, 212
Calthorpe, Peter 220
Canada
    competitions 238-9
    government buildings 26, 29–30
Canadian Embassy, Berlin 40, *41*, 42, *42*, *43*, *44*, 45, *45*
Canberra 26–7
CannonDworsky 54, *59*
    see also Dworsky Associates
Cape Girardeau, Missouri 24
Cardiff Bay Opera House *16*, 19
Carnegie Endowment 148
Carre d'Art, Nimes 170
Caruso, Adam 87, *87*
Caruso St John Architects 87, *87*
Cathedral City, California 27, 29, *30*, *31*
Cawker, Ruth 178, 180
Cesar Pelli & Associates 69
Channahon, Illinois 215
Chemetoff, Paul 9
Cheshire, Phillip Max 201
Chicago 98, 100–1
    Harold Washington Library Center 150-1, 152
    IIT McCormick Center 128, *129*, *130*, *131*, 132, *132*, *133*
    prototype schools 114, *115*, 116, *116*, *117*, *118*, *119*, *120*, *121*
Chicago Housing Authority *211*, 213, 218, *219*, 220, 221, 222-3, *222*, *223*
Chicago Westside Affordable Housing Competition 215
Chile 30
China 33

Chipperfield, David 191
Christchurch Art Gallery 182–3, 191
Ciampi, Mario J 102
Cincinnati 184, 185, 190
civic buildings see government buildings
Claiborne, Robert 87
Clark County Government Center, Las Vegas 29
Clemson University 103
Cleveland 152
Cloepfil, Brad 123, 186
Coker, Coleman 218, 219, 220
Columbus, Ohio 188
competitions 8–12, 14–15
    Australia 238
    Canada 238–9
    China 33
    criteria for entering 12–13
    Denmark 239–40
    France 240
    Germany 240–1
    invited 15–16
    Japan 241
    Latin America 241–2
    lost opportunities 17, 19, 21
    Norway 242
    Sweden 242–3
    two-stage format 16-17
    United Kingdom 243
    US 243
Contemporary Arts Center, Cincinnati 184, 185, 190
Contra Costa County Government Center 27, 46, 47, 48, 48–9, 50, 50, 51, 52, 53
Conway, William 134
Cook, Peter 212
Coop Himmelblau 184
Copenhagen
    Ørestaden Concert Hall 70, 71
    Royal Library Extension 149, 152
Cordoba, Argentina 30
Corser, Robert 202, 203
Cotti, Zita 85, 86, 87
courthouses
    Eugene, Oregon 34, 35, 36–9, 36, 37, 38, 39
    Los Angeles Federal Courthouse 54, 55, 56, 57, 58, 59
Crickhowell, Nicholas 19
Croft-Pelletier 152, 177, 180

Dallas 122, 123, 124, 124, 125, 126, 127
Daridan, Marzelle, Manescau and Steeg 224
Dartmouth University 104
Darwin T Martin House, Buffalo 217
Dattner, Richard 99
Davis Brody Bond 74, 75
Dearing, James 164
Decker, Howard 220
Decq, Odile 204
Denmark 239–40
Denver Art Museum 189, 190
Denver Civic Center 29
Denver Public Library 150–1, 152, 153
`Design Wars' (NOVA) 151
Desvignes & Dalnoky 178, 179
Deubzer, Hannelore 206
Dijon Performing Arts Centre 65, 66

Diller + Scofidio 168
Disney Concert Hall, Los Angeles 54, 62
DLR Architecture 35, 36, 37, 39
Dresden 101, 101
Duany Plater-Zyberk 88, 91, 95
Dworsky Associates 47, 48, 48–9, 50
    see also CannonDworsky

Early Childhood Facility Fund (ECFF) 100
Eaton Mahoney Architects 156, 161
Eble, Joachim 230
Edmonton, Alberta 29
educational facilities 98, 100
    Booker T Washington Arts Magnet School 122, 123, 124, 124, 125, 126, 127
    Chicago prototype schools 114, 115, 116, 116, 117, 118, 119, 120, 121
    IIT McCormick Center 128, 129, 130, 131, 132, 132, 133
    Lick-Wilmerding High School 106, 106-7, 108, 108, 109, 110, 111, 112, 113
    nonprofits' role 100–2
    School of Architecture, University of New Mexico 140, 141, 142, 143, 143, 144, 145
    universities 102-4
    University of South Dakota School of Business 134, 135, 136, 136, 137, 138, 139
Edwards, Madigan, Torzillo & Briggs 26-7
Eiffel Tower 186
Eisenman, Peter 21, 104, 133
Eizenberg, Julia 122
Elam & Bray 74
Electronic Media and Performing Arts Center, Rensselaer Polytechnic Institute 72, 73, 74, 75, 76, 77, 77
Erichsen, Anne 235
Erickson, Arthur 15, 68, 162, 164
    Harold Washington Library Center 151
    Simon Fraser University 102, 103
Escondido, California 27
Eugene, Oregon 34, 35, 36-9, 36, 37, 38, 39
Europan 224, 225, 226, 226, 227, 228, 228, 229
Evanston, Illinois 153-4

FABG/GDL/NOMADE/Yann Kersalé/Ruedi Baur 178, 180
Fairbanks, Karen 114, 115, 116
Fardjadi, Homu 100
Fehn, Sverre 11
Feiner, Edward 34, 54
Feldman, Roberta 218, 220, 223
Fentress, Curtis 21
Fentress Bradburn 24, 29
    Contra Costa County Government Center 48, 50, 53
Fifield, Michael 39
Finland 11
Fisher Friedman Associates 48, 50, 50, 51
Foreign Office Architects 21
Fort Worth 189–90
    Modern Art Museum 192, 193, 194, 194, 195, 196, 197
Foster, Norman 26, 170
Foster City, California 27
Fowle, Bruce 72
France 11–12, 71, 240
Frank, Charlotte 22–3, 26
Fremont, California 27
Fresno, California 189

Frick, Daniel 87

Garofalo, Doug 218, 220, *221*, 223
Gehry, Frank 180
    Disney Concert Hall 54, 62
    Guggenheim Museum 16, 39, 186
General Services Administration (GSA) 24, 34, 36, 37, 39
Gerkan, Meinhard von 9
German Chancellery Building, Berlin *22-3*, 26, *26*
Germany 11, 12, 240–1
Gillmor, Douglas R 42
Gluckman, Richard 194, *194*
Go Multimedia 178, *179*
Golemon, Harry 29, *29*
Golemon/Bolullo Partnership 29, *29*
Gordon, Jack L 116, *120*
government buildings 24
    Asia 33
    Canadian Embassy, Berlin 40, *41*, 42, *42*, *43*, *44*, 45, *45*
    Contra Costa County Government Center 46, *47*, 48, *48–9*, 50,
        50, *51*, *52*, *53*
    democracy and security 24–7
    Eugene, Oregon Federal Courthouse 34, *35*, 36-9, *36*, *37*, *38*, *39*
    Los Angeles Federal Courthouse 54, *55*, 56, *57*, *58*, *59*
    North and South America 27, 29–30
Grand Egyptian Museum, Cairo *190*, 191, 206
Grande Bibliothèque du Québec, Montréal 152, 176, *177*, 178, *178*,
    179, 180, *180*, *181*
Graves, Michael 21, *150–1*, 152
Grigotti, Vittorio 68
Grimshaw, Nicholas *73*, 74, 77
Groningen *225*, 226, *226*, *227*, 228, *228*, *229*
Gropius, Walter 212
Ground Zero Design Studio 116, *116*
Gruen Associates 156, *161*
Guggenheim Museum, Bilbao 16, 39, 186
Guggenheim Museum, New York City 186, 189
Guité, Gilles 152, *177*, 180
Gund, Graham 103
Gutierrez, Gabriella 143
Gwathmey, Charles 15
Gwathmey Siegel Architects 156, *161*

Hadid, Zaha
    Cardiff Bay Opera House *16*, 19
    Contemporary Arts Center, Cincinnati 184, *185*, 190
    IIT McCormick Center *133*
    Québec Library *178*, 180
Hanganau, Dan 42, 45, *45*
Hanhardt, John 204
Hanrahan, Thomas 170
Harbourside Performing Arts Centre Competition, Bristol *14*, 17
Hardy Holzman Pfeiffer 152
Hargreaves Associates 78, *83*
Harold Washington Library Center, Chicago 150–1
Hartman, Craig 21, 48, 54, *58*
Hauser, Martina 85, *86*, 87
Hays, Michael 72
Healy, Brian *210-11*, 213, 218, 220, 222, 223
Heikkinen + Komonen 21
Hellmuth Obata & Kassabaum (HOK) 48, 50, 52
Helsinki *185*, 187
Heneghan, Roisin 184
Heneghan Peng Architects *190*

Hernandez, Jorge 88, 90, 94
Herren, Daniel *9*
Hertzberger, Herman 11, 230
Herzog & Meuron 184
Herzog + Partner 230, *232*, *234*, 235, *235*, *236*, 237, *237*
High Court of Australia, Canberra 26–7
Hodgets + Fung 78, *83*
Holl, Steven 21, 122, *185*, 187, 190
Holt Hinshaw Architects 19, *20*, 21
Horn, Jerry 132
Horseshoe housing, Berlin-Britz 212
housing 212-15, 217
    Chicago Housing Authority *211*, *213*, 218, *219*, 220, *221*,
        222–3, *222*, *223*
    Europan 224, *225*, 226, *226*, *227*, 228, *228*, *229*
    Lystrup, Århus 230, *231*, *232*, 233, *234*, 235, *235*, *236*, 237, *237*
Houston 192
Huff + Gooden 168, *173*
Huidobro, Borja *9*

Ikeda, Yasushi *167*
Illinois Institute of Technology McCormick Center, Chicago 128, *129*,
    130, *131*, 132, *132*, *133*
Imperial War Museum, Manchester 188
Indiana University Art Museum 103
International Union of Architects 16, 68, 184, 191, 204, *205*
invited competitions 11–12, 15–16
    performing arts centres 69, 71
Iskala, Antii 86, 87
Isozaki, Arata *64–5*, 68, 71, 187, 188, 194, *195*, 204
Italy 25
Ithaca College 103
Ito, Toyo 11, 21, 170
Ivy, Robert 39
Iwadeyama Junior High School *99*, 102

Jackson, Sert 103
Jackson, Shirley 77
Jacksonville, Florida 152, 153
Jahn, Helmut 21, 104, *132*, 151
Jakubeit, Barbara 40, 42
James Alcorn & Associates 27, *30*
James Stirling Michael Wilford 68
Japan 8, 11, 33, 241
Jefferson National Expansion Memorial, St Louis *10*
Jewish Museum, Berlin *186*, 190–1
Jimenez, Carlos 122, 124, *125*, 194, *196*
Johnson, Jeffrey 128
Johnson, Philip 192
Johnson, Ralph 15, 21, 54, *55*, 56
Johnston, Sharon *201*, 203
Johnston, Marklee & Associates *201*, 203
Jones, Mary Margaret 48
Jorasch, Richard L 102
Jyväskylä Music and Arts Centre 84, *85*, *86*, 87, *87*

Kahn, Louis 103, 189, 192
Kansai-Kan National Diet Library 152, 162, *163*, 164, *164*, 165,
    166, *167*
Kansas City 189, 190
Kawasato Village, Japan 33
Keller, Ernst 42
Kennedy Violich/Kuth Ranieri 106, *110*
Kiasma Museum of Contemporary Art, Helsinki *185*, 187

Kim, Jin-Kyoon 204
Kimbell Art Museum, Fort Worth 189, 192, 194
Kimm, Jong Soung 204
Kitchener City Hall, Ontario 28, 29
Klein, Bruce F 220, 222
Knox Museum, Buffalo 189
Koetter, Kim & Associates 38, 38
Koning Eizenberg Architecture 116, 119
Koolhaas, Rem 104, 152, 168
    IIT McCormick Center 128, 129, 130, 131, 132
    Performing Arts Center of Greater Miami 88, 94, 95
Korean Cultural Center, Los Angeles 191
Köther and Salman 226
Kunihiko, Honjo 87
Kuwabara, Bruce 21
Kuwabara Payne McKenna Blumberg (KPMB) 28, 41, 42, 42, 43, 45

La Defense, Paris 65
La Pampa, Argentina 30
Lacroix, Yvon-André 178
Lake Erie College, Painesville 103
Lambert, Phyllis 176, 178, 180
Langdon Wilson 18
Laperrièrre, René 178
Larsen, Henning 71
Las Vegas 29, 152
Lauritzen, Vilhelm 230
Lavari, Paul 220
Le Corbusier 212
Leavitt, Jackie 213
Leddy Maytum Stacy Architects 106, 112
Lee, Eric 213
Lee, John MY 32, 33
Lee/Timchula Architects 32, 33
Leers Weinzapfel Associates
    School of Architecture, University of New Mexico 143, 145
    University of Pennsylvania Chiller Plant 104, 105
    University of South Dakota School of Business 134, 138
Leeser, Thomas 74, 75
Legorreta, Ricardo 151, 152, 194, 197
Libeskind, Daniel 186, 188, 190-1
libraries see public libraries
Library of Congress, Washington 148
Lichtenstein, Harvey 168
Lick-Wilmerding High School, San Francisco 96–7, 98, 106, 106–7, 108, 108, 109, 110, 111, 112, 113
limited design competitions 153–4
Linnemann, Bannenberg and Klaasse 226
Liskamm, William 106
Liveable Places 213, 214, 216
Lockwood, Laura 46, 47
Lohan, Dirk 151
Lomas de Zamora, Argentina 30
London 150, 152, 187, 191
Long, Mary Jane 178
Los Angeles
    Disney Music Hall 54, 62
    Federal Courthouse 54, 55, 56, 57, 58, 59
    Korean Cultural Center 191
    Liveable Places 213, 214, 216
    Low Cost Housing Competition 215
Louisville, Kentucky 98, 100
Low Cost Housing Competition, Los Angeles 215
Lubrano Ciavarra Design 116, 121

Lucerne 66
Lundberg Design 106, 113
Lutfy, Jeanne 168
Lystrup, Århus, Denmark 230, 231, 232, 233, 234, 235, 235, 236, 237, 237

Mac Scogin Merrill Elam Architects 117, 122, 124, 126
McCormick, Smith & Others 214, 216
McCormick Center, Chicago 128, 129, 130, 131, 132, 132, 133
McDonough, William 106, 111
Machado and Silvetti Associates 188, 190
Mack, Mark 198, 201
Maki, Fumihiko 8, 68, 162
Manchester 188
Manfredi, Michael 16-17
Marble Fairbanks Architecture 114, 115, 116
Maria José Araguren Lopez/José Gonzalez 71
Mariinsky State Theatre, St Petersburg 67, 71
Martin, Elizabeth 168, 170
Martin House, Buffalo 217
Martinez, California 46, 47, 48, 48-9, 50, 50, 51, 52, 53
Mayne, Thom 54, 74
Meckel, David 48
mediathèque 170
Meier, Richard 9, 65, 187
Menil Collection, Houston 192
Menkès Shooner Dagenais 178, 179
Miami, Performing Arts Center 88, 89, 90-1, 90, 91, 92, 93, 94–5, 94, 95
Miami Beach, Florida 152
Mies van der Rohe, Ludwig 128, 132, 212
Miller, George 122
Milwaukee 187
Ministère de l'Economie, des Finance et de l'Industrie, Paris 9
Minnesota 24
Mirmiran, S Hadid 162, 164
Mississauga, Ontario 29
Mitterand, François 9, 11
Miyakawa, Hiroshi 167
Mobile Government Plaza, Alabama 29, 29
Modern Art Museum, Barcelona 187
Modern Art Museum of Fort Worth 189-90, 192, 193, 194, 194, 195, 196, 197
Moller, Chris 225, 226, 226, 227, 228, 228, 229
Moneo, Rafael 54, 71
Monterey Housing 215
Montréal, Québec Library 152, 176, 177, 178, 178, 179, 180, 180, 181
Moore, Charles 27, 69, 152, 212
Moore Ruble Yudell (MRY) 69, 71
    Contra Costa County Government Center 48, 50, 50, 51
    Dartmouth University 104
    Salt Lake City Library 156, 161
    San Juan Capistrano Public Library 152
Mori, Toshikao 217
Moriyama and Teshima 42
Morphosis
    Eugene, Oregon Federal Courthouse 35, 36, 37, 39
    Rensselaer Polytechnic Electronic Media and Performing Arts Center 74, 76
Moss, Eric Owen 71
Moynihan, Daniel Patrick 11
Museum of Art and Design, New York City 184, 186
Museum of Contemporary Art, St Louis 187, 188

Museum of Modern Art, Milwaukee 187
Museum of Modern Art (MOMA), New York City 184
Museum of Modern Art, San Francisco 188
Museum of Modern Art, Stockholm 191
museums 184, 186-7
    Modern Art Museum of Fort Worth 192, *193*, 194, *194*, *195*, *196*, *197*
    Nam June Paik Museum 204, *205*, 206, *206*, *207*, *208*, *209*
    Palos Verdes Art Center 198, *199*, *200*, 201, *201*, *202*, 203, *203*
    as tourist destinations 189–91
    urban generation 187–8
MWM Architects 29, *31*
Myers, Barton
    Phoenix Municipal Government Center *18*, 19
    School of Architecture, University of New Mexico 143, *144*
    Tempe Visual & Performing Arts Center 78, *79*, 80, *80*, *81*

Nagle Hartray Associates 154
Nam June Paik Museum 191
Namba, Kazuhiko *166*
Nara Centennial Hall 162, 164, 187-8
Nashville, Tennessee 152, 153
National Endowment for the Arts (NEA) 11, 114, 154, 168, 218
National Gallery of Art, Washington 189
National Gallery, London 192
Nelson-Atkins Art Museum, Kansas City 189, 190
Netherlands 11
New Urban Housing Competition 215
New York City
    Brooklyn Public Library 152, 168, *169*, 170, *171*, *172*, *173*, *174–5*
    Museum of Art and Design 184, 186
    Museum of Modern Art 184
    schools 98, *99*
Newark, New Jersey 62
Nimes 170
Norten, Enrique 152, 168, *169*, 170, *171*
Norway 242
Nouvel, Jean 9, 21
    Brooklyn Public Library 168, *172*
    Music and Conference Centre, Lucerne 66
    Ørestaden Concert Hall, Copenhagen *70*, 71
    Tokyo Opera House 164

O'Brien, Jeffrey 203
Office of Metropolitan Architecture (OMA) 128, *129*, *130*, *131*, 132
Oh, Ki Soo 204
Okabe, Noriaki 206, *209*
Olmsted, Frederick Law 217
open competitions 68–9, 154–5
Ørestaden Concert Hall, Copenhagen *70*, 71
Oslo Opera House *68*, 71
Ott, Carlos *63*, 65–6, 71
Oud, JJP 212
Oyler, Dwayne *202*, 203

Paavilainen, Simo 84
Painesville, Ohio 103
Pallasmaa, Juhani 84
Palos Verdes Art Center, California 189, 190, 198, *199*, *200*, 201, *201*, *202*, 203, *203*
Papa, Dominic *225*, 226, *226*, *227*, 228, *228*, *229*
Paris 25, 152

Bastille Opera *63*, 65–6
Bibliotheque National 164
Cité de la Musique 62
Ministère de l'Economie, des Finance et de l'Industrie 9
Pompidou Centre 8, *12*, 170
Parris, California 27
Patkau Architects 152, *177*, 180
Pedersen, William 39
Pei, IM 65, 68, 103, 124, 189
Pei Cobb Freed 69
Pelli, Cesar 88, *89*, 90, *91*, *92*, 94
Peng, Shi-Fu 184
performing arts centres 8, 62, 65-6
    Asia 68
    yväskylä Music and Arts Centre 84, *85*, *86*, 87, *87*
    Performing Arts Center of Greater Miami 88, *89*, 90–1, *90*, *91*, *92*, *93*, 94–5, *94*, *95*
    Rensselaer Polytechnic Electronic Media and Performing Arts Center *72*, *73*, 74, *75*, *76*, 77, *77*
    Tempe Visual & Performing Arts Center 78, *79*, 80, *80*, *81*, *82*, *83*
    US 68-9, 71
Perkins & Will 54, *55*, 56
Perrault, Dominique 21, 65, *67*, 71, 164
Pfau Architecture 18, *96-7*, 106, *106–7*, *108*, *109*
Philadelphia 104, *105*
Phinney, Peter 198, 201, 203
Phoenix Municipal Government Center *18*, 19
Piano, Renzo 8, *12*, 122, 170, 192
Pompidou Centre, Paris 8, *12*, 170
Ponsi, Andrea 190, *199*, *200*, 201
Portzamparc, Christian 178, 180, *181*
Powell, Joseph 154
Prado, Spain 190, 191
Predock, Antoine 69, 80, 104, 152
    Eugene, Oregon Federal Courthouse 39, *39*
    School of Architecture, University of New Mexico 140, *141*, *142*, 143
Prescott Muir Architects 156
Prietl, Dietmar 226
Pritzker 21
public buildings see government buildings
public libraries 148-55
    Brooklyn Public Library 168, *169*, 170, *171*, *172*, *173*, *174–5*
    Kansai-Kan National Diet Library 162, *163*, 164, *164*, *165*, *166*, *167*
    Québec Library, Montréal 176, *177*, 178, *178*, *179*, 180, *180*, *181*
    Salt Lake City Library 156, *157*, *158-9*, *160*, *161*
Pudong Masterplan Competition 33
Pulitzer Museum, St Louis 188
Pyatock, Michael 215

Québec Library, Montréal 152, 176, *177*, 178, *178*, *179*, 180, *180*, *181*
Quennell, Nicholas 15
Quigley, Robert W 143, *143*

Rachofsky, Howard 122
Rancho Mirage, California 19, 27
Redwood City, California 27
Reichstag, Berlin 26
Reid, Lamarr 220
Rensselaer Polytechnic Electronic Media and Performing Arts Center *72*, *73*, 74, *75*, *76*, 77, *77*
Revell, Viljo 29
Richmond, British Columbia 29
Riley, Terence 170
Robbins, Mark 114

Robertson, Donna 132
Rock, Michael 132
Rockcastle, Garth 143
Roger Williams University School of Architecture 102
Rogers, Richard 8-9, *12*, 25, *25, 33*, 170
Rose, Charles 122, 124, *127*, 134
Rose, Deedie 122
Rose, Peter 176
Ross Barney + Jankowski Architects 116
Rosseau, Jacques 42
Rossi, Aldo 212
Route 66 140, 143
Rowan, Sean 42
Royal Library Extension, Copenhagen *149*
Ruble, John 48

S333 Studio for Architecture and Urbanism 225, 226, *226, 227,*
    228, 228, 229
Saarinen, Eero *10*
Sacher, Gerhard 226
Safdie, Moshe 21, 156, *157, 158–9*, 176
St Benno Gymnasium, Dresden 101, *101*
St John, Peter 87, *87*
St Louis *10*, 102, 187, 188
St Petersburg *67*, 71
Saitowitz, Stanley 218, 220, *222*
Sakata, Yoshio *165*
Salt Lake City *188*, 190, 215
Salt Lake City Library 153, 156, *157, 158–9, 160, 161*
San Antonio 152
San Diego Affordable Housing Competition 215
San Francisco 188, 189
    Lick-Wilmerding High School *96–7*, 98, 106, *106–7*, 108, *108,*
    109, 110, 111, 112, 113
San Jose State University 190
San Juan Capistrano Public Library 150, 152
Santa Clarita, California 27
Santa Cruz 103
Santiago 30
Sasaki Associates 134
Sattler, Christoph 42
Saucier, Gilles 42
Saucier + Perrotte 42, *44*, 45, 178, *179*
Scharoun, Hans *60–1*, 62, 71
Schemel, Kirsten 204, *205*, 206, *206, 207*
Schimek, Heimo 203, *203*
Schluntz, Roger 72, 77, 140, 143
Schmidt Hammer & Lassen (SHL)
    Lystrup housing 230, *231, 232, 233*, 235, 237
    Royal Library Extension, Copenhagen *149*
Schmidt Hammer Lassen (SHL) 71
Schneider + Sendelbach Architekten 206
School of Architecture, University of New Mexico 140, *141, 142,*
    143, *143*, 144, *145*
schools 98, 100–2
    Booker T Washington Arts Magnet School 122, *123*, 124, *124,*
    125, 126, 127
    Chicago prototypes 114, *115*, 116, *116, 117, 118, 119, 120, 121*
    Lick-Wilmerding High School 106, *106-7*, 108, *108, 109, 110,*
    111, 112, 113
Schreiber, Steve 143
Schultes, Axel 11, 21, *22–3*, 26, *26*, 189, 204, 206
Schumacher, Patrick *178*
Schwarz, David 194, *196*

Science Museum, Columbus, Ohio 188
Scofidio, Ricardo 204
Seattle 152
security 24–7, 100-1
Sendai, Japan 170
Sendelbach, Karlheinz 206
Shattuck, Roger 192
Shenzhen Citizens Centre *32, 33*
Shenzhen Cultural Centre *64–5*, 68
Shim-Sutcliffe Architects 218, 220, *223*
Shirdel, Bahram 162, 164
Siitonen, Tuomo 87
Simon, Cathy 106, 108
Simon, Roberto 204
Simon Fraser University, Vancouver 102, *103*
Skaggs, Ron 122
Skidmore, Owings & Merrill
    Brooklyn Public Library 168
    Harold Washington Library Center 151
    Los Angeles Federal Courthouse 54, *58*
    Tempe Visual & Performing Arts Center 78, *82*
Smith, Adrian 151
Smith, Garrett 143, *143*
Smith, Thomas G 29, *31*
Smith-Miller + Hawkinson Architects 74, 116, *118*
    Chicago prototype schools 116, *118*
    University of South Dakota School of Business 134, *135*, 136, *136*
Snøhetta 21
    Alexandria Library *146–7, 149*
    Kansai-Kan National Diet Library 162, *166*
    Oslo Opera House *68*, 71
Snow, Julie 134, *139*
Sobek, Werner *132*
Speck, Lawrence 122
Spreckelsen, Johann Otto von 65
Springfield, Massachusetts 34
Square of the Moneda Palace, Santiago 30
Stalder, Ivo 87
Starck, Philippe 164
Stastny, Donald 34, 37
Stern, Robert AM *20*, 21, 104, 152
Stimmen, Hans 40
Stone, Edward Durrell 184
Storey, Kim 42
Stuttgart 212
Suarez, Diego 206
Suarez, Odile 30
Sutcliffe, Howard 80
Sweden 242-3
Sydney Opera House 62, *63*

Takamatsu, Shin 184
Tange, Kenzo 68
Tate Modern 184, 187
Taut, Bruno 212
Tempe Visual & Performing Arts Center 78, *79*, 80, *80, 81, 82, 83*
TEN Arquitectos 168, *169*, 170, *171*
Testa, Coriado 30
Thoerishaus Urban Centre, Switzerland 9
Thomas Hacker & Associates 38, *38*
Thomas Petersen Hammond Architects 156
Thompson, James 72
Thompson and Rose Architects 134, 136, *137*
Thorsen, Kjetil T 162, *166*

Timchula, Michael *32*, 33
Toki, Fumio 152, *163*, *164*
Tokyo Forum 8, 68, 94, 164
Toronto City Hall 29
Troy, New York 72, *73*, 74, *75*, *76*, 77, *77*
Tschumi, Bernard 74, *77*, 104, 178, 180
two-stage format 16-17

UIA 16, 68, 184, 191, 204, *205*
UN Studio 21, 74
United Kingdom
    competitions 243
    government buildings 25
United States 11
    competitions 243
    educational facilities 98, 100-1
    government buildings 24, 25, 27, 29
    housing 212-13
    museums 189-90
    performing arts centres 62, 68–9, 71
    public libraries 148-55
    universities 102-4
universities 102-4
    IIT McCormick Center 128, *129*, *130*, *131*, 132, *132*, *133*
    School of Architecture, University of New Mexico 140, *141*, *142*, 143, *143*, *144*, *145*
    University of South Dakota School of Business 134, *135*, 136, *136*, *137*, *138*, *139*
University of California, Berkeley 102
University of California, Santa Cruz 103
University of Maryland, Performing Arts Center 69, 71
University of New Mexico, School of Architecture 140, *141*, *142*, 143, *143*, *144*, *145*
University of Pennsylvania 104, *105*
University of South Dakota School of Business 134, *135*, 136, *136*, *137*, *138*, *139*
University of Tennessee 102
University of Utah Art Museum, Salt Lake City *188*, 190
Urban Innovations Group 27
Utzon, Jørn 62, *63*

Valentiner Crane 156
van Dijk Pace Westlake Architects 78, 80, *83*
Van Lengen, Karen 143
Vancouver 102, *103*
Vandkunsten, Tegnestuen 230
Veenstra, Timothy 222
Vendrell, Xavier 218, 220, *223*
Victoria and Albert Museum, London 191
Viñoly, Rafael 8, 71
    Brooklyn Public Library 168, *174–5*
    Los Angeles Federal Courthouse 54, 57
    Tokyo Forum 68, 94, 164
Vinson, Mark 80

Wagner, Ronald E 102
Wang, Wilfried 42
Ward, Scott 198, 201
Washington, DC 189
Washington University, St Louis 102
Watson, Jill 215
Webb, Michael 198
Weiss, Marion 16–17
Weissenhof Siedlung, Stuttgart 212

Westlake, Paul 78, 80
Wheeler Kearns Architects 218, 220, *223*
Whitney Museum of American Art, New York City 186, 189
Whittome, Irene 178
Wilford, Michael 40
Williams, Terry 42
Wilson, Colin St John *150*
Windsor, New Jersey 100
Wingårdh, Gert 84
Woo, Kyu Sung 204, 206, *208*
Woodroofe, Jonathan *225*, 226, *226*, 227, 228, *228*, *229*
Wright, Eric Lloyd 201
Wright, Frank Lloyd 186, 189, 217
Wu, Jenny *202*, 203
WW 190

Yale Center for British Art 103
Yamamoto, Riken *99*, 102
Yazdani, Mehrdad 48, 54, *59*
Yost Grube Hall Architects *39*

Zane, Chad KL 203
Zumthor, Peter 84